Changing Stories
in the Chinese World

Changing Stories
in the Chinese World

Mark Elvin

STANFORD UNIVERSITY PRESS
STANFORD, CALIFORNIA

Stanford University Press
Stanford, California
©1997 by the Board of Trustees of the
Leland Stanford Junior University
Printed in the United States of America
CIP data appear at the end of the book

For Dian

Acknowledgements

Earlier versions of chapters or parts of chapters in this volume appeared in the following publications, drawing on Chinese sources still in copyright as indicated:

Chapter 1: "The Inner World of 1830" in *Daedalus* 220.2 (Spring, 1991), and "The Spectrum of Accessibility: Types of Humour in *The Destinies of the Flowers in the Mirror,*" in R. T. Ames, S. W. Chan, and M. S. Ng, eds., *Interpreting Culture Through Translation* (Hong Kong: The Chinese University Press, 1991).

Chapter 2: "Unseen Lives. The Emotions of Everyday Existence Mirrored in Chinese Popular Poetry of the Mid-Seventeenth to the Mid-Nineteenth Century," paper presented to the Conference on Self and Symbolic Expression, East-West Center, Honolulu, 1990, organized by Professor Tu Wei-ming and Dr. Wimal Dissanayake. Scheduled to appear in Wimal Dissanayake, Roger Ames, and Thomas Kasulis, eds., *Self as Image in Asian Theory and Practice* (Albany, NY: State University of New York Press, 1997).

Chapter 3: "The Crisis of Absurdity: Reflections of *Tides in the Human Sea,*" in *The Proceedings of the Conference on Eighty Years History of the Republic of China* (Taipei: Chin-tai Chung-kuo ch'u-pan-she, 1991), volume III.

Chapter 4: "Tales of *Shen* and *Xin*: Body-Person and Heart-Mind in China during the Last 150 Years," in M. Feher with R. Naddaff and N. Tazi, *Zone 4: Fragments for a History of the Human Body* (New York: Zone Books, 1989).

Chapter 5: "Secular Karma: The Communist Revolution Understood in Traditional Chinese Terms," in Mabel Lee and A. D. Syrokomla-Stefanowska, eds., *Modernization of the Chinese Past* (Sydney: Wild Peony/University of Hawaii Press, 1993). Quotations from Sima Zhongyuan, *Niezhong* (Taipei: Huangguan, 1980/ 84).

Chapter 6: "In What Sense Is It Possible to Speak of a 'Modernization' of the Emotions in Chinese Society?" in Chang Yü-fa *et al.*, eds., *Symposium on the Modernization in China, 1860–1949* (Taipei: Institute of Modern History, Academia Sinica, 1991). Quotations from Yu Guanzhong, *Fen-he ren* (Taipei: Chun wenxue, 1972/85); Li Ang, *Shafu. Lucheng gushi* (Taipei: Lianjing, 1983/ 89); and Yuan Ze'nan, *Fanfu suzi* (Taipei: Erya, 1985).

Permission from the publishers listed above to make use of these materials is most gratefully acknowledged.

For discussions of points of translation and analysis, I should particularly like to acknowledge the help of Sam Rivers (Chiang Yang-ming) and useful comments made by Dr. Warren Wan-kuo Sun and Dr. Stephen Morgan, all at various times colleagues in the Division of Pacific and Asian History of the Research School of Pacific Studies. I have valued the observations of Dr. Huang K'o-wu (Academia Sinica, Taipei) on the question of whether what I find humorous in Chinese texts is also likely to seem humorous to a Chinese reader (Chapter 2). Dr. David Kelly (now at the Australian Defence Force Academy) made stimulating comments on the philosophical question of 'absurdity' discussed in Chapter 3, and Dr. J-J. Lo (Academia Sinica, Taipei) gave me some recondite information on Ping Jinya for this same chapter. To both, my thanks. Professor Andrew Watson (of the University of Adelaide) took me to see a performance of Wedekind's *Spring Awakening*, a gesture that I much appreciated, and the consequences of which can be seen in my comments on the German playwright in Chapter 3. I should also like to thank Professor Liu Ts'un-yan for providing me with a copy of Yu Guangzhong's *Fen-he ren*.

Ramona Naddaff of *Zone* inspired the article from a part of which part of Chapter 4 is drawn with the irresistible invitation to write a piece that was as long as I wanted and contained as many illustrations as I wished. Hal Kahn has been the warmest friend and the most subtly (and usefully) mordant critic of this book as a whole.

To many other colleagues and friends who have generously given me their criticisms and comments, especially at the conferences in Hawai'i, Taipei, and Sydney where five of the six chapters first saw the light of day, I should also like to record my thanks, and hope they will understand if—partly for reasons of space and partly for fear of inadvertent omissions—I do not try to mention them all here by name.   M.E.

Contents

Note to the Reader

Abbreviations

The following abbreviations are used in parentheses in the text for citations from the works most commonly quoted. Full bibliographical details will be found on the first occasion when each one is referred to.

JHY   Li Ruzhen, *Jing hua yuan.*
GCSD   Zhang Yingchang, ed., *Guochao shiduo* =
          Qing shi duo.
RHC   Ping Jinya, *Renhai chao.*
XSEN   Hao Ran, *Xisha er-nü.*
NZ   Sima Zhongyuan, *Niezhong.*
SF   Li Ang, *Shafu. Lucheng gushi.*
FHR   Yu Guanzhong, *Fen-he ren.*
FFSZ   Yuan Ze'nan, *Fanfu suzi.*

Quotation Marks

In the main text, double quotation marks ("/") are only used for the demarcation of direct citations from an identified author or work, and to show direct speech. Single quotation marks ('/') are used for all other purposes, such as to indicate the discussion of, definition of, or literal reference to the enclosed word or phrase, or else the use of this word or phrase in a special or unusual sense, either by the present author or by a speaker being quoted. In the notes, double quotation marks also enclose the titles of journal articles, and the usual convention of alternating double and single quotation marks when one quotation is embedded in another is likewise generally observed. Concluding double quotation marks enclose phrase- or clause-terminal punctuation (such as commas and periods); single quotation marks do not, unless the punctuation is itself part of the word or phrase being referred to, or unless the single quotation marks are marking an embedded quote.

Les spécialistes d'histoire culturelle savent aujourd'hui étudier les institutions, les objets, les pratiques mais ils n'osent aborder les dispositifs affectifs dont seul la connaissance conférerait un sens à leurs patientes et fructueueses recherches. C'est qu'en ce domaine, le statut du document et la validité de la preuve posent des problèmes d'une particulière acuité.... Tout compte fait, le plus grave à mes yeux n'en demeure pas moins l'anachronisme psychologique. Le pire, c'est la tranquille, abusive et aveugle certitude de la compréhension du passé.... Répérer les mécanismes de l'émotion nouvelle ... constitue l'indispensable. Il n'est pas d'autre moyen de connaître les hommes du passé que de tenter ... de vivre leurs émotions.

—Alain Corbin, Foreword, *Le territoire du vide: L'Occident et le désir du rivage, 1750–1840* (Paris: Flammarion, 1988)

Today, specialists in cultural history know how to study institutions, objects, and practices, but they lack the knowledge to tackle those affective dispositions the knowledge of which alone can give a meaning to their patient and fruitful investigations. The reason for this is that, in this domain, the status of documents and the validity of proofs present especially difficult problems.... All things considered, to my way of thinking, the most serious failing nonetheless continues to be psychological anachronism. Worst is the calm, unwarranted, and blind certainty that one understands the past.... Indentifying the mechanisms of new emotions ... constitutes the indispensable element. There is no other way of knowing those who lived in the past except ... by trying to live their emotions oneself.

Introduction

THIS BOOK describes some of the central changes of meaning in the Chinese world since about 1800, a span of three long lifetimes.

One way to tell this story would be to discuss Chinese systems of belief in terms of their own avowed doctrines, and the acting out, and imposition, of these doctrines in social and political life. China has lost two major worldviews since encountering the modern West in the course of the nineteenth century. Scriptural Confucianism collapsed as a self-reproducing system by the early years of the twentieth century, undermined initially by an attempt to intensify its religious character and by anguish at its historical failure in the service of China.[1] Maoist Communism was strategically dead by the start of the 1980s, destroyed by cynical and murderous abuse of its own often noble ideals—as well as an obstinate oversimplification of the complexities of life. Both in their time were powerful, intelligent, and inspirational interpretations of the world, even if inappropriate for China in any reasonable future. Both have also left residues, some of them fairly certainly dead, some perhaps seeds that may come to life again. Neither, though each in its day was dominant, expressed the whole of the Chinese range of evaluative perceptions: one has only to think of Buddhism in imperial times, or natural science in recent years, to appreciate this point. But the double disavowal by which both have been successively rejected has left an emptiness at the heart of Chinese metaphysical life—the life of meanings—that no mixture of consumerism and familism, power lust and patriotism, borrowed modernism or neo-neo-Confucian revivalism, will fill satisfactorily for long.

It is an extraordinary, and important, story, told this way. In the pages that follow, however, I have taken a different approach. One that I hope is more easily accessible to the reader's emotional imagination, though less analytically systematic. I have summoned back into life again—through my own translations from a selection of popular Chinese novels and poems—some of the imagined worlds in which Chinese have passed their daily reality during the last two hundred years. I have tried to convey something of what it felt like to be a Chinese, living in Chinese society, in different settings of status, age, and gender, and how this has changed over time. For reasons of method, I have looked at a small number of organically coherent emotional spaces, contained in individual works or parts of works, and considered them in detail. I distrust the approach that strings together quotations from separate sources without concern for the contexts from which they have been taken, and without the constraints on interpretation that this concern imposes. It would be pretending to more wisdom than I have to claim that the selection I have made is the result of a rigorous intellectual winnowing process from a harvest of widespread reading in late-imperial and modern Chinese literature. Honesty compels the admission that it is more the outcome of chance, serendipity, and whatever happened to catch my imagination, for reasons that I am probably in no position to do more than guess at. And my range of real reading, as opposed to skimming, has been restricted both by time and limited linguistic ability. In so far as there has been a guiding principle behind my choices it has been the desire to show as much as the constraints of space allow of the constrasts among those in different social positions, different periods, and different ideologies.

I begin by looking at China in the early nineteenth century, before pressures from the West caused a series of transformations of feelings and perceptions. The reading of Li Ruzhen's *The Destinies of the Flowers in the Mirror* presented in the first chapter reveals a microcosm of the educated Chinese world during the last decades of an almost wholly Chinese Chinese culture. *The Flowers* is also a masterpiece of humor, fantasy, and ideological polemics not unlike *Gulliver's Travels* or Montesquieu's *Lettres persanes*, with which it has sometimes been compared. In the second chapter a florilegium of poems on everyday life from *Our Dynasty's Bell of Poesy*, collected by Zhang Yingchang, balances this emphasis on the elite with the emotional universe of peasants, women, artisans, servants, soldiers, and prisoners in so far as we can recover it from the silences of the historical record.

The third chapter, on Ping Jinya's forgotten bestseller of the 1930s, *Tides in the Human Sea*, shows the chaos and the contradictions in feelings and behavior occasioned by an ill-digested modernity. Though it has much in common with the social satire of some novels from late-traditional times, such as *The Scholars*, it is different in its sense of what might be called 'terminal absurdity', the premonition that the system itself is coming apart, and is not deserving of being reconstituted in terms of its old ideals. The resurrection of this once popular work is a reminder that the histories of 'Chinese literature' currently in circulation are far from being histories of what most people actually read, whatever their value in helping to define a canon.

The fourth chapter recalls to life a Communist masterpiece of the early 1970s, Hao Ran's *The Children of the Western Sands*, and tries to draw the reader into at least a momentary understanding of the religious idealism of the Maost faithful, and the stage-lit drama of their emotional existence—noble but also murderous on a mass scale, altruistic but contemptuous of sympathy for individual others.

The book discussed in the fifth chapter is about as different as could be imagined. *The Bastard*, by Sima Zhongyuan, one of Taiwan's best-selling writers—though this is not one of his most widely read books—interprets the tragedy of the Communist revolution in terms derived from pre-modern Chinese religion: the Maoist cataclysm is seen as a deserved punishment inflicted on the Chinese people by Heaven to chastise them for the filthy impropriety of their sexual conduct. It contrives a more powerful plausibility than one might first anticipate for this odd notion by tracing the causal links through the psychological corruption of children and teenagers. Most present-day Western readers will find it scarcely believable that such a work should have been written in the last quarter of the twentieth century, and for this reason it is a reminder that human history has no unique pattern of intelligibility. Well worth an hour or two's soul-traveling to imagine that one might imagine oneself, as a Chinese reader in the Republic of China on Taiwan, convinced by its author's savage vision.

The last chapter is about the dissolution of a distinctively Chinese understanding of the world in a modern environment. It focuses on a book of recent essays, *A Commonplace Fellow*, by Yuan Ze'nan, a Chinese-American writer who has come to the point at which his Chineseness has all but vanished, and is consciously exploring its disappearance. He shows, for example, how filial piety can become transmuted into a new form of understanding between parents and children, as it did between him and his father, or fail to, as in the case of his relations with his mother. These essays are placed in a context, only lightly sketched, of two other writers, Yu Guanzhong and Li Ang, both based in Taiwan, who have traveled some way, though less far, down this road, but have been important influences in forming Yuan's sensibility.

There are many gaps in the coverage. I would only claim to have illustrated something of the possibilities of one way of glimpsing the fugitive movie of human experience, using a handful of literary sources that serve as the stills capturing cross-sections of moments in time. It would be possible to write a parallel volume on the same two centuries of China using different literary materials, and no doubt reaching a somewhat different impression of how the experience of the many ways of being Chinese has changed through these years. There is one gap, though, that is so large and important that it deserves a comment and perhaps an apology. This is the absence of anything from the outpouring of fiction and social commentary that has occurred in the People's Republic of China since Deng Xiaoping's reforms in the late 1970s and early 1980s. For the present, and to my regret, it is beyond my competence to venture professionally into this domain. Readers who are interested in sampling what is there should look at the anthologies edited by Barmé, Minford, and Jaivin.[2]

Transitions between chapters are abrupt. The shifting of mental gears that this requires of the reader (as it has of the author) is a reminder both of the extent of the changes in China since the early nineteenth century, and the gulf that can exist between different emotional and perceptual worlds—all 'Chinese'—in recent times. The awkwardness expresses something of the substance.

The inner history explored here is not 'truer' than more conventional histories of human physical interactions with the environment, or of the evolution of economic, social, military, and political structures. Nor, however, is it less true. It is interwoven with these other histories as both cause and effect. From our point of view, as outsiders to it in time and to a variable degree in culture (depending on who we are), the value of studying it is that it helps to make intelligible past Chinese emotional reactions, past programs for action, and past decisions by individuals and collectivities that would otherwise remain opaque. This is because inner history is not merely epiphenomenal; in other words, it is not simply derivative from other sources. It has at least something of its own logic.

How?—And why use low-level literature as the means of coming to terms with it? The answer is that people live *in stories*, or *as if* they were in stories. Stories that are a social inheritance, but also in some measure self-created, or at least adapted, edited, or extended. And, these days at least, more usually a multiplicity of stories, rather than only one. Some are major, some are minor: the stories of one's tribe,[3] one's state, one's faith,[4] but also of one's political party, one's firm, or one's football club.[5] Even the myths and scandals peddled by one's newspaper or local television programs.[6] Shared stories understood in this manner give sense and coherence to a particular human group. They define the space in which it operates, its conceptualized physical landscape.[7] They structure the time in which it operates, its calendar of cyclical events,[8] and its currently remembered history. They are, presumably, subject to constraints on their natures imposed by the requirement of functionality,[9] or the pressures of competition with other stories, else they would rapidly perish. (Some do, and of course all of them vanish in the end.) If so, then this need to be functional tends to determine what they *cannot* be, but not, within the often wide range of the functionally possible, exactly what they *must* be.

Accepting that we live in stories can be difficult, especially when it relates to ourselves rather than others. An awareness of the formally arbitrarily constructed nature of a story[10] is usually incompatible with a fully involved belief in it. To draw attention, even indirectly, to the formally arbitrary nature of a major lived-in story is usually seen by those who inhabit it as an act of hostility. This is almost certainly the strongest reason why Islamic leaders were so angry with Salman Rushdie's novel *The Satanic Verses*: it repeatedly suggests that there is, ultimately, no boundary between the story told in the Holy Koran and a work of imaginative fiction.[11] Nor is there, but this is a thought that opens the abyss.

When the social perception of the world begins to differ seriously from that prescribed as 'real' by an old and once well-established major story, the phenomenon of absurdity occurs, and is almost always the prelude to the destruction or radical recasting of this story. There is a humorously savage description of this in the first part of Carlyle's *The French Revolution*, written more than a century and a half ago, as it applied to the Ancien Régime.[12] Karl Kraus did the same for Vienna at the turn of the nineteenth and twentieth centuries.[13] Analogous events occurred in China between the passing of scriptural Confucianism and the rise of Maoist Communism, and are described here in the chapter on the 'the crisis of absurdity'. A widespread sense of absurdity is a dangerous social state of mind, and has been associated, as these cases suggest, with the rise of political terrorisms and totalitarianisms.

That people live in stories is intuitively evident to me, perhaps because, for as long as I can remember, I have been moving between different countries, cultures, languages, and stories. It is the repeated experience of these transitions that is probably decisive in implanting an awareness of the story-like character of social existence. I have learned over the years, however, that for most people that we live in stories is *not* an evident truth, and that the idea can seem to them either quite implausible, or else insulting, or painful. I have no desire to offend anyone, or to hurt anyone, in saying so, but living in stories is what we are doing, all of us, all the time.

The idea that one may live one's life like a character inside a story was probably first crystallized by Cervantes in *Don Quixote*.[14] Thus: "whatever our Knight-Errant saw, thought, or imagin'd, ... appear'd to him altogether after the Manner of the Books that had perverted his imagination."[15] The knight is living in a story that he has absorbed from tales of chivalry, and which conditions his perceptions of the world about him: "his strong Fancy chang'd every thing he saw into what he desir'd to see; and thus he could not conceive that the Dust was only rais'd by two large Flocks of Sheep.... He was so positive that they were two Armies, that Sancho firmly believed him at last."[16] Thus does rationalization often impede the sensory correction of misplaced conceptions. The reader, however, accepts without difficulty that Don Quijote is living in a story because it is so splendidly ludicrous and removed from 'real' life. Truth is often only palatable when made to seem implausible. I doubt if even Don Miguel, who wrote to destroy what he saw as pernicious nonsense, was wholly conscious of the subversive message latent in his book, namely, that we are all, in our own ways, Don Quijotes.

The nature of lived-in stories as stories is often most apparent when they are in the process of disintegrating, and perhaps also when they are being born. So Carlyle comments, contemplating the failing credibility of the monarchy and the church in France during the later eighteenth century: "For ours is a most fictile world; and man is the most fingent plastic of creatures.... [I]nward sense ... is not permanent like the outward ones.... but forever growing and changing."[17] An ambivalent mixture of irony and unwilling enthusiasm infuses his view of the birth of the new French revolutionary worldview, and its story in the making, but always he is conscious of the process of fabrication: "This day [8 June, 1794], if it please

Heaven, we are to have ... a New Religion. Catholicism being burned out, and Reason-worship guillotined, was there not need of one? Incorruptible Robespierre, not unlike the Ancients, as legislator of a free people, will now also be Priest and Prophet.... Mumbo-Jumbo of the African woods seems to me venerable beside this new Deity of Robespierre; for this is a *conscious* Mumbo-Jumbo, and *knows* that he is machinery...."[18] There are obvious partial parallels here with what happened later in China, with the disintegration of the late-traditional worldview—the complex of stories within which most people lived, unaware that they were stories—and the attempts, sometimes excessively forced, under both Nationalists and Communists, to create a new one in a hurry.

At the other, relatively modest, end of the spectrum of such stories, consider the far from trivial dominion over the minds of its devotees exercised by Australian Rules football. The poet Bruce Dawe wrote, only a little ironically, of a new-born Victorian baby, that "the tides of life will be the tides of the team's fortunes."[19] According to Sandercock and Turner,"[T]o support one or other of the twelve VFL teams ... is a major part of self-identification...."[20] In a poor area, before the coming of television and the disintegration of sharply localized loyalties, "football was a source of both escape and deliverance for a hard-pressed community.... Success on the football field could transform, even transpose, the whole week: it could infuse life with purpose."[21] Many readers will be able to translate these observations into the terms of their own, different, sporting mythologies.

From another pespective, Mircea Eliade has described myths and fairy tales as "models for human behavior [that,] by that very fact, give meaning and value to life."[22] Bruno Bettelheim has argued that "the form and structure" of fairy tales "suggest images to the child by which he can structure his daydreams and with them give better direction to his life,"[23] even though in most cases the deeper meaning of these tales is at first opaque to the child. Thus the hedge of thorns around the Sleeping Beauty indicates the inappropriateness of a girl's premature sexual awakening, but the thickets will open of themselves to the right man at the right time. Bettelheim's examples are simple but important case histories that suggest the capacity of stories to structure behavior.

A 'story' may be defined for our purposes as follows. It is a coherent set of descriptions of supposedly true interlinked events relating to a cast of distinctive actors who are either human or analogous to humans in terms of communication and personality,[24] between which events there are ascribed, or at least clearly implied, patterns of causation. The key elements defining the particular character of a story are the cast and the causation, which to a large extent mutually determine each other as carriers of propensities and capacities on the one hand, and the means of the realization of these propensities and capacities on the other. A story may be said to be 'lived-in' when it is regularly and collectively accepted by a group as the basis or guide for action, though the acceptance does not have to be fully conscious on the part of all the group's members all the time. The lure of such a story is that the listener/believer is made to feel that he or she *understands*. (In fleeting, frightening, moments of honesty we know of course that we either do not understand, or understand very imperfectly.) Another attraction of the lived-in story is that it provides a role for the listener/believer to play. And if several stories, then several roles. To be without any part on the stage can be difficult for most of us to endure. A story is our metaphysical life. Per contra, to be trapped in a story that one detests, but from which one cannot escape, is to be in a terrifying invisible prison.

For practical analysis, stories have to be treated as having something of their own autonomy as actors in history. A familar example is the conflict between Jewish and Arab stories about the land of Isra'el/Palestine; a less familiar one is the resistance of the religious story lived in by the Mbya Guarani of eastern Paraguay, seeing themselves as the Last Men, to the attacks of Christianity.[25] If one compares the unassimilated Mbya with other South American Indian groups, who put up no comparable spiritual resistance, one could hypothesize that the strength of a story can in itself be a factor in social and political as well as religious history. One of the great puzzles of modern Chinese history, doubly puzzling because almost no one has been puzzled by it, is why the sophisticated and long-lived stories sustaining such a great empire of feeling and perception crumbled so easily in modern times—compared, say, to Islam, Hinduism, or Buddhism.

Finally, why use 'stories' as the means of analysis here rather than the more familiar concept of 'culture' understood in the anthropological sense of socially transmitted patterns of meaning and evaluation? In part because 'culture' is too large a unit for the scale of the subject matter of this book; in part because it is a theoretical construct not immediately identifiable by experience in a way that commands general assent; and in part because it tends to suggest a degree of internal integration, a distinctive separateness from other 'cultures', and a relative long-term stability over time that may or may not in fact have been present, but which in any case can never be justifiably assumed in advance. The 'story' is less opaque, and a modest and flexible unit more easily adapted to the articulation both of internal diversity and of conflict and change. Stories crisscross each other in space and time; and they traverse cultures, in which they interact in varying fashion with previously existing elements. A spectacular historical example is that of 'Hell' or 'Purgatory' as an institution of morally appropriate postmortem punishment. It was invented in northern India or perhaps Persia some time in the early first millennium B.C.E., and later spread both east and west until it played a major part in both Buddhism and Christianity, and numerous other faiths. A more recent example is Marxism. Both have traveled well, and found a variety of people keen to live in them in many cultures—but not all. What it was that predisposed some to infection by, but a few to resistance to, these epidemics of ideas is indeed a question of 'culture', and the answers usually far from obvious. The stories as such, at their surface level at least, are in contrast explicit and visible, and to that extent less problematic to handle.

This, then, is a book about appearances. But at times deceptive ones.

Caveat lector.

CHAPTER ONE

The Inner World of the Early Nineteenth Century

IF WE ARE TO understand what it means to be 'Chinese' today, we need some conception of what it meant to be Chinese before the invasion of Western culture in the middle of the nineteenth century.[1] This is most easily approached at two levels, that of the educated elite, and that of the less self-aware and articulate, while bearing in mind that there was no sharp discontinuity between the two. In the present chapter we summon back into a fleeting re-existence a novel that is a microcosm of the Chinese mind around the year 1828 when it was published. This is Li Ruzhen's *Destinies of the Flowers in the Mirror*.[2] In the following one we survey some of the poems of everyday life in Zhang Yingchang's mid-nineteenth-century anthology, *Our Dynasty's Bell of Poesy*,[3] verses that although not *of* the people, who have no voice of their own in any but the most elusive fragments of Chinese literature, are *about* the people in a serious, and mostly sympathetic, way.

The *Flowers* is a mixture of fantasy and realism, iconoclasm and conventionality. Irony tears at such socially accepted horrors as the binding of women's feet at the same time as a most un-ironic enthusiasm exalts accepted virtues like filial piety and loyalty to a superior. It extols Confucianism and the drama of the world history of humanity unfolding uniquely in China since the time of the sages. It devalues it by subordinating it to the vision of a reincarnational Daoism that sees our earthly lives as mere repetitive forays into the arena of illusion. Its purported setting is the reign of the usurper Empress Wu in the seventh century, but the society that it shows is that of the late eighteenth and early nineteenth centuries. The viewpoints supported by its characters often differ from one another, as the result of the author's intent, not inadvertence, and define the polarities of problems. They should not be seen, for the most part, as defining his own positions.

The book's structure is a single cycle of life, symbolizing one turn of the wheel of reincarnation. The human world is shown as embedded in a supernatural world that is all around it, yet at the same time almost wholly hidden.

The celestial story opens in Heaven. As a punishment for a misdemeanor, the spirits of the various flowers, and the Immortal of the Hundred Flowers, who rules them, are scattered to live as mortal girls in the world below. The first half of the earthly story is set in the strange 'lands beyond the seas', legendary realms that the author has transformed into sociological foils to China,[4] where Tang the Roamer, a disillusioned official now searching for immortality, gains merits by gathering together the separated flower-spirits. The second half takes place in China, the 'Land Within the Seas'. The reunited sisterhood of young ladies triumphs in the first imperial examinations for women (a historical fiction), and then celebrates at a prolonged party at the Capital, which becomes for a moment an Earthly Paradise. Their leader is Tang's own daughter, originally Little Hill, now renamed 'Servant of the Tang', and the incarnation of the once and future Immortal of the Hundred Flowers. The book closes with the war of the loyalists of the Tang dynasty against the Empress, and the breaking up of the sisterhood even as victory is being won. A few depart to illustrious careers. Many more commit virtuous suicide to follow their slain warrior-husbands. Two pass directly back to immortality. But for all, their time in the human world is done.

To take such a mixture of fantasy and polemic as a guide to psychological reality has its hazards, but the relative freedom from constraints conferred by its status as a work of the imagination makes it unusually revealing.

Causality

There was a lack of rigor in the Chinese universe. Rules could be broken precisely because they were not laws of nature. A drama of rewards and punishments based on karma[5] ran through all sentient action, human and nonhuman alike, but—in contrast to the Buddhism from which it was borrowed—was more bureaucratic than inexorable.

The Immortal of the Hundred Flowers is asked, at the birthday party of the Queen Mother of the West, to make all species of flower bloom at the same time. She refuses this as being improper:

> "God on High gives strict orders for flowers, and He checks up in the most minute detail. An illustrated register has to be submitted a month in advance, showing all the flowers supposed to open a month later. All such matters as an increase, or reduction, in the stamens or petals, or a change of colors, have to wait for His decision. God tells the Jade Maiden Cloaked in Fragrance to make an attentive decision....
>
> "If a flower has been without error, this is noted in the Cloud Tallies and the Golden Memoranda. The year following, it is moved, perhaps inside some carven balustrade, or to the front of some decorated doorway, so that it may be fed on pure soil, be watered from a clear spring, attract the admiration of poets, and give pleasure to distinguished guests....
>
> "If there are some who transgress, the Magical Inquisitor asks in a memorial that separate decrees be issued for the punishment of each. In the most serious cases, a flower ... will have to bear with people pulling it up, or snapping it off....
>
> "Since there are all these sorts of inspection, I can only pay heed, humble Immortal that I am, to the orders that I receive. I dare not act irregularly." (JHY 1:5)

Some of the other Immortals disagree, believing that it is by no means impossible to act contrary to Heaven.

With a twist characteristic of court politics, the Immortal of the Hundred Flowers is then punished for her principled disobedience by being predestined to be guilty in the future of violating the very principles she holds dear. In due course her flowers obey the order of the earthly Empress Wu to bloom all at once in winter; and for this the Immortal, who bears the responsibility though she herself gave no such command, is punished. The point is that preserving the celestial hierarchy preempts the preservation of the natural order.

This view of a universe operating through a bureaucratic, and hence somewhat capricious, causation conflicted with another conception, namely that causes worked automatically, even calculably. These two views apppear side by side in a discussion about thunder that is held during the party:

> "Mathematicians often boast without justification," said Jade Brooch, "and make everything into the opposite of what it is."
>
> "That's not true," retorted Orchid Fragrance. "I can even calculate from how many miles away this thunder is coming."
>
> [She] ... pointed to a chiming clock on the table and said: "Simply look at the second hand. Then it can be calculated."
>
> An instant later there was a flash. A short while afterwards came the rumble of thunder.
>
> "The thunder arrived here 15 seconds after the flash," observed Jade Iris. "Work it out, elder sister."
>
> Orchid Fragrance did some figuring. Then she said:
>
> "It's a fixed rule that in one second the sound of thunder travels 1285 feet and 7 inches [Chinese measure]. If we reckon on this basis, the thunder was 10 miles and 1280 feet distant [1285.5]." ...
>
> Some time later the sky became very calm. The husband of Precious Cloud's old wet-nurse had just brought two jars of Cloud-Mist tea ... so she asked him how things were at home....
>
> "If you do wicked things," the man replied, "you may fool people, but don't forget that the Thunder God can pay you back if you do wrong. There was a storm just now at Ten Mile Hamlet. A clap of thunder ... struck a man dead.... He was a bad lot, who did every sort of wickedness."
>
> "How far away is Ten Mile Hamlet?" asked White Cloud.
>
> "Only 10 miles from here," answered the wet-nurse's husband. "He was struck down a little more than half a mile outside it." (JHY 79:589–90)

The scientific method is, in a rough sense, latent in Fragrant Orchid's point of view; and this mixture of 'modern' with 'premodern' elements is characteristic of many aspects of late-imperial China.[6]

The other characters in the book are also concerned with how far future events are predetermined. They often make remarks such as 'Since the ethers and numbers [i.e., fate] were as they were, there was nothing to be done about it'. Omens are an obsession, being seen as transtemporal links between the future and the present. Much of the drama in the second half of the novel comes from the working out of the cryptic prophecies that Little Hill has found on a stele in Little Penglai, a lesser Land of the Immortals. Late in the party, a mysterious Daoist nun appears and tells the girls: "Today's gathering is in no way accidental. The karmic forces at work in it cannot be told of in a short space of time." Then she recites to them a long, riddling poem partly about the past and partly about the future. She tells them that "the slightest trifles are predetermined from the beginning," and concludes with two somewhat scientific metaphors: "In all these cases the root determines the blossoms, just as the magnet is drawn towards the iron." (JHY 90:687–88)

Many Chinese, however, believed that the otherwise fated course of events *could* be altered. One technique was that of sepulchral geomancy, that is to say, the art of improving one's own fortune by burying the remains of one's parents or grandparents in a site selected to tap the forces running in the veins of the earth. Many years often passed with the bones unburied while a descendant looked for the perfect location. Li Ruzhen has one of his characters from the Land of Gentlemen attack this practice with a typically Confucian blend of skeptical rationality, familistic ethics, concern for the prudential management of life, an appeal to the Confucian scriptures as reliable authorities for facts on which arguments could be grounded, and belief in the magical powers of moral behavior:

> "Don't men who are skilled in geomancy have parents? If they find a good location, why don't they keep it for their own use? If it is the case that, having found such a place, they can advance in the world, then consider—how many skilled in geomancy have in fact done well for themselves? ...
>
> "None of these people understand that 'if a man has been great, the ground he lies in will be magically efficacious'.... The grave-mounds of the sage-king Fuxi, of King Wen, and of Confucius all grow milfoil that

has a high degree of magical efficacy for oracular prediction [by casting its stalks]. The quality of the milfoil found elsewhere is less good, and the omen-taking not so effective....

"These days people choose a shady spot [that is, one dominated by the Dark or Female Principle] because they want their sons and grand-sons to prosper.... If we consider flourishing and decay, then in the case of the lineage of Duke Li of Chen ... there was the oracle of 'male and female phoenix in flight, singing like tinkling bells.'... Was this caused by fate, or by ground dominated by the Female Principle? Since the oracle spoke of events that were to come, it is evident that the excel-lence, or otherwise, of ground dominated by the Female Principle had no effect. In general, in the affairs of this world, only great goodness can convert a [predestined] disaster into good fortune." (JHY 12:72)

An example of this last point is provided during a later discussion of astrology by 'the response of Heaven[7] to a moral influence', with the result that the visible brightness of the constellations changes, and the otherwise correctly predicted demise of Empress Wu is postponed for a few years. (JHY 57:426–27) Even a generation or so after the *Flowers* was written the real Chinese emperor was still issuing decrees that apologetically linked bad weather to his own lack of virtuous conduct.

Morality had a magical power to affect the fate of the individual. According to Seafarer Lin, Tang the Roamer's brother-in-law, if a man is eaten by a tiger this is always because "his previous lives have determined that he should suffer in the tiger's jaws." The helmsman-scholar Duo the Ninth disagrees, arguing that tigers only eat men if the immoral behavior of the latter, in this life, has made them the equivalent of beasts. If the virtuous appear to suffer, this can only be because their outward goodness is a sham that hides a secret wrongdoing. (JHY 10:61)

Later, though, Job's problem is confronted in a different way. The following conversation takes place between the Daoist nun and Little Spring:

> *Little Spring*: If all of us sisters are going to die so many sorts of ill-omened death, can it really be that every one of us has done some sin in her lifetime great enough to meet with such retribution?
>
> *Nun*: If it is tragic to be disembowelled, would you argue that in an-

cient times Lord Gan of Bi [put to death by the evil last emperor of the Shang on account of his honest criticisms] also committed some sin? To those in this universe who are endowed with feelings of loyalty and purity, the question of whether they live or die is irrelevant.

Little Spring: There are always many good people in this world who, even so, do not come to a good end, and some bad people enjoy excellent fortunes. What does this mean?

Nun: It is said in the *Analects* that the "superior person's anxiety is that he may die without leaving a good name behind him." ... If one merely schemes to save one's own neck, one leaves behind a foul repute for many years afterwards.... Isn't it better to meet death with a smile, and leave behind a good name in perpetuity? (JHY 90:687–88)

Others of the girls join in the debate, but the issue is not resolved.

Virtue had its powers. Helmsman Duo recounts how his filial great-grandfather cured the dysentery of his great-great-grandmother by the time-honored means of making her a soup from flesh cut from his thigh, and how his filial self-torture later obtained from an immortal on a nearby mountain a cure when she relapsed. (JHY 27:195) The hagiographical chapters of the local histories of the later empire are full of such tales of devotion. These *miracula* had the social status of facts, and were ethically 'rational'.

The character of the interaction between the physical world and human actions, moral or immoral, remained controversial. During the Han dynasty, a Judas tree belonging to the Tian family was said to have withered when they were on the point of dividing up the family property and separating, an offense against the ideals of kinship; but to have recovered when they changed their minds and stayed together. Orchid Talk comments:

> "You can hardly argue that the tree had a certain knowledge of human affairs, and died merely because they were about to split up the family property. It happened simply as the result of a blast of perversely violent energy[8] that emanated from the Tian family on this occasion." (JHY 71:522)

Purple Mushroom counters with the more conventional view that "the Judas tree ... itself desired to die, so as to warn them." Orchid Talk reasserts her materialism based on the idea of energy:

"From ancient times down to the present day, a great deal of family property has been divided up. Why have we never heard of other families having a tree warn them not to do it?... Even if trees and grasses have the power of consciousness, they are definitely not going to put an end to their own lives to 'rescue others by falling into the well themselves'."

Purple Mushroom then asks why violent energy has not been emitted when other families have divided up their property. Orchid Talk replies that these things are unknowable, as "violent energy is something without form," but the fact that the tree later came back to life shows that "harmonious energy causes good fortune." (JHY 71:522)

The weakness in the analysis made by the young ladies is not a lack of rationality, but an inadequate repertoire of facts, and an inadequate notion of what a 'fact' might be. They work as best they can with historical and scriptural data that they cannot validate, and with their own experiences. A 'fact' was a complex cultural creation that only fully emerged in the West during the seventeenth century,[9] and its absence in China may have been linked with different conceptions of 'trial' and 'evidence' in the two cultures.

Ethical rationality was, however, incomplete. Magical powers could emanate from evil sources, not just from good ones; and good and bad could be mixed up in ways that a Westerner can find confusing. Little Hill (who is the reincarnated Immortal of the Hundred Flowers) and her companions are captured by four demons who intend to ferment them into 'naked-body wine'. They are rescued by a nun who is the Immortal of the Hundred Fruits, a close friend from a previous life, in disguise. She reveals that the demons are the emanations of four fruit pips that once lodged in the mouths of, respectively, a *femme fatale* of ancient times, a catamite minister, a virtuous and many-talented statesman, and a disciple of Confucius. The quasi-magical influences of two depraved and two moral historical figures have alike nourished evil. The only difference is that the first two demons can assume the actual faces of the personages who "used their physical beauty to seduce their lords into delusion," whereas the others have to be content with faces that resemble an orange and a date. (JHY 46:336–37)

Particular evils were not seen as manifestations of a central source of Evil. They were widespread and harmful, like diseases or dangerous animals. There was no Master-Adversary behind them. Yanluo, or Yama, who ruled the Chinese hells, was not a tempter but a judge, and part of a single supernatural bureaucracy that was infernal as well as celestial.

If the source of moral destruction lay anywhere it was deep in the individual as a sort of 'original weakness'. This can be seen at the novel's end, when the loyalist warriors, who have married the flower-spirits, attempt to overthrow the Empress Wu. To reach the Capital they have to pass through four enchantments of 'self-destruction' conjured up against them by the Empress's brothers. These four are wine, anger, women, and money. Most of the warriors cannot resist these temptations, and so bring their deaths upon themselves. When Hero Lin loses his temper with an insolent waiter in a restaurant (conjured up for this purpose by the brothers), "in an instant the nameless fires inside him drew forth the evil in the enchantment.... He tripped, toppled over, and lost consciousness." (JHY 98:751–52) In the fourth enchantment, beneath an immense golden coin suspended in space there is a multitude of people of all classes engaged in every sort of evil for the sake of gain, and the corpses of the destroyed lie about in heaps. In some respects the scene resembles Bunyan's Vanity Fair, but what is different is that it is an illusion, and power to resist the spell can come only from a lonely personal moral fortitude, or the piercing vision of an enlightened understanding. (JHY 99:757) Delusion is the principal proximate cause of evil. The Daoist nun tells the girls at the party:

> "The life of a person in this world is a thousand schemes, a thousand anxieties. He gambles for victory and struggles to be the strongest. Illusion follows illusion as he dies and is born again. It is no more than a game of chess. Because he cannot see through this soul-befuddling spell, he is deluded by it." (JHY 90:689)

And this, she adds of the novel itself, is the "main theme of this dream."

The last problem is that of free will. One immortal tells the Immortal of the Hundred Flowers that she was punished because she neither controlled herself nor fulfilled her duties, (JHY 6:33) and this implies that she had the freedom to do so. Nonetheless, individuals come into the world with different 'predestined affinities' (*yuan*) bequeathed to them from their previous existences. The concept of 'predestined affinity' is many-sided. Someone seeking immortality needs a predestined affinity with the magic foods that confer longevity or eating them will only make him sick. The banishment of the flower-spirits to the earth below is their "predestined affinity with the dust." (JHY 88:666) Little Hill escapes from the fruit demons because of her predestined affinity with the Immortal of the Hundred Fruits. Likewise, she can read an inscription that tells of the future, whereas her friend Flowerlike, without the appropriate predestined affinity, sees only incomprehensible archaic characters. Flowerlike asserts, however, that it is better to have the "freedom" that comes from being without the burden of predestination. (JHY 49:361) In short, the Chinese believed that underlying the complexities of life, and its seemingly capricious turns, lay a skein of these predestined affinities linking lives once lived and lives yet to come, bonds across time between past, present, and future.

The Confucian Inspiration

The central cultural dream of traditional Chinese society was that China was the center of world civilization, the only place where life was lived properly, in its full humanity, and that the influence of her values and learning radiated out to all other nations, transforming them for the better. In the Land of the Black Teeth, Tang the Roamer and Helmsman Duo observe that the modest and proper demeanor of its people is due to the influence of the neighboring Land of Gentlemen, which in turn owes its high moral quality to China. "The fact of the matter is," declares Duo, "that our

China must be regarded as the root of all other countries." (JHY 16:109) The modern West, simply by making China conscious of the West's existence, was to destroy this self-ennobling vision, and so to devalue a history. The comparatively rational and this-worldly justification of Confucian beliefs—since Heaven-Nature, when It responded, responded only here below—made it doubly vulnerable to apparent empirical failure.

Educated Chinese in late-imperial times thus saw themselves as participants in the latest chapter of a story that was, essentially, the story of civilization. This civilization depended on a pattern of human relations that, internally, connected humanity with itself, and, externally, with the normal and in a sense normative pattern of natural forces—the dependably turning constellations and the dependably recurring seasons on which the human calendar was predicated. This pattern was precious and fragile, and in need of fine tuning every few hundred years as times altered. (JHY 52:383) Confucianism was the body of doctrines and practices responsible for the maintenance and renewal of this pattern.

The characters of the *Flowers* devote many pages to enthusiastic discussion of ritually correct behavior; and it is close to impossible for a reader who has not spent years of self-induction into premodern Chinese ways of thought to share their concern for the almost countless specific details. What he (or she) can perhaps imagine is the Chinese sense of how superficially small deviations by the ruler or other leaders could undermine the psychological orientations on which the system depended. Thus Servant of the Tang declares, "In the case of Duke Wen of Lu [who ruled in the second quarter of the first millennium B.C.E., and] who sacrificed improperly in his ancestral temple by placing his father's soul-tablet above that of his father's predecessor [since his father, although *the elder brother*, had only been *the son of a concubine*, and had first served as the minister of his younger brother, *the previous ruler*, and the son of the *principal wife*] ... the rituals of mourning were done away with." (JHY 52:385) The preservation of the proper human hierarchy required an almost scientific precision, like the movements of the stars or the sequence in which plants flowered.

Two virtues were preeminent in Confucianism, namely filial devotion and loyalty to the lord whom one served (rather than to an ideal or a collectivity). A third virtue, the fidelity of a widow to her deceased husband, grew in importance during the last few centuries of the empire. Li Ruzhen celebrates the first two; the third he takes for granted. An unusual shift of perspective, and one that has made parts of his book famous to the exclusion of others, is that filiality is embodied not in sons but in daughters who perform heroic feats that would normally have been thought more suitable for boys. Thus one girl kills tigers in order to avenge her mother's death in the jaws of one of these beasts. The late-traditional reader could relish conventional morality displayed in an unconventional setting.

Little Hill makes two dangerous voyages, inspired by the filial desire to find her father, now an immortal in the quasi-paradise of Little Penglai. The author's intention seems to be to convey admiration for her determination but at the same time to indicate covertly that the significance of this quest is no more than a creation of her imagination. "There is nothing," observes Duo, "that is not made what it is by the mind."[10] (JHY 43:320–21) The quest has no sense in the world of the immortals.

The nobility of the burden of loyalty touched Li deeply. Here is the aged Tang loyalist, Governor Wen Yin, speaking to his nephew:

> "As to myself, I am old, sick, and debilitated. I seem no more than a candle that gutters in the wind.... If you want to know why I prolong my last few breaths in office, to no good use ... it is, first of all, because His Majesty has not yet been restored to his throne, and second, because internal disorder has not yet been suppressed. If I were to retire, I would not share my sovereign's sorrow during my years of life, and would so fail in the pure fidelity required of ministers. Even after my death, how could I face the rulers of the past in the world below? ... Every time my thoughts turn to His Majesty, before I know it, my internal organs seem to be on fire! Since not long is now left to me in the world of men, ... I can only urge my descendants to take up my purpose as their inheritance." (JHY 57:425)

All three virtues, in their premodern forms, were to vanish in the modern era. Belief in the fidelity of widows went the soonest, and was gone by the middle of the present century. The ideal of personal loyalty was to a great extent transmuted into loyalty to the 'ancestral country' or a cause. Rigorous devotion to filial piety, that had once allowed the State with good conscience to inflict punishments like flaying alive on a son who had slapped his mother, or to exile a son at the mere request of his father, softened into social insistence on filial respect and filial support for aged parents. What little is now left of these old virtues is of slight intensity compared to what once was.

The Individual

The Chinese 'self' had two aspects. In the Confucian domain one was one's parents' child. One came into the world with obligations defined by what was, ideally at least, a unique place in a network of ascendant and descendant kin. As life progressed, one acquired further obligations toward teachers, friends, and relatives by marriage. A 'person' in this Confucian sense was defined by his or her relationships, which created a field of obligations and feelings in which the self found its orientation and hence its meaning.

One was also a reincarnated soul. As such one's links with one's earthly kin were contingent, though conditioned by the karma acquired in past lives. Destiny was individual, pursued through rebirth after rebirth, with the status of an 'immortal' as the ultimate goal.

Sometimes the two aspects clashed. When Tang the Roamer has eaten a magical herb that seems not to be agreeing with him, Seafarer Lin says wryly:

> "You'll be an immortal before long, brother-in-law. Why have you suddenly begun to frown and look unhappy? Surely you don't mean to say that you can't give up family and homeplace, and are scared to play the part of a deathless spirit?" (JHY 9:4)

Not infrequently Li Ruzhen makes it clear how the search by one person for immortality wounds the hearts of those who are left behind at home. Tang's wife loses both her husband and her daughter in this way. Li's personal view, though, may be close to that expressed by Purple Twig:

> "From the point of view of human affections ... when husband and wife are united together, and so are father and son ... then the chief matters of human life have been fulfilled. But—to my way of thinking—what happens after ... people have taken this delight in being together? Once a few tens of years have passed they all go to their extinction. As the moment approaches, who can escape the grave-mound?" (JHY 94:724)

She says she wishes to "escape from the bitter sea," so indicating a yearning for immortality or enlightenment.

Lin, the merchant, represents the average sensual Chinese, except perhaps in his heightened level of self-awareness. "I know well enough," he says, "that a man's life in this world is like a dream.... At ordinary times, when I hear people talking about this, I, like them, can feel a cold indifference. But, when some critical chance appears for grabbing a little prestige, or a little profit, my heart cannot help being led astray. I rush forward with my mind bent on nothing else, as if I were going to live for an eternity." (JHY 16:107) His realistic comments often serve as a foil to the idealism of his traveling companions. When they later admire a mountain pheasant that dashes out its brains against a rock after being defeated by a peacock in a display of dancing, Lin demurs. "If all human beings had the same heroic spirit," he observes, "think how many would die! As I see it, the best thing to do is to be hard-boiled about matters of face. Then one can muddle through." (JHY 20:143) The grander Confucian aspirations for life are summed up by Tingting, the girl-scholar of genius, as her companions weep at the ending of the party:

> "If I and my three sisters were to stay in China, or to go back to our own countries, that would be unbearably commonplace—lives passed in emptiness. Today we have received the Empress's decree to accompany Flowerlike back [to the Land of Women]. This sort of opportunity occurs but rarely in a thousand years.... We shall assist her to be a worthy sovereign, and leave behind for ourselves a fine name as famous lady ministers.... Even if we stayed together for another few decades, it would not be better than it is now.... There are no feasts in the world that do not break up some time." (JHY 68:504–5)

The well-managed Confucian private existence required a subtle combination of regard for principle, delicacy, and ingenuity. This is shown in an intricate conversation between Tang the Roamer and his former tutor Yin Yuan, in which they each agree to arrange the marriages of each other's children. (JHY 15:101–2) It is too long to quote here, but it shows how an individual Chinese orchestrated his actions in society. Each move was based on an awareness of the relative statuses of the participants, and this was continually expressed in the language, notably by terms of address and self-description. Each status carried its particular rights and obligations. In this conversation, Tang and Yin assume quite comfortably that elders have the right and duty to arrange the lives of their juniors. Tang suavely switches around his son's prospective wife for another when it seems strategically preferable to do so, with no concern for the boy's possible feelings. He does, though, pay close attention to the proprieties, raising the question of the possible conflict in status terms that could arise if the daughter and son of his teacher, who is defined as his senior, become junior relatives of his through marriage, but Yin dismisses this. It is also of major importance to Tang that his own future daughter-in-law be filial.

Both of them act by mobilizing their connections into a pattern of social choreography. Tasks are entrusted to those with whom they have the appropriate links, and who owe them some obligation. It is understood that a return request may in due course be made. All these negotiations are conducted with a diplomatic *politesse*, but each proposal is supported by a socially underwritten sense of what is proper, and a concern to maintain a warm field of mutual rapport, and thus carries more force than is apparent at first sight.

By early-modern European standards, the late-imperial Chinese world was relatively free of any ingrained sense of guilt or self-disgust, though exceptions can be found, and such practices as the examination of one's conscience and confessions were not unknown. In general, though, the person was worth cherishing and preserving. This was evident in the Confucian goal of refining one's character throughout one's lifetime, and the somewhat more Daoist concern with the cultivation of physical health—sometimes to a point that can seem to us hypochondriacal—and the quest for longevity.

Chinese believed that qualities of character had physical correlates that were hard to counterfeit. When Seafarer Lin has been obliged by circumstances to "make a pretence of Confucian elegance" in the land of the cultivated Black Teeth, he observes as he recovers, "Who would have thought that merely trying to put on airs would have given me backache, blurred vision, a sore neck, a dizzy head, a parched tongue, and a dried-out mouth?" (JHY 19:131) Conversely, defects of personality are liable to lead to bodily deformity. Those who are lazy and greedy develop lumps in their breasts; gluttonous fisherfolk grow preternaturally long arms; and the heads of the winged people swell "from their love of compliments and flattery." (JHY 27:191) Ideally, at least, moral worth is physically visible, as is illustrated by the Country of the Great, where people ride on clouds whose color corresponds to their inner nature. Shame is a pressure for self-reform, since "a black cloud is shameful." (JHY 14:91)

The author of the *Flowers*—and so, presumably, many of his readers—was obsessed with diet, medicines, and health. Tea is attacked as a slow-acting poison. Herbal remedies are listed with all their ingredients and proper proportions. Physical exercise is extolled, so long as it is done in the proper way. The wrong style and use of inner energy, and a faulty posture, can, on the other hand, be debilitating. (JHY 79:586) The effects of 'burn-out', a real danger in a society already overcompetititive, are warned against by Duo in a passage on the Land of the Intelligent:

> "They are addicted to astrology, divination, trigonometrical calculations, ... and every kind of mechanical art. They compete against each other, and take risks to come off best. They use all their mental powers in their determination to surpass others, with anxious thoughts and ill-intentioned cogitations.... From the beginning of the day to its end they are only concerned with scheming until, eventually, the forces of their minds are worn out.... For this reason none of them reaches a great age." (JHY 32:229)

Another cautionary tale is that of the Land of the Worried, who fear that falling asleep will prove fatal, and go to the greatest and most painful lengths to stay awake, eventually perishing "like lamps that have used up their oil." Tang the Roamer resolves, after hearing this, that he will "banish all care from this time on, and, with the relaxed attitude that comes from content, live for many more years." (JHY 27:193–94) The Chinese were unashamedly concerned with looking after themselves both physically and mentally.

Society

The Chinese of late-imperial times could also look at themselves with an anthropological self-awareness. Li Ruzhen caricatured the society of his day. Sometimes he does this directly in the form of his fictitious societies 'beyond the seas'. At other times he has the members of these exotic societies use Chinese theoretical standards to pass critical comments on actual Chinese practice. The tragic vision is not as deep as that in the last part of *Gulliver's Travels*, nor is the ideological subversion as radical as that of the *Lettres persanes*, but there is more than a little of the nature of both of these works in his pages.

His perception of cultural relativity is apparent in the account of the visit that Tang, Lin, and Duo make to the Land of Women, where physical differences between the sexes are the same as elsewhere, but everything else is reversed: dress, social and economic roles, and political power. When Tang comments that women in men's clothes seem to him a "perversion," Duo retorts, "I only fear that when they look at us they'll say, for their part, that *we* don't make very good women, and are perverted in playing the roles of men." (JHY 32:231) Almost immediately afterwards, they are warned by a male 'woman' that their impropriety risks causing them to be flogged half to death. Li's point is that while conventions may be culturally arbitrary, they can be dangerous if not respected.

Li's disgust at the way women were turned into merely pretty objects without being permitted a full personality, or control over what happened to their bodies, is displayed in his account of what happens to Lin when he is captured for the female 'king's' harem. His feet are bound, his ears are pierced, his intimate bodily functions monitored by palace 'maids' with moustaches, and he is tortured—including by being hung upside down—until his spirit is broken and he submits to the degrading process of being beautified for the royal bed. (JHY 33–34:237–41) In the Country of Gentlemen, one Confucian worthy comments on footbinding: "I thought these girls had in all likelihood committed some improper action, and that their mothers, unable to bear putting them to death, had therefore used this method to punish them. Who would have thought that it was done to make them *beautiful* to look at?!" (JHY 12:78)

Other social vices—as Li defines them—are attacked in the *Flowers*, some predictable, others less so. Thus, in the eyes of the Confucians of the Country of Gentlemen, both the stepmother and the widower who self-indulgently marries her, are figures of evil:

> "She falsely accuses the [deceased former wife's] daughter of not listening to her instructions, or she falsely accuses the [previous wife's] son of disobeying her.... She lays every sort of trap.... How can one count the numbers who have died from such ordeals ... or perished from a broken heart?" (JHY 12:77)

Likewise, the habit of dedicating children to be celibate monks and nuns undermines the perpetuation of the family, runs contrary to the proper pattern for the mating of the sexes, and leads to adulterous liaisons by the majority who have no religious vocation. Li is haunted by the fear that uncontrolled sexuality will dissolve the bonds of society, and he denounces the female confidence tricksters, saleswomen, midwives, and others who arrange covert sexual affairs—since in China, even an affair needed a go-between. (JHY 12:76)

Other targets for his satire are snobbery, hypocrisy, and the quest for social prestige. The dishonesty behind the external *politesse*, the manners linked to a surface show of morality, is symbolized by the Country of the Two-Faced. The visible countenance of these people is charming, at least toward those who are elegantly dressed, but they have a second set of features at the back, hidden under a scarf, with rat-like eyes, a hawk-like nose, a frown of disgust for anyone not judged important, and a mouth spewing foul vapor. (JHY 25:178–79) The waste of money on banquets in the interests of conspicuous ostentation, rather than delectable cuisine for the pleasure of the guests, offends Li, and he has one of his Confucians conclude that "in the end it will become impossible to afford even a single banquet. One will be obliged to roast pearls, boil jades, simmer gold, or stew silver for the *pièce de résistance*." (JHY 12:76) Lying disgusts him, and he has Duo the Helmsman observe that liars have become so numerous since the passing of the Golden Age that the regular hell cannot hold them all, and that they have since been reincarnated—the worst cases only excepted—in a new location called Pigsnout Land, where they have the snouts of pigs and live on slop. (JHY 27:192) Many of these criticisms coincide with those made by Arthur Smith, one of the sharpest of missionary observers, in his *Chinese Characteristics*.[11]

Li was moved by what might be called 'the romance of kinship', a feeling so little known in the West that there is no word for it. It is a delight among the Chinese to extend the network of one's relations, whether through marriage, adoption, the rediscovery of long-lost kin, or sworn brotherhood or sisterhood. The ever expanding sorority of the flower-spirits takes particular pleasure in always sitting at banquets in the proper order of seniority, with the same partners always next to each other, except on the rare and precious occasions when a new member has been added. (JHY 53:397, 62:458) The abuse that corresponds to this delight is the forging of spurious kinship bonds. Li denounces the prevalent vice of neglecting one's poorer relatives, and creating fictitious relationships with the powerful and the well-to-do, as a form of social climbing, which is now, says one of his characters, "a common practice." (JHY 39:275)

Finally, Li was convinced that animals, no less than people, were moral beings. His travelers on one occasion save some mermaids and are later rescued from a fire attack on their ship by these, or similar beings, repaying a debt of gratitude. He therefore deplores the butchering of beasts for food, especially the plow oxen to whom farmers owe so much, and describes it as an act that lays up a heavy burden of bad karma for its perpetrators. (JHY 12:74–75; 26:185–86)

Politics

The ideal Chinese state was one in which social status and moral worth were publicly labeled, and the ruler was the supreme labeling authority. This is both portrayed and gently satirized in the Land of the Pure Scholars. Here all respectable citizens have passed at least one public examination and wear the dress of men of letters, subdivided by colors according to grade. Most of the houses are adorned by placards, bestowed by the king, on which golden characters proclaim such legends as 'Understanding the Scriptures, Filial and Frugal'. A few bear black lettering and announce such themes as 'Reforming Our Faults and Renewing Ourselves'. These latter, the travelers learn from an old man, can only be removed if "the neighbors in the district where they live submit a petition on their behalf, or if the officials determine the facts of the case by a public enquiry." (JHY 4:170) Here is that mania for moralism that gripped the Chinese mind in its Confucian mode, the importance of group approval in giving it effect, and the assumption that it was the state's obligation to define and induce in its subjects a sort of externally supported conscience.

The public-service examinations became an obsession with the educated classes, a romance and an agony that combined the individual quest for glory, the state's praiseworthy search for talented and upright officials, and the excitement of a sporting occasion. When the girl-scholar Honghong tells Servant of the Tang that in the Land of the Black Teeth success in the examinations depends on social position and intrigue, the latter is shocked and assures her friend that this never happens in China. "If anyone were to obtain a place by means of intrigue," she avers, "that would inevitably entail doing wrong to someone of real talent. If this were to happen, how would posterity be able to flourish?" (JHY 51:378) Li Ruzhen then devotes the next thirty pages or so to describing an examination fraud in China. The brilliant but elderly Mrs. Black flouts the age restrictions for the women's examinations and takes first place at the prefectural level, but has then to feign sickness in order to avoid being detected. What is typical of Li's treatment of these events is the way in which indirect cynical comment on the true state of affairs, and hints about why China may be decaying, are interwoven with an implied defence of these examinations as, above all, a way of determining the moral character of the candidates, and not, in the first instance, their knowledge. The two examiners are shown to be skilled readers of the heart, and sensitive to Mrs. Black's "concentrated truthfulness and expression of experience" that "did not seem to come from the hand of a young person." (JHY 56:417) As so often, Li's criticisms serve an idealistic conservatism.

The actual process of politics was thought of in terms of the interaction of a leader and the masses. There was no ideologically acceptable form of opposition. At most, subordinates could venture loyal protests on grounds of principle. Examples of both good and bad leadership, and of hostile and favorable popular response, can be found in the episode where Tang tries to have Lin released from the harem of the 'king' of the country of Women.

He begins by stirring up a crowd with promises of what he can do for their flood-stricken country as a water-control expert. "If you want the waterways to be controlled," he declares to them, "you must go to the Court and appeal there with your tears. If he is set free, I shall start the work at once." The mob gives a great shout and moves off to the palace. (JHY 35:247) Lust for Lin the Seafarer has, however, diminished the 'king's' sense of responsibility for her subjects' welfare. She orders the 'Royal Uncle' to lie to the masses. 'He' tells them it is too late. The marriage has been consummated. They are not convinced and begin to enter the palace. The 'king' then turns on them:

> Stirred by an impulse of hatred ... she ordered the commandant on duty to exterminate the mob as rebels without further ado ... No sound was heard but the thundering of muskets and cannon ... [but] the throng of commoners was in no mood to back off....

> The 'Royal Uncle' saw that the situation created by the people might become ... a rebellion. So she told the troops ... not to hurt anyone. Then she repeatedly urged the commoners with these words:
>
> "You must disperse. I shall of course present your case to 'His Majesty' on your behalf and make sure that the person who took down the proclamation [offering a reward for solving the flood problem] will be detained here to repair the waterways...."
>
> When the crowd heard this, they slowly scattered. (JHY 35:248)

The public-spirited leadership given by Tang evokes, in contrast, an enthusiastic mass response:

> Since they had been afflicted by flooding for year after year, the inhabitants of the entire country came to contribute their efforts when the work was started.... Tang gave the directions and supervised the operations. When the common people saw that he rose early in the morning and returned late, making painful efforts day and night, they were moved to admiration. Before long a few old 'men' subscribed money to have an image made of Tang. A shrine to a living person was set up for him, on which they erected an inscription in large golden characters that read 'To whom the marshlands pay their tribute and whose mastery is acknowledged by the rivers'. (JHY 36:256)

Here, long before Chinese communism, is the paradigm of the ideal of Chinese communist leadership, both in its justification as being 'for the service of the people' and its cult of personality. On the darker side, this episode also contains several choice examples of bland-faced Chinese administrative lying. Thus the 'Royal Uncle' tells Tang that "Your relative [Lin] suddenly caught a severe illness while selling her goods in the palace.... The talk about 'her' having been made a Royal Consort is a lie spread about by the lower orders of society." (JHY 35:251) It is not surprising that the people are shown as disinclined to believe what their rulers say to them.

The Discipline System

Traditional China, seen from a Western perspective, lacked a social and an intellectual dimension—that of law, justice, and jurisprudence. Courts had little conception of the weighing and testing of evidence. Conviction required confession; and—unless protected by privileged status—accused and witnesses were tortured. There was no legal profession in the sense of qualified advocates who were heard by courts on behalf of litigants. Those who offered advice outside the courtrooms were regarded as social nuisances. In practice, the contents of a great part of the 'law' and of 'legal' precedents were inaccessible to those who were not officials. Subjects of the emperor were not equal before the law, such as it was, and this was most notably the case as regards seniors and juniors in a kinship structure.

The objective of the system was not justice—a term for which there is no satisfactory traditional Chinese translation—but social discipline and the maintenance of the social structure, as it is with the rules governing a Western army, school, or church.[12] Those who came nearest to pursuing justice in China were the so-called knights-errant, who were moved by a "public-spirited righteousness" and "a heart-mind set on the Way of the General Good." (JHY 60:444) They were, almost by definition, impulsive and heroic beings outside the established system of social discipline.

There is only one trial in the *Flowers*. Two immortals pass judgement on Sinful Dragon for abducting Little Hill, the daughter of Tang the Roamer, and on Great Oyster for inciting him to do so. The case is too intricate for summary here, and in any case a fantasy. What is interesting is that it shows common ground between the West and China in the concept of the offenses committed, namely abduction, incitement to abduct, and the corruption of the mind of another, while different standards are applied to the different creatures over whom Heaven rules. The Oyster, we learn, was motivated by the desire to be revenged for his son, murdered and robbed of his pearl by "the filial daughter of the Lian family" so it could be presented as a gift to Tang after he had saved her life. Only at the trial does the Oyster learn, belatedly, that Heaven has been using the girl as Its means of executing his son, whose gluttony had made him "the bane of the sea creatures." (JHY 45:330–31) Both the girl, who was unaware that Heaven was using her, and the Oyster had culpable intent; and the Oyster had arguably better grounds for mitigation of sentence; but they are treated differently, only the latter being punished. Heaven, like the emperor, was more concerned with discipline than fairness.

Technology and Economics

A delight in technology runs through the *Flowers*. Duo steers across the ocean with a magnetic compass. Several warriors carry the 'linked-pearls musket', a kind of primitive machine gun. (JHY 95:731) The 'king' of the Country of Women consults a striking clock to see if it is time for her nuptial banquet with Seafarer Lin. Seagoing ships, chronometers, and firearms were European speci-alities in early modern times. They were not, however, European monopolies.

The Chinese were proud of what they saw as their technological superiority to other nations, and the notion of Chinese technical assistance to less advanced peoples took Li Ruzhen's fancy. In the Country of Women, Tang the Roamer teaches the female inhabi-tants how to make cast-iron tools and delivers a lecture on hydrau-lics. He explains that "when one wishes to use the flow of the wa-ter to scour away the silt deposited in a waterway, its course must be as straight as an arrow. Only then can the silt be carried down-stream with the current.... Where you want it to be scoured away, the watercourse must become narrower, ... and have a downward gradient." He explains that it is a common error to think that "the wider it is, the more freely it will flow," since in fact "when water flows from narrow places to broad ones, it spreads itself and loses its power." (JHY 36:255) There follows a detailed account of the method of dredging using temporary cross-dikes and baskets on pulleys for hauling up the mud removed.

Ingenious machinery had a romantic appeal. When Flowerlike has to return in a hurry to the Country of Women to become its new monarch, she and three companions travel in 'flying carriages':

> [The pilots] raised the keys and set the mechanism in motion. All that could be seen were copper wheels, some upright, some horizontal, turning furiously. Some were the size of millstones, others of pulley-wheels. [The carriages] seemed like pinwheels,[13] and each one rose up

spinning. In an instant they were a few feet off the ground. Then they rose straight up to a height of more than a hundred feet and headed due west. (JHY 94:722)

The romance falls under the shadow of the awareness that changes in China's accustomed technology could have disruptive economic effects. Pleasant muses: "If I could get hold of a flying carriage, then—if I wanted to go somewhere—I wouldn't have to stop for a meal or stay overnight in hostels." Little Spring then observes that "if this were so, the assistants in the hostels would have nothing to live on." (JHY 66:486–87)

For Li, economics was a zero-sum game. One person's gain was another's loss. He does not conceive of the possibility of a general progress, sustaining itself with internal positive feedback. In Shaman Land, for example, we learn that the people had originally dressed in cotton, but that two girls had then arrived bringing with them silkworm eggs and the techniques of silk manufacture. Since the country has an abundance of mulberry trees, silk production has expanded, and families who once lived by producing cotton now face bankruptcy. The travelers save the life of one of the girls who has introduced sericulture, when she is attacked by a man ruined (he says) by these "poisonous worms" and the spread of "these evil arts." "Half of the households that used to grow [cotton]," he tells them, "have lost the livelihood that they possessed for generations past." (JHY 28:198)

This passage, with its humor based on inversion—silk, a luxury item, becoming a social scourge by becoming commonplace—also expresses the view that circumstances determine value. Seafarer Lin expounds the merchant's philosophy that, wherever one is, "one has to look and see what they're short of, and make those items expensive." For Lin, as for most Chinese businessmen, the essence of trade is arbitrage, not a regular relationship; and the highest skill is the opportunism that lets one "get an advantage without making an effort to do so." (JHY 32:230–31; 20:139)

Scholarship

In some respects late-traditional Chinese scholarship was like a certain type of television quiz. It required memorizing vast amounts of information, and to a great degree the answers were thought of as being either right or wrong. Exchanges between scholars, though conducted with surface politeness, were covertly aimed at establishing an academic pecking order, and could be enjoyed by the onlookers as a form of intellectual fencing match.

The *Flowers* is obsessed with scholarship, and the reader is entertained with competitions like that between Helmsman Duo and Tingting over the pronunciations of a certain Chinese character. (JHY 16:111–12) But behind these displays of erudition, Li has a serious purpose. He is telling his reader to value the argument, and not the social standing of the person who puts it forth, and also to approach the scriptures with an open mind, using reason rather than authority to unravel their meaning. He drives this point home by repeatedly using Tingting, who is young, foreign, and female, as well as having a black face (all aspects of a manifest inferiority according to the notions of this time) to discomfit Duo, who is elderly, Chinese, male, and the holder of an academic degree. When Duo cannot disprove her contention that characters were pronounced differently in ancient times,[14] the best riposte he can make only causes him to appear ludicrous:

> "You would have to find some men from ancient times so that I could talk with them, and hear what sort of a pronunciation they really had.... If not, your lofty theory will have to wait till that time in the future when you have discovered some people from the past and spoken with them." (JHY 17:115)

Even more important is Li's rational approach to the Confucian scriptures as historical documents. His attitude, typical of much eighteenth-century scholarship, was the first stage in an unintended process of desacralization that began long before modern Western ideas began to impinge upon Chinese culture. An example of this orientation can be found in the dispute between Duo and Tingting over how to gloss a sentence in the *Analects*, namely, "Yan Lu asked Confucius for his carriage, so that he could make it into a *guo* [the term at issue]."

> *Duo* (smiling): All the commentators, ancient and modern, say that when Yan Yuan [Confucius's favorite pupil] died, his father Yan Lu was too poor *to buy an outer coffin*. He asked Confucius *to sell his carriage* so that he could buy one. They all say this. On what do you need instruction?
>
> *Tingting*: Although Confucian scholars from former times explain it like this, do you have an alternative view, eminent worthy?
>
> *Duo*: In my opinion, that is all there is to it. How should I presume to make a reckless show of cleverness, or give voice to disorderly disputation on this point? ...
>
> *Tingting*: ... There would seem to be a different sense. If one explains it as Yan Lu being *too poor to buy an outer coffin*, he ought to have asked the Master for financial help. Why should he specifically indicate that he wanted him *to sell his carriage*? Is it plausible to suppose he thought there was nothing in Confucius's home, apart from this carriage, that could be sold?
>
> It's the same today. When people ask for financial help, they request assistance. How could it be proper for them to point, specifically, at the object they want someone to sell in order to furnish them with this assistance? Even a commonplace idiot wouldn't make such a remark. How much less a worthy man who was the disciple of a sage!
>
> When Confucius responded to this request he said that when previously his own son, Li, had passed away, he had only had an inner coffin and no *guo*. "I am not willing," he declared "to go on foot to provide him with one." If we interpret this according to the commentaries you've quoted, this must in the same way have referred to *selling a carriage in order to buy an outer coffin*. How could it be that when Yan Yuan died his father boldly asked for the selfsame carriage that Confucius had earlier considered selling on behalf of his own son [but had decided not to]?
>
> An outer coffin is not all that valuable or rare. Even an expensive one does not cost more than twice the price of an inner one.... What is more, the lavish burials of disciples are described in the later chapters. Why were the funds for these not used to buy an outer coffin? Why was it necessary to oblige Confucius to sell his carriage? ... On the contrary, it would seem that what was meant was *using the timbers of the carriage* to construct *an outer surround for the coffin* [as a sort of memorial]. (JHY 17:116–17, emphasis added)

Faced with this logical onslaught, Duo can only say—fatuously—

that if the meaning was not that Confucius had been asked to sell his carriage, "what need would there have been for the men of earlier times to write explanatory notes to that effect?"

Li's criticism is the discontent of the believer who still ascribes an intrinsic importance to the scriptures, and who wishes to use the powers of scholarly reason to understand them better. The potential for dissolving faith that was latent in the quest for the historical Confucius was as hidden from him as it is visible to us.

Intellectual Recreations

The educated Chinese relished amusements that challenged mind and memory. Above all they delighted in complexity, and the exercise of that mixture of literary, literal, and analogical thinking that is used in the West today to solve crossword puzzles and was used in the China of this time to unravel the so-called 'lantern riddles'. (JHY 32:229)

The supreme example of this kind of thought was the two-dimensional poetic palindrome. The Chinese language usually uses one syllable per unit of meaning, represented by a single written character. This, and the lack of inflections, makes it possible to construct matrices of characters that can be read as rhyming poems from right to left and left to right, downwards and upwards, along diagonals and around circumferences, and even alternately backwards and forwards. Li devotes almost thirty pages to his elucidation of the proper reading of the most famous of all these palindromes, the 29 x 29 word-square, with the graph for 'heart' in its center, composed in the fourth century C.E. by Lady Su Hui in the attempt to win back her husband's affections from a concubine.[15] Here, by way of illustration, are two of the shortest poems, taken from a 6 x 6 submatrix. In Chinese they consist of exactly the same characters, but read in opposite directions:

> Alas! I sigh for my cherished one
> And the norms he has forsaken!
> Distant the road, and empty.
> Wounded my inmost feelings!

> Our family—without its lord.
> Chaste the room within the curtains.
>
> Its painted splendor shining back
> —My face within the looking-glass.
> Fallen pell-mell my sparkling jewels,
> And luster gleaming from my pearls.
> But with thoughts of *him* before me—
> What price *their* glory?

Reversed, this becomes:

> What, then, is glory,
> With thoughts of him so many?
> The loveliness of my lucent pearls?
> The sparkle of my scattered jewels?
> The shining mirror that shows back
> My face embellished and bedecked?
> Loveless within, the curtained room!
> And my lord without his kin.
> Inside my feelings, deep the wound
> Empty the road that winds away.
> Through places where he was I pass,
> And in my mind-heart sigh "Alas!"
>   (JHY 41:293)

The effect is like that of shaking a kaleidoscope. And the above are but two out of an alleged two thousand coherent poems in the matrix.

But the Chinese could also think analytically. Li himself was a keen phonetician, and his characters in the *Flowers* are made to wrestle, and his readers likewise, with the deciphering of a system of phonetic 'spelling' used by the Double-Tongues. The method, when its details are finally divulged, turns out to be a grid along whose vertical and horizontal axes are characters containing all the possible initial and final sounds for the syllables of the Chinese language. The idea is not original in its essentials, going back to the Tang dynasty and having parallels in certain Morse Code–like drum signals used in Li's own day. (JHY 28–31:200–225 *passim*) What it shows is that the method of accounting for a wide range of phenomena by means of a limited set of elements plus a set of derivational rules was established in the Chinese intellectual domain before the introduction of modern science and modern logic.

Humor

Humor gains its effect by drawing attention to the ways of thought that a particular group of people have in common, but only acknowledge publicly to a limited degree, if at all. The smile or laugh evoked in response is the reaffirmation by the recipients of the humor that they share the unspoken perceptions and values of the person making the joke. The absence of the explicit statement of these assumptions is of the essence. Only by leaving what is central unmentioned, in other words 'the point' that has to be 'seen', can members of the group reassure themselves that they really see the world in the same way as each other. The need to 'explain' a joke is the symptom of a failure in communication, and it cuts, as it were, the flow of the psychological current that makes it 'funny'.[16] From a philosophical point of view, humor presents a sort of practical resolution to the problem of 'other minds', in the sense that though one cannot share someone else's pain, one can, under suitable circumstances, share a joke.

Humorous response to particular jokes is restricted to specific social groups. Much humor from an unfamiliar culture is totally inaccessible without a skilled explanation.[17] (And such explanation does not make it funny, but merely provides a certain cold understanding of how it *might* seem to be comical to those inside the other system.) Hence it is unlikely that there is any subject matter that is intrinsically and universally funny. Rather, the accessibility of a particular type of humor defines a community of communication, and its use is a form of circuit-testing of this communication. There are many such communities, and in the modern world at least they overlap, since some jokes touch on themes that are common to much of humanity, and some appeal to cross-cutting collectivities defined—for example—by a shared faith, ethnicity, sexual orientation, profession, life style, or age-group, whereas other jokes at the other end of the spectrum are restricted to a family or even to just two individuals.

The *Flowers* is a masterpiece of humor, and features a spectrum of jokes running from wordplay and tall tales through the scatological and the sexual to social satire, and the ironic self-revelation of their inner nature by the characters. At the least accessible end are forms like literary parody, and the gossamer-thin teasing backchat in which the flower-spirits reincarnated as girls engage. Let us look at samples of these various types in sequence.

Li enjoyed puns of a labored Shakespearean awfulness. In the Land of Winged People the women lay eggs (*dàn*). Seafarer Lin therefore suggests to his companions that they buy a few such man-eggs and sell them to actors on their return to China. Why actors? his friends ask. Lin explains: small eggs (*xiâo dàn*) will hatch into male theatrical impersonators of young females (*xiâo dàn*), while old eggs (*lâo dàn*) will hatch into male impersonators of old females (*lâo dàn*). (JHY 27:191)

Paul Bunyanesque extravagances were equally loved. Duo chats on one occasion with some old men who are vying with each other in telling stories about the tall men they have seen. One mentions a man with a body a thousand miles long who drank 500 gallons of the magical dew called 'celestial wine' every day. Another tells of a man so huge that he was as high as a mountain when he lay on the ground, and could block a river by simply putting his body in its way. A third says of his tall man:

> "Long ago, when a gown was made for him, he bought up all the cotton cloth in the world. What's more, every single tailor worked on it. Several years were needed for it to be finished.... One tailor stole a piece of cloth from the under-lapel, and used it to go into the cotton cloth trade instead.... This man was exactly 193,500 miles tall."

The others clamor to know how he can be so precise. He answers:

> "The men of old said that this was the height of Heaven above the Earth. When he trod on the Earth, it so happened that he reached to

Heaven.... He not only had a body this tall, but his big lips also loved to tell tall tales."

The others remain skeptical:

> "We have heard that the solid wind that constitutes Heaven's surface is extremely hard, and that birds who fly too high are blown to shreds. If this tall fellow's head reaches to Heaven, why isn't his face blown to shreds?"

The old man retorts that his giant is thick-skinned. When they demand to know how he knows, he replies:

> "If he wasn't thick-skinned, how could he spend all his time telling tall tales, and never worry that people might laugh him to shame?"

Q.E.D. In this particular case, by fortunate accident, the key words—'tall' and 'thick-skinned'—carry the same double senses in both English and Chinese. (JHY 24:138–39)

Li uses scatological humor for social criticism. In his account of the Land of the People Without Guts, there is a savage inversion of categories:

> *Duo*: Before they eat something, they first find a place where they can excrete. Once they consume, they have to shit out. It's like when you've drunk too much wine and have to 'give a return banquet' with your lower parts at once.... Once something's been ingested, it goes straight through them.... They spend huge sums on food and drink every day. You'll laugh when I tell you how rich families pare down their budgets. Because the food they gorge passes directly through their bellies, you can call it 'shit' if you like, but since it isn't retained in the gut it doesn't get putrid and smelly. That's why they store this sort of 'shit' carefully and keep it to feed their servants....
> *Lin*: Do they devour it themselves?
> *Duo*: This delicious stuff doesn't cost them a penny. How could they not be willing to do just that?
> *Tang*: ... It's going too far to make their servants of both sexes wolf down such muck.
> *Duo*: They not only oblige their servants to put up with being so poorly fed, they force them to eat *and then re-eat* shit that has gone through three or four times. Only when it hurts the servants to the point that they vomit it up, and food and shit can't be told apart, do they start the process over again from the beginning. (JHY 14:94–95)

Meals, for the Chinese, were the supreme social activity, but here they are depicted almost as a form of solitary vice.

The main sexual merriment revolves around the subject of bound female feet. Blue Brooch, trying to stop a ball that has been thrown in her direction, accidentally kicks off her shoe. After the giggles and blushes have died away, Purple Mushroom says that the shoe flying through the air reminds her of the famous tune *Floating on a Raft along the Milky Way*. This is a tease, suggesting that "Blue Brooch's honorable feet must be a couple of steersmen"— gross rather than properly petite. This provokes convulsions of mirth, and Blue Brooch retaliates. There was a gourmet once, she says. His greed caused him to be reincarnated first as a dog's lips and then as a monkey's asshole. For the latter there was only one deodorant powerful enough—*a purple mushroom*. (JHY 80:598, 81:600)

The shoe theme reappears as a joke throughout the next fifty pages, and provides material for parodies of the Confucian scriptures. The *Songs*, that venerable medley of love ditties, celebratory odes, flytings, and plaints from the early first millennium B.C.E., is mocked with this quatrain:

> Wind-borne is the vasty shoe
> O'er that bank so high.
> Uncovered is the mighty foot
> That smells so fragrantly!
> (JHY 87:653)

The *Questions to the King of Chu* is likewise mimicked:

> Nine thousand miles upwards strikes the Great Shoe,
> Clouds cleaving and rainbows,
> Ent'ring blue empyrean,
> Flying aloft above endless darkness!
> —How could a commonplace shoe
> Mark out, in this fashion, Heav'n's height above Earth?
> (JHY 87:652)

Other respected classics were also lampooned. The following spoof oracular judgement was attributed to *The Scripture of the Changes*:

> Going on sandals brings good fortune. This is the proper way of walk-ing. Flying brings ill fortune. This is lifting the feet too high. (JHY 87:653)

A furious Blue Brooch declares that "insulting the sacred words" will bring down retribution on her tormentors. One wonders if Holy Writ could have been treated in this fashion by a novelist in early Victorian Britain, though the Indian tradition seems to have had a rich vein of scriptural parody.[18]

Li also exploits the clash between the different modes of behav-ior thought appropriate for the different classes in society. When Lin sees that Tang, a scholar who has become a Daoist adept, is about to be transformed into an immortal and able to walk on air, he makes a typical merchant's remark: "Won't that save you quite a bit on shoes and socks?" (JHY 9:52) In the Land of Gentlemen traders and their customers engage in anti-bargaining. The buyer pleads to be allowed to pay more, while the seller urges his cus-tomer to pay less. (JHY 11:66–67) The point of this satire is that one cannot be a gentleman when shopping, and that there is a form of behavior appropriate to particular situations. The waiter in the teahouse who addresses his customers in the formally courteous language of the classics is merely ridiculous. (JHY 23:165)

Another conversation between Tang and Lin contrasts the im-mortal's view of the world, the scholar's search for reputation, and the practicality of the merchant. Tang has just eaten a magical red herb—the macrobiotic route to immortality—and finds that for a moment he can remember everything he has ever written:

> "I feel a pain in my stomach now," said Tang. "Why, I don't know."
> Before he had finished speaking there was a noise inside his belly, followed by a down-draught of foul vapors and a slight sound.
> "... Can you still remember the poems and essays you wrote in the past?"
> Tang hung his head and thought a moment.
> "... I can't call to mind more than a tenth of them," he confessed.
> "The nine-tenths you can't remember," said Seafarer Lin, "are that blast of foul air to which you gave vent just now. The red herb disliked their smell and expelled them. They have already revealed their true

nature and penetrated into my nose.... If, in the future, you want to have your student writings printed ... there's no need to entrust someone else with the job of making the selection. Just cut out the nine-tenths you can't remember today, and only have the printing-blocks cut for the tenth you can recall. I will bet you that those are the good ones! It's a pity this herb is so rare. If we took some home and gave it to people to eat, think how much work could be saved for the cutters of printing-blocks!" (JHY 9:54–5)

Lin's marketplace pragmatism converts the mysteries of literary criticism and of transcendental bodily transformation into a useful saving of time and money effected by farting.

The humor both of class and of character is most fully developed with respect to Lin's pretensions to scholarship. In the Land of Pure Scholars, for example, he joins a class of students being drilled by a pedant in how to write conventional antithetical couplets. The teacher has set them as their first line 'The goose in the clouds'. The students match this with uninspired offerings like 'The seagull on the water' and 'The fish under the water'. Lin is asked to contribute and suggests 'The fowling-piece shoots it down!' This is funny in that it shows up the narrowness of the accepted aesthetic conventions for this genre: Lin's line is both highly appropriate, in one sense, and in another quite unacceptable. The students press him to justify his unorthodoxy. Lin says that his second line has more of the required 'connections' with the goose in the clouds than their proposals. One student then wonders if perhaps their distinguished guest may not have been basing himself on a line from the Daoist scripture *Master Zhuang*: "Looking at the bolt of the crossbow and expecting roast owl." Lin, who has had no such reference in mind, quick-wittedly compliments him on his perception. (Li Ruzhen is here taking a swipe at what we might call 'citationism': one classical reference and all is forgiven.)

Lin then pushes his luck. No doubt, he observes, he would have baffled them had he drawn on *The Old Master*, most renowned of the Daoist scriptures, or on *The Young Master*. This latter is an invention on the spur of the moment, like a *Middle Testament* for the

Bible, perhaps. The disbelieving students will not let him go till he explains. Lin coolly concocts an imaginary scripture well suited to the title, a handbook for the well-to-do young gentleman:

> "*The Old Master* ... discussed primality, emptiness, and mysterious subtlety. Although *The Young Master* takes recreations and amusements as its matter, yet—secretly lodged within it—is the intention of urging people to goodness. [This is a dig at the cant with which books of pornography like *The Prayermat of Flesh* justified themselves: the reader, surfeited with images of fleshly indulgence, would come to see them as illusion through a sort of aversion therapy.]... It contains a full account of famous personalities, flora and fauna, calligraphy and painting, the seven-stringed zither, Chinese chess, medicine, divination, astrology and prediction based on the physiognomy, not to mention the Tang-dynasty rhymes for poetry, and methods for doing calculations. It has in addition all sorts of riddles of the type written on lampshades with prizes for the answers, every kind of game and forfeit for wine-drinking parties, as well as the Double-Six board-game for two players racing black and white wooden horses with dice, the four-handed tablet-game Madiao [a forerunner of Mahjong], target-shooting, football, ... pitching arrows into a pot for forfeits, and every type of diversion able to banish the Demon of Sleepiness, and make people spit out their food with laughter. I've brought a lot of these books along with me. If you don't disdain to soil your eyes with them, I'll slip back to my ship to fetch them." (JHY 23:164–65)

Human nature triumphs over pretensions to scholarly purity. They eagerly let him go, and he escapes. The reader meanwhile smiles at the understanding he shares with Lin of the true character of young men.

On another occasion Lin boasts that it was his ability to repress his fiery sexual urges that saved him from the 'king' of the Country of Women. Had the marriage been consummated, his friends could not have secured his release from the harem. Tang the Roamer, with mock solemnity, likens him to Hui of Liuxia, whose legendary self-restraint was such that a homeless girl could sit safely on his lap all night. Lin then congratulates himself on having kept off alcohol during his captivity in the 'king's' palace, although wine is normally his "lifeline." Tang compares him to the sage-king Yu, who banned the best-quality liquor for fear that it might besot one of his successors on the throne. Still unaware that he is being teased, Lin next brags that though the female 'king' loaded him with jewels, he looked on them as mere "shit." Bravo! says Tang, just like Wang Yan, who was famed for never letting the word 'money' pass his lips, even when his exasperated wife built a wall of coins around their bed. Last of all, Lin vaunts himself for having endured the "devilish torments" of having his ears pierced, his feet bound, and being flogged—routine afflictions for women at this time, and which the reader will remember had caused Lin to scream. "I don't imagine," he adds nonetheless, "that you could find many men from ancient times who could have endured this sort of humiliation as I did." With feigned awe, Tang draws a parallel with a renowned general who, when his brothers spat on him, just let the spittle dry on his face. Duo adds, mischievously, that Lin is certain to become an immortal now. Perhaps his title will be 'The Bound-Foot Immortal'? (JHY 38:266–67) The tendency to self-deluding self-aggrandizement that is satirized here was regarded by the modern writer Lu Xun as a serious defect in the Chinese character, and one he attacked in his famous story of the layabout Ah Q.

The *badinage* engaged in by the young ladies is more subtle and difficult to capture. A heavy-handed example will have to suffice. One of them criticizes Little Spring for her habit of making difficulties for those who overuse conventional phrases: "If one remarks to her 'Oh, we must have met in a previous life,' she is sure to reply, 'Then it must have been at the gates of hell.'" (JHY 62:458) This is less nasty than it would be in a Christian context, since the Buddhist and Daoist hells were only temporary purgatories, not permanent. In another joke about hell, a drunkard's spewing and puking is described as so revolting the Infernal Officials that they send him back to the world above to go on living. When his relieved wives adjure him to reform, he tells them they are mistaken: "If I become sober, I'll die!" (JHY 93:715)

Most of the anecdotes depend for their effect on a specifically Chinese cultural component that has to be understood if they are to raise a smile. Thus Purple Mushroom tells a tale about a disobedient donkey. Not only won't he budge when his impatient master lashes him, but strikes out in all directions with his hooves. "Isn't it more than enough," says the disgusted man, "that you won't get a move on, but have to play guess-fingers with me as well?" This is a visual pun in words. The donkey's flailing kicks are compared to the game of guess-fingers in which the participants thrust out various numbers of fingers at the same time, and at great speed, while simultaneously guessing aloud the total number of fingers shown by all those playing. (JHY 85:579)

At a more philosophical level is Starbright's deflation of the empty profundities of some Zen masters. She recounts the story of a Confucian pedant who visits the hermitage of a celebrated monk. The monk does not rise to greet him, and the pedant is offended. "Your attainments in the Way are profound," he observes, "so you should understand proper behavior." "In my *not* rising," answers the monk, "is contained an essential point of Zen.... My *not* standing up *is* my standing up." The pedant then gives the monk a furious thwack on his bald pate. "Why, Sir, do you strike me?" asks the monk. "I, too, have an essential point of Zen," murmurs the pedant. "When I strike you, that is my *not* striking you." (JHY 85:637) It is worth recording, with respect to the communities that are defined by humor, that a Japanese professor—a serious Zen Buddhist—to whom I told this story did not see it as a joke but as an anecdote with a serious religious point.

Li Ruzhen's sense of the comic is thus extraordinarily varied, reflecting almost all the types of humor found in life. He does not, however, like Montesquieu, mock the foundations of conventional faith,[19] nor is he haunted, as was Dean Swift, by the all but irremediable inadequacies of mankind.[20] Beneath his laughter lies a respect for the Confucian pieties and proprieties, and deeper still a Daoist vision of the universe and our lives in it as a sort of endless riddle, whose clues are a web of predestined affinities hidden from most people's sight for most of the time. What his work does show us, however, is that the educated Chinese of late-imperial times could look at themselves with an element of both self-criticism and of an almost anthropological self-understanding.

CHAPTER TWO

Unseen Lives

U NLIKE THE ELITE, the common people have almost
no one to speak for them. They are easy to forget. Yet
the massiveness of their presence bends every line that runs
through the social space-time of China. If we are not to have a per-
vasively false impression of China and the Chinese we have to find
some way of giving them a voice.

The two thousand or so pieces in *Our Dynasty's Bell of Poesy*
provide a partial if indirect answer to the problem. Although they
are written by literati, they touch on aspects of life that, so far as
we can tell, touched most Chinese deeply. If the reader can be patient with their awkwardnesses, their simplicities, and their sentimentality, they open a window into the heart.

The contexts in which they were written vary. Some were written to soften the attitudes of officials. Others, like those against
female infanticide, were designed as propaganda. Others were
meant to serve as memorials of events, or as descriptions of interesting customs, and found an appropriate home in local gazetteers.
Many were the simple upwelling of emotion. Their language is
workaday literary Chinese, seasoned with occasional erudite refer-
ences. They are not in the diction of the common people. Compared with the earlier poets of the middle empire who wrote about
the lives of ordinary people, writers such as Nie Yizhong and Du
Xunhe, and Du Fu, the greatest of them all, there is a detectable
shift in emotional tonality. To me, this change feels like a movement from a sympathy that is without much real understanding to
an empathy that is possessed of an acute understanding, even if it

may at times lack warmth, probably because of its sense of realities. Several scholars whose views I respect dispute this interpretation of the change. One symptom that perhaps argues in favor of my intuition is the new and not infrequent tension between the writer's sense of identification with his humble subject matter and his awareness as an educated person of the need to take a wider and more ideologically proper view from the outside, with corresponding shifts in tone as one or the other perspective dominates.

Almost all of the poems rhyme, and a translation without rhyme falsifies them. Faced with the difficulties of the English language, which is as short of rhymes as Chinese abounds in them, I have therefore used vowel rhymes on the final stressed syllables as a substitute. As an illustration of this technique we can take the following translation of Zhang Yun'ao's *Selling a Daughter* (GCSD 17:567), with the vowel rhymes in bold type to show the ABAB pattern:

> The little girl is seven years old,
> Born and raised in a thatched hut.
> Her daddy died a year ago.
> Her mother cannot bring her up.
>
> Girls sell for several strings of cash
> —Enough for more supplies of gruel.
> You get some money in your hands
> —Lose someone who is part of you.
>
> The girl's tears fill a palm's inside,
> The mother's money two palms, cupped.
> Before her daughter's tears are dry,
> The mother's money's all used up.

No similarly simple technical solution is available for rendering the effect of the five-syllable or seven-syllable lines that form crystalline structures of extreme regularity in most of the poems. The mid-line caesura—most commonly after the fourth syllable in seven-syllable lines—has, however, been reproduced in most of the translations that follow. An example is the *Tea-plucking Song* by the poetess Wu Lan below (GCSD 6:179), in which the break, read as a momentary pause, is marked by a vertical bar '|' :

Daughter of folk in the mountains, | her raven hair coiled at her
　　temples,
She picks the new leaves from the shrubs, | before, and then after, the
　　showers.
The pools in the rock-bounded streams | seem like mirrors that,
　　shaking, unsteady,
Reflect, as she wades through their ripples, her face |—like a flower.

Before a full basket's been plucked, | she releases a long drawn-out
　　sigh.
To whom can she speak of the pain | of these three long months of the
　　spring?
Whenever she offers her tea | to grand households, they won't meet
　　her price.
Yet for leaves for one bowl of 'Spring Snow' | she must roam through a
　　thousand hills.

Where the reading rhythm is not immediately obvious, I have
sometimes used a long dash '—' to show a mid-line or other pause.

By strict standards the translations are free, and incorporate,
where useful, both glosses by the original authors and my own
amplifications.

Patterns of Peasant Expectation

At the back of each peasant's mind there was the ideal of a
prosperous normality in which seasonal weather and seasonal activities were interwoven with a sequence of festivals. This was but-
tressed with the concept of a political order that was beyond his
power to change in its essentials, and that he accepted, even if with
no enthusiasm, provided it was administered with fairness. Something of this vision is expressed in a versified farmer's calendar for
the southernmost province, Guangdong, written by Xu Rong
(GCSD 5:150-2). It is a testament to the bedrock beliefs of the
Chinese as to proper human relationships with nature, with each
other—whether dead, living, or unborn—and with the gods:

First Moon
The wind rising out of the east takes us into the coming year.
The life-breath from off the sea blows through the leaves' mild greens,

Over the hazy expanses of coastal salt-rice fields,
And groups of cottages crouched—under their banyan trees.

The thirteenth-day lamps are lit. Our neighbors have come together
To drink of the new-warmed wine for those who have new-born sons.
The old men, under the city walls, are foretelling this year's harvest,
Watching the beans—tossed into the air—and the rice of varying colors.

This year the pottery ox is stuffed, full up with the lucky yellow.
—No need to pick out the popcorn puffs to determine what's to come.

We must see that the soil by the roots of the trees has been thoroughly
    turned over,
Take care that a proper job's been made of fixing up the sluices.
From the almanac a lucky day will tomorrow have to be chosen
For sending our son off to take his place in our community school.

We farmers, too, are preoccupied, from this time of the year forwards.
So swiftly past the days fly by, they seem to be importunate.

The use of the pronoun 'we' is a translator's choice. It would be
equally proper as a translation to use 'they', and to treat the poem
as a description from the outside, but the poet's local chauvinism,
which is particularly explicit in the stanzas for twelfth lunar month
(translated below), supports opting for an insider's perspective.
Other points to note are that the 'pottery ox' was carried in a procession to welcome the spring, and that during the 'Rainwater' period, in the second half of the first lunar month, rice was roasted in
an iron pan and people would pick out puffs as a way of telling
their fortune for the year ahead.

Second Moon

The Earth God's Sacrifice Master moves through the fields in
    procession,
Not tasting the water pertaining to the clay spring ox of last year;
But now, as the dawn is breaking, he drinks the new shower's
    refreshment
And in their fullness the hidden springs of the life-force are released.

The lines of pottery basins are laid there in preparation,
Now that the moment has come for steeping the seeds in nutrients.
There go the ducks' heads, quacking, moving across the lake,
And swallows wheeling, in serried groups, above the mud in platoons.

When, on the south-facing slopes, the wheat stands ready for reaping,
And the high-lying fields must be soaked, to receive the early rice,
Once the spring plowing is over, hand-harrowing's also needed.
Long ago, already—books say—this was what life was like.

Ox of last year! Your vital force has still not been destroyed,
But finds its end in this glory—in this surge of life's resumption.
They are calling—do you not hear them?—Those are the wood-pigeons'
    voices
Answering one to another one, in the deep-shaded cotton shrubs.

The Sacrifice Master did not drink 'old water' on the day of the
ceremony in order to ensure (by these magical means) that it would
rain.

Third Moon

The spring will not be warm—until the equinox—
Our rice will not be sturdy—until transplanted out.
How swiftly the Visit to the Graves, and the Cold Food Feast, come
    on.
In paddy after paddy we transfer our seedling sprouts.

We load our fertilizer up—into the plain wooden tubs,
We carry our rice-plants out in trugs, plaited from yellow withies.
Each bunch is given a dip, and then it is pushed in upright.
The rows lie aligned in patterns, faultless in their precision.

With backs stooped over and bent, like cranes with heads down
    pecking,
We are anxious at every instant lest we strain a muscle or joint.
Our families come out to be with us, when the noon sun's overhead.
Up drifts the aroma of fish, from the rice that they have boiled.

The better-off among us own several yoke of buffalo.
So hiring a plow-team by the day costs little, and is effective.
Nothing is sweeter than work done briskly, without the need to
    struggle.
When one eats from one's own exertions, no other taste's so relished.

The spring visit to the graves up in the hills was the time when the
family reported the year's happenings to the ancestors and ate a
meal of cold food.

Fourth Moon

Once the Plow's-Tail and Pig's-Tail stars have gone,[1] we sow in the hilly
    land,
But do not plant in the tidal fields—till the start of the rainy season.
Then punts, with seedlings on board, move down to the flooded
    paddies,
But have hardly come before they've left, they work at such a speed.

One household's hardly finished—with boiling their salt from brine,
When another's scythed the foreshore clear, where the grasses grew, for
    hay.
Limitless the horizon seems, opening out on all sides,
And foaming the trampling crests of the waves—like thousands of acres
    of snowplain.

The silt-fields' tenants' leader, puffed up with his self-importance,
Gives sharp, and strict, instructions for all of their activities:
They must sprinkle lime, to deter the crabs, at the time the tide's
    withdrawn,
So neither they—nor the molluscs either—damage the rice with their
    mischief.

They offer up pig's pettitoes to the Wife of Grains, their goddess,
And drunk on her afflatus, their spirits swell delighted.
Next year, when settling sediment has formed new silt-deposits,
Singing, and swinging lanterns, they will thank her for her kindness.

The Wife of Grains may have been the mother of the god of agriculture. The peasants are said to have had the custom of "setting up
pavilions and presenting limitless offerings."[2] In some writers the
last verse would be ironical, and a mockery of popular superstition,
since the deposition of alluvium was a natural event for which no
god needed thanking; but Xu Rong seems to have been writing in a
celebratory mode, not a critical one.

Fifth Moon

The fifth moon is for weeding, so—we make our way out
Among the stalks of rice grown tall—each one to an equal height,
While, ever restless, the wind—has swept the sky of clouds
And in each field the water is like a clear glaze, shining.

The sun is above us now, burning down on our backs.
Below we're submerged in mud. It swallows our upper legs.

The colorless rain comes suddenly, dousing us with its splattering,
And so our bodies are cooked—in each others' steam—instead.

How can I show you how it is? How bring to life this scene
Where we do not dare feel weary, our task no matter how hopeless.
From those who pass by on the road we get no pitying feelings,
Nor do we seek of the bureaucrats that *they* take any notice.

Then one among us turns. He says to his eldest boy:
"This field here's yours, your inheritance, that your ancestors bestowed.
They wanted no more for you than this: that you get your chance to toil
A lifetime here, as *you* see *me*, laboring at this moment."

The complex of emotions in the last verse expresses the intertwining of an individual's belonging to the land, and to his ascendants and descendants, and his commitment to a certain way of working, a technology, and his socially acknowledged right to do so. Property was more than the simple commercial commodity that it has become in modern times.

Sixth Moon

Before the mid-point of the year, the first of our harvests' completed.
We can see that our yields this year will be—a little better than usual.
Where the rivers flow together, the lychee-trees are sweetening,
And water-chestnuts, and lotus-roots, are growing in profusion.

Precious beyond any lucre, the worth of a farmland's fruits!
In furrow on furrow, on furrow, across all the width of our acres
Both Mild-Warmth and Great-Warmth Rices are flourishing
    luxuriously,
Each ear is hanging bowed down, half-seen in the haze of daybreak.

We have sickled and gathered in. What joy this labor is over!
We sample our new-cut crop. We do just whatever we like.
The taro-frames by the wall that is facing the east are opened,
And we focus our thoughts on the taro's taste, eaten chopped up with
    rice.

It's the honor of modest folk, like us, to know how much is enough.
What need do we have for dishes that reek of onions and meat?
Small economy after economy leads to a constant abundance.
*Heaven-Nature can more than meet its match in the efforts of
    human beings.*

The last sentence speaks of the active, even aggressive, attitude taken in practice by Chinese toward the environment before modern times, whatever archaic philosophy may have said about restraint and harmony.

Seventh Moon

The best grain has to be paid away, into the government's granaries.
The next best that is taken's to fill private granges up,
The gleanings forgotten, out of doors, lying there in the paddies;
And when we feed the cranes—why even they grow plump!

Everyone munches long'ans and betel, for the Feast of the Hungry
    Ghosts.
In one village after another the boys—shrill Harvest-Home reed
    whistles.
But how can it ever come to be—that farmwork's really over?
Plowing for our second crop has still to be persisted with.

We soften the straw by soaking it, we separate out the rice-shoots,
And savor, too, the cloudless sun, still shining here above us.
How soon before autumn winds blow in? How soon before their
    coolness
Does battle with the lingering warmth—of our ebbing Indian summer?

The resin-scented cypress trees cast their criss-crossing shadows,
Over brooks flowing by for several miles, unmuddied and undisturbed,
While we work on. —And at moments, now, relax,
Cold-weather cicadas overhead giving their muted chirps.

Eighth Moon

....

Spreading the paddies with muck is something we've done already.
So now, but not for long, we can take it easy and idle.
It was yesterday we celebrated the Mid-Autumnal Festival,
Today's the day that we renew the Ancestral Temple sacrifice.

How long the two generation-lines formed by our forefathers' tablets!
Who gave their trust respectfully to Heaven-Nature's essence.
Modest offerings of meat bring favor from the ancestors
That spread equitably out upon all of their descendants.

Throughout the sun-filled evenings we hold wine-flushed conversations,
In happiness so perfect it's not easy to describe,
Yet, sadly, family members who've gone off to make money from trading
Have departed our community, and left us—their kin—behind.

Ninth Moon

We do not know of the cold, in our river-basin region,
Where the hills, under their cloud-caps, are verdant throughout the
    year.
Once a faint frost has altered—the somber hue of the cedars,
We are touched by an intimation of the first autumnal feeling.

We step outdoors. We go walking—through earthen-colored mists,
The earth itself being hidden, under their spreading immensity.
While on the incoming tide the incoming ships' keels sing,
And crawlers are washed back, dazed, by the ebb-flow into our nets.

Yellow, the siskins are blown along, by the western wind, in hundreds,
Transformed from shoals of yellowfish, or so it's said, and flapping
Across and over the crests of the waves, their wings incessantly
    fluttering
To seize their chance of a feast—on our ears of rain-smirred paddy.

Bird-snarers would trample those crops. Crops that we want abundant.
So, birds, feel free to peck and drink, for we'll not catch you in nets.
Once we've taken the omens for frost-fall, we'll be starting on the
    cutting,
Though first we must see that the yards where we thresh and winnow
    are ready.

The 'crawlers' had the shape of silkworms and were an inch or two
in length. They emerged from the rice-stalks and if a high tide
broke into a coastal field they would escape on its ebb into the sea.
The peasants suspended funnel-shaped nets from rafts to catch
them, after which they were eaten.[3] There was a belief that in the
eighth lunar month a certain kind of fish changed into a siskin,
changing back in the tenth month to a fish. There were also 'au-
tumn-wind birds' in Leizhou, the prefecture of which the poet is
writing, and these too were thought to derive from fish. The two
ideas seem to have been conflated.[4]

Tenth Moon

By winter's onset the principal crop is mature enough to be reaped,
So now comes the time of the year when the season's last harvest
    commences.
We drag field-barrows behind us that teeter on single wheels,
And pole along village skiffs curled up like slices of melon.

We bundle the sheaves up at sundown—and make our way back home.
We stack them, sweet-smelling, in layers—up under the eaves.
Our produce is more than enough to give even the widows a bonus:
From the handfuls of stalks left behind, to be gleaned.

And it's not just the better-off now who have their grand storehouses
    stuffed.
We've not suffered a shortfall, ourselves, for stocking our Local
    Reserve.
Look at the fields! At how thickly they're covered with stubble,
Which means that our kitchens, till year's end, have plenty to burn.

What good fortune to live in an age so well off!
People's bellies bulge drum-like. They're happy. Relaxed.
Responding with songs and with dances to blessings sent down by the
    gods,
Nor tardy parading their statues around—to show thanks.

Eleventh Moon
....

First of all there's winter mud that has to be turned over,
And old dikes, likewise, that have to be refurbished.
People prate about the happiness enjoyed by farming folk,
But such happiness as we enjoy is based on bitter work.

That neighbor over there. He's an idler and a waster.
His bedding, and his clothes, are meager shreds of hemp.
This year was the year that his land went up for sale.
So his children will have nothing left, except what they remember.

At the level of their social class, men and women have to marry,
Then struggle unremittingly to keep their households going.
Do not take exception to our uncouth country manners—
Things have been like this since times remote.

Twelfth Moon

How warm is the soil's vital force, on the southern side of Leizhou,
Where pestilence-expelling drums throb softly on the eighth![5]
Its steamed fermented rice for wine's well-suited to the old:
The alcohol's no sooner brewed than it slips straight through the
    strainer.

How magnificent the fishes from draining dry our pools!
Our oranges and pomelos taste sweeter than any outside.
And when sons and grandsons are gathered, around us, in a group,
How their faces shine with light, as each one starts to smile!

Between Lei prefecture and Qiong, or so the folklore tells us,
It's now that new rice-seedling clumps are taken from their seed-beds.
Why begrudge others their fertile tilth? We put before all else
Tending with diligence the fields our ancestors bequeathed us.

We spend our leisure moments replacing tiles on rooftops.
Repairs to plows and harrows wait likewise to be started,
While last year's thunder-force moves on—to the thunder of the future,
A presage that when spring arrives, we shall reap an autumn's harvest!

It was thought to be possible to divine the quality of the harvest from the nature of the thunder at the crossover from the old year to the new. Here it is asserted that the subsidiary harvest in the spring will be as plentiful as the main one in the autumn.

The vision was optimistic, convinced of the ultimate benevolence of Heaven or Nature; but underlying it at all times was the fear that the anticipated pattern of prosperous normality might be disrupted. Some lines in Tu Zhuo's *A Warm Spell in Winter* (GCSD 1:2), put into the mouth of an old man, express the fear that unseasonably hot sunshine in winter, pleasant though it is, betokens future disaster:

"No rain for long days in winter, nor any snowfall either,
Make the Two Forces[6] weaken and swell, in confused, inappropriate
    fashion.
I dread that, in the year to come, this prevent the spring's revival.
Don't you recall how, in 'fifty-six, the spring snow caused catastrophe,
A cold that killed the older trees, leaving hundreds and thousands
    dying?"

Sometimes even the benevolence of Heaven was called into question. You Tong's poem *The Old Farmer*, from the later seventeenth century, depicts a peasant who speaks of first unceasing rains, and then drought (GCSD 6:156):

"For mile after mile there was nothing but wastes, and a sky without a
    cloud,
Only the red sun burning, high over our reed-thatched cottages."

He begs the poet:

"Would you be willing, on my behalf, to speak to Heaven-Nature?
To ask why It should play these tricks on the poor and unsupported?

Inflicting only on country-folk their total ruination,
And hardly cutting, if at all, into county officials' resources?"

You Tong presents himself as answering with a blunt bureaucratic realism:

"Think! How many acres of farmland does a common person have?
Yet he worries about them and whimpers, his forehead puckered in
　　wrinkles.
While Qin to the west and Chu to the south are filled with our
　　battalions,
While robbers and brigands pitch camp overnight in our deserted cities,
While the hummocked ruins of townships are half bleached over with
　　bones—
Who is going to be concerned if *your* quick and slow millets are
　　growing?"

The poet was sensitive to the peasant's sufferings, but also aware of another perspective.[7]

A similar attitude of critical superiority can be found in Shen Lan's *Sacrificial Processions for the Fields* (GCSD 6:161) that begins:

The Soil God determines the weather—clear or cloudy—that's to
　　come.
There are prayer-processions in spring and fall, when sheep and pigs are
　　killed.
In the morning the canton headman appears, to make sure that we're all
　　of us dunned,
And the shrine of the God is fronted by a high brocaded pavilion ...

but ends, after denouncing the waste of money on puppet shows and banquets, with an ironic coda:

There will be no rice this fall. The spring fields have tortoise-shell
　　cracks.
You can see, can you not, the potent effects worked by the Soil God's
　　magic?

There was a fault line here in the belief system. To a significant extent the hypatotheistic-agnostic Confucian elite[8] and the polytheistic common people, forever seeking favors from their divinities, did not share the same religion; and this made a contrast with most comparable societies—such as those in the worlds of Islam and Catholic Christianity—before modern times.

The peasants had an acute sense of their economic vulnerability to conscription, taxes, rents, and bullying. Here is Wang Zunmei's *Old Peasant* (GCSD 6:153):

> His son's been conscripted. To work in the city. He's left,
>   No more coming home with the evening.
> His elderly father's obliged—to tug the door shut by himself,
>   In their cottage beside the stream.
>
> The wind is blowing. Impatient. The moon sinks fast in the sky.
>   Their room fills with frost.
> He strikes on a flintstone to kindle the fire,
>   Then offers their yearling its fodder.
>
> His body is chilly as iron, under its thin linen covers,
>   Unquilted, unpatched.
> The atmosphere's heavy with damp. His sick bones
>   Ache, as if wanting to snap.
>
> Wine that he ventures not taste
>   Brims in their earthenware vats.
> Come the springtime he'll have to exchange it for grain
>   To settle their tax.

Li Tianqian's *Reaping Wheat* (GCSD 6:160) tells the story of an area where seizure for nonpayment of taxes has left so few able-bodied men that women are doing almost all the farmwork. An old man describes to the poet the behavior of the tax collectors:

> "Now at dead of night they come to a village. They seize and tie up
>   their victims.
> We tremble like people with fever, when we go past the magistrate's
>   court.
> Our guts, burning with hunger, turn round inside like a windlass,
> As we drive our bodies—on and on—in terror of being tortured...."

He himself is dragged off, at the end of the poem, by the men "with black ropes in their hands."

The more powerful landlords also used violence to enforce their claims on defaulters, as lines from Shen Lan's *Rent Deadline* bear witness (GCSD 6.162):

> The instant the third asking's past, the strong-arm boys pay you a visit.
> The family's turned topsy-turvy, the dogs and the poultry scared
>   witless.
>
> If you've curly-haired daughters, or little sons, who cling on tight to
>   your bedstead,
> They've no place to hide. The thugs haul them out. And take them
>   away to sell them.
>
> State taxes are merciful. Private rents are cruel.
> How, ever, can Heaven-Nature's eye alight on the homes of the poor?

The absence of strong natural village communities in north China often obliged peasants to hire gangs of bullies to protect their ripening crops, and these protectors tended to become another form of predator.[9] Liu Shan's *Crop-watching* evokes the rage that this inspired (GCSD 6:168):

> The crafty rogues from the market-towns, who swagger about in gangs,
> Come to play checkers with empty hands, but leave loaded like gods
>   with cash.
> When they go down to the countryside to 'watch over the grain in ear',
> They share out the land into territories, each run by a separate team.
>
> Their left hands grasp their measures for grain. Their right hands
>   shoulder their baskets.
> "You'll depend on us for your proper quota—of rice, and legumes, and
>   wheat.
> We'll be taking three bushels of crop," they add, "for every ten you
>   harvest,"
> And point out in advance the square field-plots they're not going to let
>   *us* reap.
>   ...
>
> They'll seize much more than their due, if a peck or a pint is short,
> Then turn back and, for extra measure, rip a whole field of vegetables
>   up.
> It's heartbreak to reach the end of the year, with your palms callussed
>   and worn,

To find you must still borrow grain for seed if your tax-grain's to be
    enough.

Half goes to fill the bottomless pit of that leviathan greed—
The self-important, mincing, canton clerks,
Whose hats dance with tassels above their black gowns and long sleeves,
So even the village dogs wag their tails.—And don't bark.

It's their practice, if times are good, as now, to ask for further sums.
Struck dumb, how can we counter this, when they do it all of a sudden?
The canton clerks and the market rogues—they're claws and teeth for
    each other,
Doing their utmost to ferret and scratch, till our flesh and bones are
    dust.

These market blackguards take our cash for clerks' birthday
    congratulations.
Or to dedicate wine and fattened lambs for parades of deities' statues.
Alas! "There are rats on our altars. On our city walls, there are foxes."
As scorpions' curved-over tails sting feet, they hook the common folks'
    bodies.

How, then, can we get our hands—onto thorn-spiked brambles of iron,
To batter such people as these to death, to exterminate such tyrants?

This sense of being preyed upon, of almost literally being eaten to
death, ran deep in the lower levels of society. It engendered many
reactions: rage, eagerness for revenge, the formation of organiza-
tions to resist and even to prey upon others, and—sometimes—
dreams of a millenarian Great Well-Being rising out of a disaster-
struck world.

Women

Women in late-imperial China, with only a few exceptions, were
excluded from participating in the world of public affairs. As
adults, they were defined in terms of the family into which they
had been married. If a woman did have any 'public' standing it was
most likely to be as a widow acting by default as the head of her
household. Among the exceptions were the leaders and members of
Buddhist and Daoist nunneries, and those belonging to professions

dominated by females such as midwifery, the arranging of marriages, some kinds of healing, and perhaps to some degree the organization of entertainment and prostitution. In the far south there were also sororities of girls who never married, and who clubbed together to help and support each other.

The usual domain of a woman's existence was 'the inside', the home of her husband's family. Here she was subject to codes of propriety and fidelity that were, in general terms, common to most pre-modern agrarian-urban societies. These codes served to hold the family together as the basic economic enterprise and locus of social decisions, and to assure males that there was a high probability that they were investing in the support, education, and endowment of their own genetic offspring. In the specifically Chinese case, considerable importance was also attached to ensuring that so far as possible relatives were only related to each other in a single way, in order to preserve an unambiguous pattern of domination and subordination throughout a complex kinship network. This requirement (in so far as it was observed) had implications for who was allowed to marry whom, and tended to isolate newly married brides, and deprive them of the chance to bring with them into their marriage any form of social support existing before the marriage (as can be the case elsewhere, for example, when marriage between cousins is encouraged, and a father may also be a husband's uncle).

Within the constraints just outlined, a Chinese woman's life is best thought of as a progression from being a relatively devalued child (as compared to her brothers), via a position of almost total helplessness as a new bride subject to her parents-in-law, to becoming a matriarch who could wield formidable power, especially if she had grown-up sons, daughters-in-law under her orders, and a well-established network of alliances in her community. The poems presented below roughly follow this progression. It is useful to begin, however, with the catechism of orthodox beliefs expounded by Li Yuqing in her *Injunctions to Wives* (GCSD 22:786–87):

I

We leave our homes to marry, and serve our parents-in-law
With the duty we once owed parents. Like parents, in-laws are kind.
You ask, Why do we serve the fathers and mothers of others? Because
Our existence now consists in being these others' wives.

It is Heaven-Nature's conjunctions that cause our lives to be thus.
Things will go well for us, or ill, as allotted fortune has it.
Men who feel love for their sons will give their sons' wives love,
And, eight or nine times out of ten, will show us kind compassion.

It is normal, as human feelings go, for love to be expected,
And if this love is missing?—That is our own bad luck.
We may not put the question, Do they show us any affection?
But only, do we obey them, as every son's wife must?

If we've given our all to serve them, given our all to be helpful,
Then, so we may anticipate, no fault will be held against us,
Respectful in all our actions, sustaining our husband's elders,
Unstinting in every way in the care we show his parents.

Reverent, at nuptial ancestral worship, our wormwood and waterplant
    offerings,[10]
And when we feast his guests—pure the wine in our drinking cups.
To wear herself out in service is the married woman's lot,
And never grow weary—ever—of using the dustpan and brush.

To our husband's elder brothers' wives we must show a compliant face.
With his younger brothers and sisters we should not chatter too much,
Careful, in handling our person, to be frugal and restrained,
Yet, when helping other people, to be generous in abundance.

Obeying father, then spouse, then son, is the emblem of woman's
    virtue.
Our first concern in all we do must be for filial reverence.
If we act well, then Heaven-Nature gives happiness in return,
And the blessings that we stockpile mean wealth for our descendants.

II

A husband guides his wife, as the lead-rope guides the net,
Yet there is parity as well between a wife and spouse.
Married couples match each other in a balanced complement,
Their feeling affectionate and kind not being in any doubt.

Once matrimony's crimson thread is bound about her foot,
She may not take another man until her life is ended.
Keeping the Sages' teaching, she does everything she should.
Perfect obedience gives her sign 'Receptive Earth' its splendor.[11]

What's to be honored in a man is an unyielding firmness.
But that which suits a woman best is to show a soft compliance.
She should urge *him* at cockcrow, "It's time to be up and doing!"
Serving him food, she should lift the tray, until it's held at eye-height.
  ...

When in unbroken concord she has happily grown old with him,
She will not, beside his death-bed, be touched by selfish motives,
But shift to the self-restraint that becomes a faithful widow,
Making her nature adamant, till it seems like frozen snow.

Since days now long gone by, great numbers of virtuous beauties
Have bequeathed to us, one by one, their sweet examples showing
That the rise of men of courage, and devotion to moral duty,
Has been half due to the character instilled in them at home.

The span of our human existence is no more than a generation.
A hundred years is the limit that cannot be exceeded.
Only by leaving behind us undying reputations
Can we remain beyond change throughout uncounted aeons.

III

We grieve that our filial obedience is never expressed enough.
We fear in maternal affection we may show ourselves excessive.
Isn't lavishing loving feelings tirelessly onto the young
Merely fit, at best, to be called—no more than brute-like or bestial?

Our daughters are made to apply themselves to the task of spinning
    thread.
Our sons are set to studying the scriptures of *Songs* and *Documents*.
Both boys and girls must be obliged to be diligent in these lessons,
And between a father's and mother's concern no difference is proper.

Even a towering building must rise from basement-level,
Nor be stable unless, at the start, foundations are truly laid.
When Mencius forgot to study, his mother chided his negligence.
Thrice she slashed at the cloth she wove, and moved to another place.[12]

With firmness the virtuous mother instills—the sense of what is right,
Wholeheartedly determined her child's moral will develops.

While her son labors at bookwork, devoted she stands at his side,
And displays in her self-restraint an exquisite female exemplar.

Thus above she can answer the ancestors, when they call her to
    account,
While here she makes, in this world below, her family renowned.

Such was the ideal, but a girl's life might be ended by infanticide
before it had even properly begun. Since she was destined to leave
her own family, any investment in her was often seen as unreward-
ing. In some parts of China, the heavy demands of the family of the
husband added to the costs of marrying her off; and moralists attacked this custom as indirectly further encouraging female infanticide. Wu Zhao's *Basin of Water—Against the Drowning of Daughters* (GCSD 26:970–71) is devoted to this theme, but only the
opening and closing lines are quoted here, since the details of the
obligatory present-giving are of secondary interest. Wu was an edu-
cational official in southern Jiangxi. Here he adopted the *persona* of
a woman for these verses:

From inside that basin of water comes a bleating sound, she's crying,
Her baby hair fluffy and downy, her still unopened eyes—
Her pink flesh and wrinkled skin, hands and feet clenched like fists....
Who could give birth to a baby girl and then have the heart to kill her?

Gentlemen listen, please, to the words of a humble wife:
The customs of our countryside are only fit for loathing.
That little girl will grow up. There will come a time
When she waits in the women's apartments for the news of her
    betrothal.

    ...

So mothers coldly resolve, when they first give birth to a child.
That they will not help another house to maintain its family line.

Even before you have heard me out, or sighed three times in regret,
In one home after another, girls are no sooner born than dead.

—Oh, grief!
High officials have plastered announcements on every city street,
But who will send the bailiffs out to check on the country people?

Even if the decision had been taken to bring up a daughter, she could still be sold off later if the family was too poor to support her. Ironically, almost the only time in China when girls were more valuable than boys was when being sold.[13] But rearing girls could also be made into a paying proposition. In Shao Changheng's *The Sale of Daughters* (GCSD 17:573–74) he describes the customs of some of the families who lived in the lower Yangzi valley (the area known as 'Wu'):

> What a commotion they make in Wu when they've given birth to a
>   daughter!
> But not because they hope, one day, she'll run some family's house.
> They bathe her young complexion in douches of peach-flower water,
> And pray her youthful movements cause lusts to be aroused.
>
> She's only just eleven when she puts on rouge and powder,
> Twelve when her fingers are caressing the tunes from silken strings.
> At fourteen years her tresses have come tumbling down her shoulders,
> And her moth's antennae eyebrows—can bewitch.
>
> Mommy lets herself indulge in a smile of satisfaction:
> The minx will fetch a thousand shoes, of silver, to the ounce,
> The finest class of clients will demand her hand in marriage,
> And splash out lavish fortunes for this belle bred in the South.
>
> Just let one of them hear rumors of this darling's reputation,
> And there he'll be, outside the door, to offer his respects.
> Out she'll come to meet him, then, and kneel down in obeisance,
> Gently steadied by her go-between as she sinks to genuflect.
>
> She'll brush her skirts back after that, to unveil her dainty feet.
> While the circlets on her wrists—will offset her ice-cool flesh.
> He'll ask her, "Do you understand how to pluck on the strings
>   sweetly?"
> When she'll tune her zither's bridges, and play Li Bo's *Crows at Rest.*[14]
>
> He'll ask, "Have you been trained as well to use the brush and
>   inkstone?"
> Like surges breaking over are the verses she'll invent.
> "Any good with the pieces?" is the next thing that he'll think of,
> And, facing one another, they will try a game of chess.
>
> The client is enraptured. He assures the virgin's mother:
> "No way at all could one regard a thousand as too much!"

Let tonight, he says, become the night that decides a lifetime's love.
He amasses golden clasps for her, and bangles, up and up.

Ecstatically they interlock beneath the red silk canopy,
The tassels at the corners swinging back and forth like pendula.
The scent wafts off her body like the odor of marsh-orchids,
As she twines herself around him like the dodder-plant's tendrils.

So the master and his purchase relish night-time nuptial fucking.
Next morning child and parent must exchange a last goodbye.
But no affection's entertained by the daughter for her mother.
And her mother is no different. She is not disposed to cry.

Off they go, not in the least concerned, with no warmth toward their
    families.
Once a chick's become a grown-up, she'll be making her own way.
Flesh and blood mean nothing.—Money is what matters.
When one's taken this to heart, it fills one with dismay.

The shift in tone at the end is evident. The tension between the lip-smacking sensuality of the body of the poem and the disapproving Confucian orthodoxy with which it ends may have been a genuine reflection of many people's complex feelings. As one colleague said to me, "Has the mother really done so badly by her daughter?—She is educated, beautiful, rich...."

Families who regarded themselves as respectable held unauthorized love-making by their women in horror. It was felt to menace the honor, authority, and cohesion of the family. Qian Mei's *Mandarin Ducks Mirror* (GCSD 22:823–74) expresses the feeling that only a magical force—here embodied in an antique Han-dynasty mirror—could arouse a heat of passion that a respectable unmarried girl should, otherwise, have been able to subdue. A young man sweet-talks his way as follows into the affections of a girl:

"I live quite near you," he said. "We're both of us from the same village.
You're old enough, dear, for the pin in the hair that shows marriage is
    now envisaged.
So there's nothing amiss if we were to arrange—a surreptitious tryst.
Only be wary that nothing you do rouses foxy-minded suspicions!"

She tells him to get a mirror from a chest in her house, probably one given to her by her late parents to give to her future husband,

since there is a pair of mandarin ducks on the back, symbol of conjugal faithfulness, and agrees to meet him the next day at her family's ancestral temple. By accident a traveler, caught overnight
without a bed, is trying to sleep in the temple. He finds himself
witnessing a family trial held there by the ghosts of the ancestors:

> He'd borrowed the place to sleep in, but couldn't drift off into dreams,
> For the moonlight was cold, and a wind—*from the other world*—was
> blowing.
> He saw an old man before him there, and an old woman, seated
> In the twin places of honor, both with their mouths slewed open,
>
> Angrily calling two others to come, and make their appearance before
> them.
> These two were prostrated, shrunken with terror, upon the courtyard
> steps.
> "That daughter you bore," the elders said, "grows worthless and
> insubordinate.
> She is plotting in secret to bring disgrace on the house of our
> descendants.
>
> "Your wretched home has failed in its duty to inculcate moral tenets.
> You have been convicted before the law, and deserve to get a flogging."
> Like lictors they seemed, those serried lines of terrifying attendants
> Who laid the lash on the culprits' backs as these made a piteous
> sobbing.

The shades of the accused parents make a plea for mercy:

> "We should like to shatter the mirror that was part of our bequest,
> For when that mirror's smashed, then, too, their passionate craving
> breaks.
> May *this* atone for our sins. May it be that we, who are dead,
> Have a way of escape, if fate permits, from the whips and the bamboo
> canes."

The traveler, hairs standing up on his body, sees the elders nod. He
gasps; and at this noise the ghostly court vanishes. The next morning he sees a young man with a mirror go into the temple. Suddenly
the glass slips from the young man's hands, and shatters. As the latter stands contemplating it in melancholy dismay, the traveler tells
him of the scene he has witnessed during the night, adding that

"The dim world of the shades is difficult to trick." What is more,

> "If even the dead may be condemned for their wrongdoing in this way,
> It's certain the actions of the living are only too well known."
> The color of the young man's face had paled to a muddy grey.
> A terrified shivering seized him, that was out of his control.
>
> ...
>
> Then he contemplated the mirror that she'd given him for his own,
> Its daemonic brightness fragmented, and scattered about pell-mell,
> Tossed hither and thither upon the mosses that were growing between
>   the stones,
> And a chilling gust of vitality-energy ran through his mortal flesh.
>
> How sad the devoted couple, the mandarin duck and drake,
> Had disintegrated and flown away, like no more than weightless dust!
> A looking-glass that is full of light will reflect the outward shape,
> Distinguishing in its clarity the beautiful from the ugly,
>
> But the ghosts of the dead, and the spirits, can mirror the heart and
>   mind
> With a candle lighting up the depths of the hidden and illicit.
>
> ...

Teenage love affairs could destroy individuals in this society.

Marriages had to be arranged, and this too could be the cause of a lifetime's tragedy. Chen Chunxiao's *The Flower-seller* (GCSD 23:839–40) describes the anguish caused by a greedy and heartless marriage broker:

> The flower-selling lady—
> Though in the autumn of her age, her eyes still sparkle like waves.
>
> In the latest hair-style and make-up, she goes walking along the
>   pavements,
> Elegant, slender and graceful, swaying her southern waist.
>
> Since her youth she's passed, as a matter of course, through great
>   houses' vermilion portals,
> Where her winsome, smiling deportment always spreads a happy
>   euphoria.
>
> By peddling her blooms, it may happen, she earns herself a few cash,
> But to Old Man Moon, God of Marriage, she dedicates most of her
>   chatter!

...

Her plausible tongue runs bubbling over, like a mouth-organ's suasive
  notes—
But if you're a skilled marriage-broker, that's what the job imposes.

For his daughter, it seems to the family head, that to get a groom
  straightaway's best.
He observes that he's heard it be said Madam's skillful at knotting these
  threads.

So the card of engagement's dispatched. Off it goes! And comes back—
As in all her three lives[15] arranging a marriage whose happiness hangs
  upon hazard.

...

Who'd have thought that our phoenix, in glory, would have to obey a
  crow's orders?
A girl who is joined with a man that's flawed will be crushed by his
  bullying scorn.

The pearl on our palm's thrown away.—Our daughter. *And our
  mistake.*
That matchmaker's self-serving phrases should be spat back into her
  face!

The marriage we'd hoped to be proud of—corrupted to one that is foul!
But the lady, still peddling her flowers, has moved on to another house.

The marriage ceremony itself often cost far more than the families
could easily afford, and was sometimes denounced by poets on this
account.[16] The lewd horseplay that accompanied weddings in some
areas, and whose function may have been to accustom the bride to
her new sexually active status, also came in for criticism, sometimes with the ambiguous tonality, part prurient and part puritanical, that we have met with in other contexts. A few lines from
Chen Chunxiao's *Wedding Horseplay* gives an impression of the
poets' treatment of this theme (GCSD 23:840):

The young bucks kick up a shindig. Their behavior is reckless and wild.
Their lewd tricks lack any feeling. Their conduct is loose and unbridled.

Like Liu Zhen they ogle her straight in the eye, which causes her no end
    of misery.
Like Shunyu Kun they fondle her fingers. Distraught, she forgets who
    she is.[17]
    ...

In couples and triples they wallow about on the bed meant for marital
    pleasures,
Or snore, with their feet on the horn-inlaid pillows, and sprawling out
    at full length.
    ...

The paterfamilias sits in his hall, resolved he is going to say nothing,
Convinced that the more of this bedlam there is, the more it is lucky.

But anger arises from shame, and can turn one-time friends into
    enemies.
These folkways one finds in Hangzhou and Yuyao are something that *I*
    deem contemptible.

An alternative mode of marriage was the adopting of a young
girl, at ages that varied but always well before puberty, to be 'a little daughter-in-law'. She would be brought up rather as if she were
her future husband's sister, and it seems likely that feelings akin to
an incest taboo reduced the fertility of such unions.[18] Zheng Xie's
The Mother-in-Law's Hatred (GCSD 25:943) portrays a pathologi-
cal case of this arrangement. The mother-in-law's cruelty has its
roots in her jealousy of the girl's attractiveness to her son:

The 'little wife' is a mere eleven years old.
She's left her home to serve her in-laws' comfort.
Unknown to her the passions that rule conjugal devotion.
—She just calls her future husband 'elder brother'.
    ...

Her mother-in-law insists that chores, of all vexing sorts, be done.
She's to go across, chopper in hand, into the central kitchen,
And slice the meat into strips, taking care she doesn't cut chunks,
Then stack them in layered rows, onto the serving-dishes.

She concocts a meat-stock broth—but its flavor is insipid,
With neither sour nor pepper taste having a sharp definition.

She chops at the logs till her hands, still soft, are splitting where they're
    blistered.
She supervises the blazing fires till her fingers are all shriveled.

Her father-in-law observes of her, "She's little more than a kid.
Surely teaching her and training her ought both to be done more
    gently?"
The mother-in-law retorts to this: "If we don't break her in
When she's young, who'll keep her in check, once she is past
    adolescence?"
    ...

She swallows her sobs. She turns her eyes to face the wall in the
    shadows,
Her snivelling only broken by a barely audible muttering.
The mother-in-law rasps back at her, "Cursing me, are you, you
    baggage?!"
And grips a rod to flog her with—and a blade to cut her.

"There are still a few slices left—for me to carve out of your flesh!
It's not yet had time to waste away, being more than a little plump.
Just as hairs are *still* dangling down from your head—
But, when I've yanked them out, why then—you'll look like an autumn
    pumpkin!

"We can't both of us live in this world. *That* is just *not* possible.
If you're to survive, then, in that case—it's *my* life that is doomed."
The mother's shape is crabbed with age, her features are demonic.
Her eyes, brimming over with hate, bespeak a murderous cruelty.

When her husband-to-be gives his future wife the slightest of
    attentions,
"How can you be so lacking in shame?" is his mother's curt rebuke.
When her father-in-law encourages her with the least of interventions,
His wife lashes out at him with her tongue, and calls him a senile fool.
    ...

If Heaven-Nature ever attends to the pleading of the humble,
Why's It not touched by the grievances of which she makes complaint?

If, in this world of human beings, you serve as a 'little wife',
You will sink in pain, and be the butt of slander and of enmity.
Each time her stomach is filled, she pays—with another cut of the
    knife.
They make her act for them as their sow, their milch-ewe, and their
    heifer.
    ...

Here, as often in the old China, the worst direct exploiter of a woman was another woman.

Women worked at a great variety of tasks outside their usual family duties, and we find accounts of them farming, rearing silk-worms, spinning thread and weaving textiles, and providing public entertainment. The evidence for this is substantial but raises some problems as regards its interpretation, because the poets were at-tracted to these topics, and had been at least since the days of Du Fu, in part because they were to some degree unusual.[19] A simple example is Guo Jiuhui's *Farming Family*, which was written in the later seventeenth century and probably refers to northern Zhejiang (GCSD 6:154). A farmer has told his wife and two young sons that they are going under economically. Only if all of them work in the fields have they a chance to survive:

Hearing this, his wife gave a sigh.—A sigh long drawn-out and rueful.
But out of her startled spirit there emerged a determined excitement.
So now her hair is disheveled, and both of her feet are shoeless.
She does not make herself up any more, as she did when staying inside.

Instead, through the middle part of the day, she wields the hoe and the plow,
And totes tubs of manure on her carrying-pole during the hours after.
Since her younger son doesn't yet possess this sort of physical power,
He seats himself on their ox's back, and directs him out to the pasture.
...

The older lad has a second task, that of gathering fuel for burning,
So he picks up the dried-out stalks of reeds and withered branches of mulberry.

The wife is out and about in the wind. Out under the rain and the heat.
With nothing but patches to baste together her tattered jacket and trousers.
Her farmer husband bustles around, fired with fresh vigor and speed,
Busy non-stop, turning over the furrows, and getting weeds rooted out.

Neither begrudges, not one nor the other, transforming their sweat-drops to grain.
What makes them suffer is 'cutting the flesh merely to doctor a sore'.

Their burdensome toil, in my humble opinion, is bitter and distasteful,
But the sting of the whip on the debtor's back is even less easily borne.

The modern reader is inclined to applaud their successful joint
struggle, but maybe Guo is arguing that it should never have been
necessary. It is my guess that the technologies of production became to some degree degendered during the Qing, under the pressure of economic necessity, as here. But the inherent difficulty of
interpreting evidence such as this poem must indicate extreme
caution in coming to any conclusion.

The fullest description in The Bell of women at work in the
fields is Ji Qiguang's Farming Women, which depicts conditions in
the environmentally degraded valley of the western Huai River
(GCSD 6:155-6):

...

From time to time an old man calls out, as they toil at the edge of the
    trenches:
"Store that millet in panniers, now!" "Shift that firewood!" "Sickle
    those grasses!"
While their suckling babies grizzle and fret, with only bare earth for
    bedding.
They've brought them along, like the stoneware jars, and the woven
    bamboo baskets.

Up-and-over the high field-ridges they clamber. Lower ones—they just
    straddle.
Even tough women move with a staggering gait. The weaker ones all
    limp,
Sickles and hoes tucked in at their waists, and infants slung on their
    backs.
Face after face is running with sweat. Their shoulderblades are
    dripping.

They cut the mulberry leaves. Chop hemp.—Pick and lift up the
    melons.
Lofty chestnuts, and white-leaved aspens, resound to the rooks' sad
    cawing.
Then in wind, or in passing gusts, the dust rises, swirling and yellow,
Till every inch of their skin is thick—with the moist and sandy soil.

In the sky burns the unforgiving sun, with a heat that seems like a
  furnace.
Elbows poke through their jacket holes, their heads are shielded by
  scarves.
Hands cupped, they sip from the stream in the grove, when they're
  suffering from thirst.
Hungry, they munch boiled wheat, sitting down, at the verge of the
  fields, on the path.

  ...

When you talk of their 'bitter affliction', these words—*can not* convey
  the idea
Of not having *one* extra kernel of corn, not *one* single width of fabric,
Nor the weeds, nor the walls—tumbling rubble—around the beds
  where they sleep,
Nor the tears, nor the howling of storms in late fall, nor the sound of
  the night-rain—pattering.

  ...

How much women's additional labor on the farms may have contributed to feeding the greatly increased population of Qing times,
or at least that proportion of it on a lowland land base that had not
expanded to a comparable extent, is an important and unanswered
question.

Work is a major concern of these Chinese poets, and it has its
own mystique: the gift of work shows more than anything else that
you care for the person to whom you give it. Many verses tell of
the life-saving contribution made to the budget by the wife's spinning and weaving (though men also wove). The patient everyday
sacrifice made by a mother for her family is evoked by Wang
Mengjuan's *Spinning at Night* (GCSD 7:207):

Through the cracks in the paper pane, the wind spies her out. She's
  alone,
Head bent over, intent on her task, concerned not to snap the roving.

Her fingers have chilblains from cold. The spinning wheel squeaks
  around urgently.
Getting even a handful of expenses—means unlimited exertions.
Already the oil in her lamp's used up.—The last dregs will not burn.

The millet porridge that stood on the stove has every last mouthful
    been eaten.
Nothing's cooked ready for the morrow.—She's no cash to buy the
    ingredients.
So she has to be off, her yarn in her hand, to the market to find a deal.

As the golden cockerels chorus at daybreak, as the night-watch
    drumbeats finish,
She calls to her husband "It's time to be up!" while her son and her
    daughter whimper.

The obsessive care that was shown by the women engaged in sericulture is described by Zhu Yizeng's *Song of the Silkwives* (GCSD
7:184):

For the purchase of extra mulberry leaves, they pawn both hairpins and
    clothes.
Being only concerned to have the leaves, they take no account of
    expense.
Senior sister-in-law has disheveled hair, unkempt, and untouched by
    the comb,
And the junior forgets, in her distress, to redden her lips with
    cosmetics.

The elderly wife gives the worms their food, her hair knotted up in a
    bun.
She never removes her outer garb. Her body is never relaxed.
During daylight hours she takes good care her worms don't suffer from
    hunger,
And she keeps a look-out, the long night through, to see they're not
    bitten by rats.

They protect the worms as if they were babes, taking suck at the breast,
    whom they cherished.
They don't leave them alone on their own a moment, while they
    themselves go off.
After the third sleep's over, the silkworms become strong and heavy,
So the women burn paper money and pray, begging their worms will
    prosper.
To buy beasts for sacrifices and wine, they go to the money-lenders,
Whole families down on their knees beseech—these favors from the
    gods.

The results are spectacular:

The reeling-machine turns round like a spinning-wheel, rotating its
    frame wound with silver,
And in hundreds of bubbles the boiling froth tumbles cocoons about in
    its vat.
Elder sister-in-law, with her slender fingers, teases loose one end of a
    filament,
And the length she pulls out from this single strand extends for a
    thousand fathoms.

Alas! prices are too low. After their silk has been marketed, they "have not been paid back for their gifts to the gods, nor their cash spent on buying leaves." The end result is that "all their slaving has only left them bankrupt." The economic tragedy of ordinary people, such as that expressed here, was a theme that touched Chinese poets deeply—unlike most of their western counterparts, at least until the days of George Crabbe and Thomas Hood.

The higher the social level of a family, the less its female members appeared in the public view. Lovely women visible in public were seen as a danger to themselves and others. Hu Ben, in *The Blaze of Beauties* (GCSD 25:950–51), tells how the sight of more than a thousand women attending a theatrical performance out of doors, engendered "the miasma of sexual enchantment and the vapors of seduction" to the point where an enraged God of Fire sent the Wind God and the Candle Dragon to burn down the multistoreyed theater boxes in retribution. It seems likely that this sense of the impropriety in female display limited the growth of fashion, which was weak in late-imperial China as compared to early-modern Europe, where it both symbolized and perhaps even helped to induce the taste for constant innovation.

Nonetheless women entertainers were common, and a source of fascination, even as the poets—as enthralled as everyone else— felt obliged to preserve their own appearance of respectability by expressing regret that these artistes had no other way to earn a living. Here is Zhu Peng's *Song of the Tightrope Walker* (GCSD 25:951):

Her husband leads the way in front. He beats a bronze gong ear-
    shatteringly.
At his shoulder, behind, his missus bends, under her trussed-up pack.

Where three roads come together, he shouts—"Tightrope acrobatics!"
And boys tumble out to welcome them, delightedly clapping their
    hands.

Keen for the show, folk gather around. Fees are collected swiftly.
Onlookers perch themselves on walls, as they try to press closer
    together.
She appears from one side! The crowd is about her. She takes a hold on
    the cloud-rings,[20]
And, seeming about to soar skywards, turns head-over-heels and stands
    there erect !

She glances about her. She leaps in the air, like a spirit with powers
    unequaled,
Provoking a chorus of gasps—from the disbelieving spectators.
Only she, of all there, seems composed, with her calm, disdainful
    demeanor.
Then, with the movement of willows in wind, she lightly sways her
    waist.

Next with high-stepping gait, and lofty carriage, she walks as on a
    straight path,
And during this time she seems unaware there is any rope beneath her,
Then back and forth, in continuous motion, she speeds as though
    Zephyrus startled,
When one loss of balance, when one foot put wrong, would be certain
    to see her go over.

She hand-stands. Then hangs upside-down, as a monkey would from a
    tree-limb,
With the merest half inch of tapering foot suspending her hooked
    round the rope.
She seesaws in space. Like a pulley she suddenly spins!
Gyrations merge into a blur—and one's eyes are glazed over.

Others admire this consummate skill, this technique that admits of no
    rival.
They do not agree with the view that I take, namely, that it's
    regrettable
Plowing and weeding, and spinning of thread, are all put away to one
    side
While she thinks that the risk of her life for their profit has very much
    more to be said for it.

She answers me: "Most respected official, don't scorn me, and do not
    rebuff me!
The life of a wandering mendicant is not the life I'd aspire to.
Our land by the riverbank yields little rice. Once taxes are levied, we've
    nothing.
Our food, our clothing, all, all, depend—upon this length of tightrope."

Once again the tone shifts, from the virtuoso description of virtuos-
ity to the puritanical physiocratic platitudes of Confucian orthodoxy. One has the suspicion that in some respects orthodoxy already rested—or maybe always had rested—on shifting psychological sands.

We turn now from the public world to the private one. There is
darkness, a warm, self-absorbed and self-absorbing darkness, at the
heart of every family into which not even the closest friend can
penetrate. For the ordinary Chinese, unless perhaps he or she had
found some other relationship with life through Buddhism or Daoism, this was infinitely precious; and it was a state that many believed perdured after death. At the center of every such family nu-
cleus was the woman who had created it as a wife and mother.
Psychologically she was often the strongest member. Something of
this is conveyed by Li Fuqing's *Ballad of Date-tree Lane* (GCSD
26:963):

...

A poverty-stricken married couple, then living in Date-tree Lane,
Set off to the county capital market, to dispose of their only son.
To feel affection for one's child is only human nature,
But when taxes have to be paid to the state, what else is there to be
    done?

When halfway there their hunger—stopped them going on ahead.
She felt exhaustion crushing her, but her heart still stirred with resolve.
So she could purchase from an inn two left-over loaves of boiled bread,
She handed in her own torn clothes, as a pledge, at a pawnbroker's
    shop.

"To look at my husband's tragic face devastates my own feelings.
To see that my son is crying cuts at something in my guts.

These loaves are for husband and son to eat. They're easily conceded.
Taste them myself? No, that's an act for which I have no stomach.

"If I am to have no son, then our lineage comes to an end.
If I am to have no husband, then I shall be left by myself.
A wife must grow accustomed to never being fed,
Undeterred that she may hear complaints that rise from her empty
    belly."

So she addressed her husband, using gentle words to urge him.
He and the boy, she intimated, should go on a little in front.
There were excellent mulberry trees just there, along the roadside
    verges.
She'd stop, herself, and pick some leaves, then later catch them up.

Agreeing, he took their son by the hand. They went off in advance,
The two of them strolling on ahead for a third of a mile, together.
He saw no sign of his wife, however, as evening was growing dark,
So they turned, to return to meet her, swiftly retracing their steps.

They soon got back, one leading the other, to where they'd seen her
    last.
Here, too, as before, they could catch no sound of any human note.
But, from a grove of trees, there came—rooks' voices, cawing harshly.
They found her then. *Already hanged.* At the end of a silken rope.

Sick with his grief, he hugged and hugged his motherless son in his
    arms.
Without restraint their tears poured down and not a word passed
    between them.
To be with *her*, in their last home, the two of them also departed.
Three bodies hung there, from the branch.—Under the mulberry trees.

*Like wings that support each other in flight they soar now in Heaven
    above.*
*On this Earth beneath they are linked, each with each, like intertwining
    branches.*
*The physical souls of their essences keep—forever—in touch with each
    other,*
Which far surpasses just living on—if they'd had to live apart.[21]

To enter into a state of empathy with the feeling that suicide can
be affectionate, gentle, and even beautiful under such cruel circumstances is difficult for the European mind, which has been reared

on different metaphysical beliefs. It is also part of understanding China.

At the end of the road was widowhood. Faithful widows, that is, those bereaved when still young but who virtuously refused to re-marry, were a source of admiration and awe in late-imperial times. They could also work certain minor miracles through the force of their virtue. The prose introduction to Feng Jing's *Cutting Off Both Ears* (GCSD 20:711) describes the agony and triumph of such a widow in Fujian province in the eighteenth century:

[Her late husband's] younger brother, Wenfang, made sexual advances to her. In her rage she cut off her left ear and denounced him to the head of the clan, who had him flogged. Wenfang then fabricated a libel about her and inserted it into her son's document-case. She was out-raged and cut off her right ear. Her father sued Wenfang in court and the Governor ordered the miscreant to be lashed. He was displayed in public, his buttocks pouring blood, and wearing a punitive wooden col-lar round his neck. This took place at the time of the summer heat, but on this particular day there was a heavy fall of rain, and both her ears suddenly regenerated themselves. Heaven was making manifest her ex-ceptional fidelity.

The poet then tells us that "her surging moral energy filled the em-pyrean," that "the passion of her anger stilled the hearts of the mob with awe," and that "the life-force drained away from those who were poisoned with lust like toads." The feeling that improper sex-ual urges and acts could infect society in a general way is a belief that our more tolerant age finds hard to imagine, but its intensity of belief should not be underestimated.

Virtuous widowhood could also be rewarded by great happiness. Xu Zongyan's *The Late Lady Wang, Faithful and Filial Mother of the Zhang Family* (GCSD 20:721–22) is as ploddingly prosaic as its title, but it is also a celebration of patient merit. Lady Wang first prays to the gods to take her life instead of that of her dying hus-band. When her wish is not granted, and she is widowed, she cares for her sick mother-in-law and her late husband's senior wife, who is also afflicted with illness, besides bringing up this wife's children

as well as her own with a loving impartiality. Heaven rewards her
with a life so long that she can see, before her, no less than five
generations of her living descendants. And she was clearly a re-
markable person, for the poet observes that

> Whenever one went to her household
> It seemed that somehow a load
> Had been lifted off of one's shoulders.

An observation that suddenly makes her come alive. One has
known people like that. A few.

The feelings of widows who committed suicide to follow their
husbands 'under the ground' may be intuited from the death verses
written by Zeng Rulan. (GCSD 20:726–27) She made two unsuc-
cessful attempts at suicide after her husband had died, in order to
keep the vow that she had pledged to him. The county magistrate
then told her to desist, to have a son adopted as an heir, and to look
after her father-in-law. Once the old gentleman had passed away,
however, she told her sisters-in-law that she now intended to fulfil
her promise. "She bowed in farewell to Heaven and to Earth, and
to the Ancestors." Then she seated herself, faultlessly dressed, and
composed the poem that follows. In a strange way, it is a love
poem:

> Like the water-chestnut's blossoms, cold my face in the looking-glass,
> And never, through these last three years, have my tears been dried
>   away.
> In the fullness of old age, my parents-in-law have departed.
> Once more I taste the frost and snow, the chill of the widow's estate.
>
> But now I myself am returning, to that place for all time my home.
> You, whom I leave behind me, don't think I'm heroic.—Not so.
> Under the faith-keeping pines and cedars that rise on the Western
>   Slopes,[22]
> Husband and wife, we roam together, where delight has bidden us go.

This written, and her share of immortality won (*because you are
reading her lines at this moment*), she flung aside the writing-brush,
swallowed a little metal ball prepared beforehand, and passed
away.

Servants, Conscripts, and Prisoners

At the lowest level of society were those directly prevented by their fellow human beings from leading a fully human life. These were people who, for one reason or another, and in one way or another, had little or no choice as to their activities—sometimes temporarily, sometimes permanently. Chen Yin's poem *Servants*, probably written toward the end of the eighteenth century, expresses his sense of the injustice that this represented (GCSD 26:976):

> When the Creator of Things made men, they were, at first, of one kind.
> When did those of 'honor' get access to Court, unlike the 'base' who
>   did not?
> Both share the same body-structure. Their five sense are all alike.
> And yet male slaves and serving-maids are designated 'helots'.[23]
>
> They come to their masters through contracts, signed in a single day,
> But must, till they die, give others—the toil of their hands and feet,
> Generation following generation, grandsons still in this status
> —Something our laws on family life have stated to be illegal.

He goes on to point out that servants tended to assimilate to the social status of the families they served, comparing them to "clouds that follow the breeze." When a master rose to a position of power, his servitors rose with him:

> Few of their former cronies, then, will be able to keep their
>   acquaintance,
> With their bulging eyes, distended guts, and contempt for other folk,
> Abusing position and pocketing bribes, with which they are never sated,
> Promoting their kin by leaps and bounds, until they resemble nobles.

The serfs of the less well-off, he says, have "no way to compete,"

> Those half-starved lads with sallow faces, acting as gate-house porters,
> Those maids who go on their shopping rounds in worn-out clothes and
>   bare feet.

But even the retainers of the rich, he adds, were whipped and "trampled upon like mud" by their masters. There is a note of outrage in Chen's lines that suggests a different underlying attitude from the passive humanism and merely philosophical reflection of, for example, Du Fu when he wrote on a similar theme a millennium earlier. This is a point that can merely be suggested here. A subtle sea-change of this sort would take an extraordinary labor to establish properly. Consider, nonetheless, by way of illustration the following lines from Du's *Describing My Feelings*:

> Were honor and status abolished, however, the serf would feel no
>   disgrace.
> Without the rich the poor would relish their poverty-stricken estate.
> From times remote we have, all of us, shared a similar bodily frame.
> Songs of joy shift from house to house—and so do tearful complaints.

The sense of acceptance, the feeling that what will be will be, is stronger here than in the later writer and his contemporaries.

Sometimes servants and serfs (a term that seems appropriate when purchase was involved) could not live in a family of their own, and they might even be blocked from forming one. Lin Yunming, who came from the province of Anhui in the seventeenth century, protested against the custom practised by the merchants there of never finding husbands for the female serfs who waited on their wives, probably because, with long absences from home, they did not care to have other men left alone in the household with their spouses. Here are some lines from his *Old Maid's Song* (GCSD 26:972):

> It was daybreak over Haiyang. A woman was drawing water,
> Her feet were bare, and, around her, her skirts were hanging, torn.
> Her hands kept a grip of the well-rope, as she leant on the winch's
>   support,
> Head bent over the icy spring, covertly letting tears fall.

> I held back the whip from my horse. "Why," I asked, "are you
>   grieving?"
> She answered me: "I was a daughter, once born to a family of freemen,
> But when I was twelve I was sold. To my present master. Since then
> I come mornings to draw up the water they need to cook their
>   breakfast.

"I shoulder their firewood throughout the day. They never give me time
   off.
I assist with the weaving, the shuttle flying. And so my toil grinds on.
How pitiful are my tangled tresses! I am twenty-nine years old.
Only Moon, my one friend, wanes faster still, as I lie in my bed alone."

She goes on to relate how her master's wife has deceived her with
promises, year after year, to find her a husband, while her charms
faded "like dried-out blossoms falling." She ends, bitterly,

"Oh, like swallows that make their nests in our beams, that's what I'd
   like to be,
As each with her mate, pair following pair, flits through our hall roofed
   high,
Or else, with my trail of bubbles behind me, I'd like to be a fish
Who appears, then disappears, with her spouse, out of, then into the
   silt!

"But in human form, all I want to be is building timber, and plaster,
My feelings extinguished, and conscious no longer of pain that wounds
   my heart."

Lin, shocked, wonders if she will ever find a husband after "nine
years neglect and maladjustment." In the Chinese view, being married was essential to living a fully human life.

Family life was also difficult for soldiers. Gao Zhuo's *Listening
to the Words of the Old Soldier* (GCSD 12:381), which was presumably written in the seventeenth century, since it refers to the
Shuixi uprising of 1664, and hence to a particularly hard period,
evokes this problem:

"I saw combat in war, and suffered from it, for all of thirty years.
My one son died by drowning.—He fell in the Sanggan River.
My wife's dead, too, but where she perished I still have no idea.
Mother's passed on. Her lonely grave is crumbling into bits."

He goes on to talk about the hardships of some of his campaigns:

"Mornings we'd make our way stumbling, over the pebbles and
   mudflats,
At night find a place in the swamp-plants, where we could pitch our
   bivouac ...

> We trudged through water-logged dunes, with no complaint of
>   exhaustion,
> We earned our scars from arrowhead wounds—to uphold the
>   Emperor's authority."

The poet concludes, sententiously, but justly enough that

> Though generals' strategic achievements may earn them exceptional
>   merits,
> It's the rank and file who've got the guts to face the hard slog and the
>   terrors.

Here again is what might be called a 'democratic' tone. In this, as in
many of the other poems of the period, there is a concern with the
'ordinary' people as the makers of history, that is subtly but no-
ticeably different from what one finds in the writings of poets five
hundred or a thousand years earlier.

The extreme form of semi-human existence was that of the
small number of jail-house prisoners, but in practice the much
more numerous conscript laborers suffered from conditions that
were sometimes hardly better. Although labor-conscription was
only for a limited task or period, a number of the young men forcibly enrolled to haul boats, build fortifications and ships, repair hy-
draulic systems, and do similar services, died on the job. This was
especially so early in the Qing dynasty, it seems, when conditions
were exceptionally harsh.

The mistreatment of prisoners could be horrendous, if we are to
believe Jin Shi's *Lament for the Prisons of Shandong* (GCSD 10:
267), where he describes how the warders strapped the inmates to
planks at night, so that they were immobilized. He speaks of "a
hell, right here, among humanity." Li Lunxuan, an official in the
Board of Punishments who had been born into a relatively poor
family during the later eighteenth century, describes his efforts to
reform the worst abuses of a sadistic jail system in his *Verses of a
Superintendent of Prisons.* (GCSD 10:276–78) He calls it "an ocean
that is black and vast, and whose depths sink down bottomless":

> How utterly dispirited, these multitudes shut up in prison
> With fetters clamped upon them, dragging themselves along limping!

There were even a few among them—some ten, perhaps, or a dozen—
Strung up in the air spreadeagled, between a couple of ridgebeams,

Having no way to get their buttocks to support their weight on the
     ground,
And their heads, like a ram's in a thicket, not moving that way or this,
Choked with asphyxiation, their life-breath all but out,
And hardly an inch unlacerated—anywhere—on their skin.

Since these disciplinary tortures are all unspeakably cruel,
Sights that indignant pity turns its eyes from in aversion,
I called the warders together and told told them that, in the future,
They were forbidden. None of them was to practise such perversions.

He brings a sharp eye to the checking of malpractices in the distri-
bution of the prisoners' food, making unannounced inspections:

One bowlful of cooked rice per man.—That was the portion dispensed.
The screws looked on with glaring eyes. Their attitude was vicious.
Artful old lags got bowls filled full, or at least filled more or less,
But they only doled half-helpings out to those who were slow-witted.

I wanted to stop this villainy, which lacked principle or fairness,
So I watched each helping ladled out, as bowls passed before my eyes.
Then, giving no warning, I took a mouthful—to see if it had any taste,
And, unintended, welled up inside me the saddest of heavy sighs.

In Our Imperial Majesty's granaries, chests in their tens of thousands
Hold rice within that sparkles, in the whiteness of its purity,
Since prison grain is also grain from our imperial storehouse,
Why should it be, unlike the rest, that it's grimed with mold and dirty?

A prisoner pushed forward then, and presented their complaint:
"Your Honor, these corruptions are matters for *you* to judge,
But gouging's a habit of these sly warders to which they give free rein.
They use no coal, nor charcoal either, when boiling our rations up.

"Instead they jumble some horse's dung together with rotten firewood,
Which if combustible at all will not give a flame that burns freely.
Then, just as the moment approaches to finish cooking our rice,
They give it a thorough sousing, with water that's not been heated.

"Why do they give it a sousing? you ask. There's a reason for it. It's this:
Each kernel of grain counts double when put on the scales for
     reckoning."

When I'd heard what he had to tell me, my mind was filled with pity.
Rules are made a mockery of, if we supervise them neglectfully.

It is the Buddhist sense of compassion informing Li's actions that is
the most interesting feature of his poem. For him the prisoners are
"children, like us, of human beings," even if caught in the meshes of
the law. He watches their sufferings:

How protracted is their agony through the days of blazing summer!
The sweat pours off their bodies more copiously than broth.
In every corner, the jail-house—is filled with blue-bottles, buzzing,
A din too loud to fight against, for continuous talk to be possible.

At night they're crushed more tightly, side pressed hard against side,
Than the short-legged *bei* [24]who has to squat propped up on the rump
   of a wolf.
Across their bodies, dragging long tails, crawl hungry jail-house lice
Sucking their blood as one might sink one's teeth in the pulp of a gourd.

And he asks:

Convicts, what crimes in previous lives are you now paying for?
Wherever I look I see only souls who stumble in ignorant blindness.
   ...

How can we enlighten them, without wasting another moment?
So Mercy's Boat float them, on *dharma*'s rains, across to the Other
   Side,
And the thrice thousand realms of which our Cosmos is composed
Be pure throughout unmoving Space, and calm throughout moving
   Time?[25]

After an evocation of the equally horrifying conditions in winter,

Alas! for you who are prisoners, locked up here in detention,
Your fingers splitting with chilblains, your flesh raw and chapped,
Unable to cover your naked frames with a single twist of thread,
Stripped bare, but still erect, the way dead tree-trunks stand,

he entreats his friends to send him contributions to improve food,
clothing, and heating. The poem is one of the most powerful beg-
ging-letters ever written, and he ends by telling his correspondents
that, if they help him, then "likewise Hell's demonic legions will
feel compassion for you." In other places he tells of his efforts to

arrange medical care for the convicts and to arrange twice-monthly family visits for those serving long sentences. Buddhist salvationist metaphysics, the Buddhist emotion of nondiscriminatory empathy, and Buddhist motivation for altruistic good works, thus constituted still another important aspect of the world of late-imperial China, one more spontaneous and generous perhaps than the prescribed dutifulness of Confucianism.

The sufferings of those impressed for labor services are summed up by the opening lines of Liang Qingbiao's *Boat-hauling Song* (GCSD 8:226):

> On the official haling-way, the dust comes off best.
> On the official haling-way is no place for men.
> The dust gets trampled on *once*, but then it has time to rest.
> Men's strength gets exhausted, their bodies done to death.[26]

Qian Chenzhi, the philosopher-poet and Ming-dynasty loyalist, describes the afflictions of the conscripted boatmen in his *The Boatmen's Ballad* (GCSD 8:225), which obviously has to be understood in the context of his anti-Manchu bias:

> The boatmen live, along the banks, beside the Yangzi River,
> Being impressed, year following year, for the transports of the military.
>
> They've traveled up-river, traveled down, too often to be told,
> And all they see is vessels come, impress a crew, and go.
>
> From each ten households, for one trip, one boatman is assigned,
> Not grumbling at what lies ahead, whether it's death, or life.
>
> He may be lashed and beaten, until his skin's all broken.
> And if the boat still goes too slow, their swords and arrows goad him.
>
> Those with blades stuck in their belts, and quivers gripped in their fists,
> Respect as much a human life as they would a dog's, or pig's.
>
> Those shot to death lie this way and that, their corpses blocking the path,
> But who they are is the question—that no one dares to ask.
>
> Your fathers and mothers brought you up, till adult strength was acquired,
> They saw you off, when you went away, and leant on their doorposts, crying.

Though the time's long past since your rotting flesh fed the crows' and
  the kites' voracity,
Your families watch, still full of hope, for their boatmen coming back.

Sometimes craftsmen, too, were conscripted to perform work in
places remote from their homes. Yao Shiji's *Song of the Artisans'
Carts* (GCSD 8:229) tells of a boat builder who is being ordered to
the Korean frontier to built military vessels to sail on the Yalu
River, and is terrified of what he has heard about the northern re-
gions from a returned soldier.

....

"And yesterday he let me know: not one of their seasons is summer.
Ice and snow—uninterrupted—have reposed there since time eternal.
When the spring thaw quickens, the topsoil floats, and often horses go
  under.
The sunbeams fall in the depths of the forests, unable to pierce to the
  earth,
And bears are heard roaring in open day across the desolate uplands.
...

"When my father and mother gave me birth,
They dreamt I'd be skilled at my craft, that I'd make their old age
  happy.
Today, I've no prospect of return.
I am leaving them while they are living, afflicting those who once
  carried me...

"Will my shade, in the earth, ever see that day when its grievances get a
  hearing?
How can it? For year after year
My ghost's fire will glimmer out there. On the cold frontier."

He feels he is being torn from his homeland, where filial obligations
can be fulfilled, and thrust into a world beyond the confines of
civilization where even after death his soul will flicker like a will-o'-
the-wisp, the typical fate, in the old Chinese view, of soldiers who
die on campaign.

This was the world of the emotions, then, as sketched in the
foregoing two chapters, in which Chinese lived during the closing

century of the traditional empire, down to about the middle of the nineteenth century. To talk about it as 'Confucian China' is a blurred oversimplification due to too coarse a focus. It was characterized by a complex and sophisticated premodernity, with many internal tensions and contradictory scenarios. Overall, though, it provided the stories with which to make a sort of sense of human existence, one way or another: stories we can understand even if we do not always like what we encounter. The problem we confront in the next chapter is why most of them dissolved so swiftly when they began to interact with those from the West.

CHAPTER THREE

The Crisis of Absurdity

NO ONE DISPUTES that there was a crisis affecting the legitimacy of political institutions in China early in the twentieth century.[1] The Empire collapsed in 1911–12, and the experiments in democracy that had been started in the preceding years never succeeded in putting down strong roots. It is almost equally agreed that, while the small modern sector of the economy on the coast absorbed Western technology at an impressive rate and grew vigorously during these years, the much larger farming sector only approximately matched the substantial increase in population,[2] except for Manchuria and Taiwan, which fared notably better; and that this failure to generalize modern economic growth was at the root of many of the country's problems then and later. The crisis in the values of what may be called 'the high culture', beginning with the collapse of scriptural Confucianism in the early years of the century, and developing in the New Culture Movement during the late 'teens and 'twenties, is likewise familiar territory for all those interested in China's modern history.[3] What has not been so clearly perceived is that there was also a diffuse psychological crisis among sensitive and aware Chinese that may be summed up by saying that life as it was being lived in the 1920s and 1930s had become for them in many respects absurd.[4]

A sense that one is living an absurdity is a dangerous emotion, and an emotion that may have contributed, through the desire for its denial and suppression, to the rise of National Socialism in Vienna and Germany, where the sense of absurdity was strongly developed. The German-speaking world of Karl Kraus (in Austria) and

Frank Wedekind (in Germany) suffered from what was, *mutatis mutandis*, the same malaise. Kraus had the gift of writing about the commonplace things in Viennese life—such as the omnipresent and undeterrable wretches who earned their living solely from tips received for opening the doors of other people's carriages—and transmuting them into a nightmare of meaninglessness that somehow seemed to apply to eveything else. Wedekind, in Germany, was likewise able, for example in his play *Frühlings Erwachen* [Spring Awakening], written in 1903, to make obscenity touching, social respectability disgusting, and the juxtaposed combination absurd. Timms, in his recent book on Kraus, has pointed to "the contradiction between the given social structure and the forms of consciousness in which it was apprehended" as the mechanism that produces a sense of absurdity.[5]

The Austrian and German parallels suggest why the topic is of more than literary importance. As Sartre has written, "un homme, c'est toujours un conteur d'histoires, il vit entouré de ses histoires et des histoires d'autrui, il voit tout ce qui lui arrive à travers elles; et il cherche à vivre sa vie comme s'il la racontait."[6] Since life is *lived as a story* by societies and individuals, there is almost nothing more important, in the domain over which human beings have some control, than a change in the story.

The concept of 'absurdity' adopted here is essentially the everyday one rather than the philosophic one used, for example, by Sartre, when he suggests that "the world of explanations and of reasons is not that of existence," and hence all existence is, in so far as it is just itself (and not placed in a context of humanly created meaning), absurd.[7] Everyday absurdity is a feature of the transitional stage in the breakdown of a pattern of meaning, in which the old beliefs still retain some hold over the minds of some people, or over a part of their minds, but whose underlying lack of meaning has become to a certain degree apparent. Its essence is a suddenly visible sideslip between a surface sense that has a conventional or traditional social backing and a newly emerging non-sense that is increasingly intuited by individuals—a sort of semantic black hole.

The present chapter is a detailed examination of one volume of a once popular novel that has since been largely forgotten. This is Ping Jinya's *Tides in the Human Sea* , which he published in 1935 under the pen-name of 'Web-Spinning Spider.'[8] It is shown that absurdity is perceived by the author, and by extension his readers, as an all but ubiquitous aspect of life—not an accidental and merely entertaining attribute of certain incidents. To demonstrate this it is necessary to look at the fabric of the story in order to establish that the sequences of social causality, traced with a precision that betrays Ping's other profession, that of a lawyer, depend essentially on misunderstanding, lying, stupidity, malice, and ludicrously improbable happenstance. In so far as the last factor—happenstance—is at work, there is an unraveling of the old structure of meaningful karma by a meaningless contingency.

A *caveat* is in order. The volume that has been chosen is almost entirely about the countryside. It is therefore to some extent a part of the literature of the 1920s and '30s written by city dwellers for city dwellers about the country. This literature took varying views of the rural scene, ranging from a contempt for its idiocy to an idealization of its imagined Arcadian innocence. Ping is unusual in that, in a certain sense, he presents the case for both of these views, though Arcadia appears as a momentary external impression, which is both illusory and, perhaps also a lost possibility—what could have been, but was not. Yet it is precisely the fact that the countryside has become, partly, a sort of foreign country to urban Chinese that makes the sense of its absurdity so strong.

In the end the confidence that one places in a particular reading of a text is always a matter of judgement. What seems absurd to a Western, or even a Chinese, reader in the 1990s may not have appeared in the same light to a Chinese reader in the 1930s. Rightly or wrongly, however, I hear a tone of voice in *Tides* that I cannot imagine possible in China before the late nineteenth century, at the earliest. Whatever exactly it may be—perhaps the apprehension of systemic rather than transient absurdity, of the terminal rather than curable disintegration of traditional interpretations of life—something has changed.

"This Is How Families Make People Cry"

The abraded quality of the relationships within a farming family is conveyed by the way in which Big Jin, of the village of Paxville,[9] creates a quarrel with his wife and thirteen-year-old daughter in order to work off a grudge. His subsequent use of conventional sayings and superstitious formulae to buttress his case is shown up by the author as fraudulent. By implication they undermine the worldview from which they come.

One day, at the beginning of the tenth month, Big Jin and his family were eating round the table. It so happened that his daughter, Silver Pearl, picked out a grain of rice and dropped it on the floor. When Big Jin noticed this, he set his own bowl down on the table, let his eyes grow round, and abused her:

"You there! Don't despise the Five Grains! There are no hens *now* to come along and pick it up if you drop it on the ground.... If you want to die, that's fine! Why make Old Man Heaven do the killing?"

As he was saying this, he pointed his chopsticks straight at Silver Pearl's shining black eyes and made her cry.

... As Big Jin's wife found this too much to bear, she bent down and picked up the grain. Then she popped it into her mouth, remarking as she did so, "If a grain's been dropped, so—it's been dropped. What's all the fuss about?"

"One kernel of grain," replied Big Jin, "where do you think it came from if it wasn't hard work? Look at the two of you, mother and daughter, with your frivolous chatter and vulgar natures, unable to tell apart what really matters from what doesn't! You stuff yourselves till your blue veins bulge. You don't give a damn if the head of the household lives or dies.... But Old Man Heaven will not let you off so lightly."

"When we were harvesting the fields," said Big Jin's wife, "we dropped more grains than I can remember, and who saw Heaven killing anyone?"

Big Jin became annoyed.

"At that time," he said, "there were more than ten chickens to peck them up.... But where have these chickens gone now? Let me just ask you that!"

Big Jin's wife would not answer, so he banged down his chopsticks on the table. Then he took up his bowl of rice in one hand and moistened it with a couple of spoonfuls of beansprout sauce. He was on the point of eating it when he noticed that his wife was not uttering a word, and that tears were streaming down his daughter's face into her rice-bowl.

This was more than he could stand. He gave the girl a real tongue-lashing. The sound of her whimpering became less and less restrained until all she could do was to drop her bowl and run to a place in front of the stove, where she blubbered without interruption....

Big Jin ... downed three bowls without saying anything, pulled on his cotton waistcoat, tied a wrap-round apron (of the kind worn by men in the countryside)[10] around his middle, pursed his lips, and went into the next room, where he groped about for a while in a jar.

It was completely empty. All that remained in it was rice-chaff dust. Big Jin drew in a cold breath and walked outside.

Usually there were hen's eggs kept in this crock, and every day, after finishing his lunch, he was accustomed to taking five or six of them off to town to pay for his wine. Third Matron had opened a little wineshop in Prosperton, and Big Jin could be reckoned to be one of her regulars. He would have three cups of sorghum wine every evening, an egg pick-led in brine, a bowl of clover, and a couple of packets of peanuts. All to-gether, these cost over one hundred cash, and were exactly met by six eggs. He would drink until sundown and then stagger home, where he would either beat up his daughter or swear at his wife. This could be regarded as the fixed pattern of Big Jin's day-to-day existence.

The day before yesterday, however, his wife's younger sister had married into the family of Boss You of Prosperton. A twelve-table ban-quet had been ordered ... resulting in a temporary shortage of chickens. Big Jin's wife had lent all of the eight she had reared herself to her mother's family to be slaughtered. So it was that the supply of eggs had been cut off.

Big Jin groped around twice in the empty jar. Then his mind became inflamed. In no way was he going to go without his evening drink of sorghum wine! Parvula, who was Third Matron's daughter, had already entered two credits against his name in the day ledger; and it would be even harder to ask for credit again today. It was this that he had been pondering when suddenly he'd seen Silver Pearl drop that grain of rice, and it had served as a pretext for him to lose his temper....

When Big Jin's wife saw he'd gone, ... she observed: "What a bitter fate for you, my child, to fall into the hands of this Heaven-accursed man! It's even hard to live on from one day to the next!" (RHC 13)

This is Ping Jinya's view of the central institution of Chinese life, the family, among the common people. It is an irrational torture-chamber to be escaped from. The mother is in fact already planning to join her sister-in-law in Shanghai.

Gossip and the Cobbler

Human social life is a tissue woven from individual strands of, among others, ill-requited kindnesses, addictions, obsession with 'face', misunderstandings, malicious gossip, and mistakes. Running through the old cloth of karma are new threads of contingency to which Ping often draws attention by such asides as "The affairs of the world are sometimes perversely affected by this sort of happenstance," (RHC 12) or "all the troubles in the world are born from people changing their minds." (RHC 13) At a workaday level this can be seen in the following sequence of events:

The young widowed daughter-in-law of the Paxville village headman, Brightstrider Qin, accosts her neighbor Big Jin as he sets off for his drink in Prosperton. Will he take a pair of her father-in-law's shoes into town to be mended? They are wrapped in a handkerchief that is later to cause serious trouble. Being a good fellow in some respects, Big Jin agrees.

In Prosperton he asks an itinerant cobbler to fix them, and shouts after him that they belong to the young widow Qin. "Young widow Qin is waiting for you to do [them]! Do [them]! Do [them] at once!" (RHC 8) In his thick rural accent, the word 'do' (*shàng*) sounds like 'do' in a sexual sense, that is 'to defile' (*zàng*). It sounds—given the absence of the appropriate pronouns in the Chinese—as if he is inciting the cobbler to have sexual intercourse with the widow.

Meanwhile Big Jin hears that his second brother's wife is returning from Shanghai, and persuades himself that she is bound to be bringing enough money to pay off his wine bill. So he goes into the wine-shop and starts drinking again—with his pockets empty. He is, in a certain sense, rescued from his financial predicament by Brighthard Qin, Brightstrider's powerfully built younger brother, who storms in and drags him off by his pigtail.[11]

For no reason he could think of, Big Jin found himself hauled by this fellow into a tea-house. Brightstrider was sitting there, exactly at the center of a table, with the teacher Quartus Wang at his side. Wang was still laughingly urging him to let some matter drop.

The instant Brightstrider set eyes on Big Jin, he rushed across and gave him a flying kick that nearly killed him.

Big Jin was bewildered. He asked what it was all about.

Brightstrider swore at him.

"You thieving cur! Playing dumb are you? What was it you were shouting just now on the street?"

Big Jin was quite unable to recall.

A bystander broke in at this point.

"You were at the entrance to Toto Ding's tea-house. Didn't you bawl something like 'Young widow Qin is waiting to be *done*! *Do* her! *Do* her!' ?"

"His daughter-in-law entrusted me with a pair of shoes to be mended," Big Jin argued back. There's nothing wrong with my telling him to get on with it...."

At this point teacher Wang intervened.

"Your fault is no fault at all," he said, "and I am not blaming you. It is simply that if you will reflect carefully on what you said just now, you will see that it's offensive, and that bystanders who overhear you will want to get you into trouble. Be rather more careful how you speak...."

Brightstrider contemplated Big Jin's face all puckered with unhappiness, and the tears streaming down it, and his hair disheveled. So he said nothing more. The large man at his side just barked "Scram!" and Big Jin made off at a run. (RHC 14)

It appears that Brightstrider was goaded into this rage by the local barber who had said to him, "smiling all over his pockmarked face": "I heard someone yelling on the street just now, 'Widow Qin is waiting to be *done*!' But is she waiting for you, her father-in-law, or is she waiting for someone else?" After Big Jin has left, Brightstrider continues to denounce him for "showing no concern for other people's reputations." Then, as the conversation turns to other matters, he observes to Quartus that the reason that Second Jin had quarreled with his wife was that she had been 'chapthieving', or in other words having an affair. The author adds, sarcastically, that "when a holder of the first academic degree [like Brightstrider] says something of this sort, it cannot be deemed to have any relation to the moral reputation of others." (RHC 15) Thus the network of gossip poisons relations between people.[12]

The immediate victim is, however, the cobbler:

> He had put down his pack at the side of an alleyway, and was squatting there like a baboon. Two pig's bristles were stuck in his mouth, while his hands were busy tugging on two hemp threads. Out of the corner of one of his eyes, he glimpsed Brightstrider Qin coming along, and wanted to call on him to stop, to ask if the shoes were his. Because there was no room in his mouth and he was afraid that, if he spat out the bristles, Brightstrider would have hurried past in the meantime, he hastily stuck out his right leg, with the intention of blocking his way.
>
> —Readers! try to visualize how narrow the streets are in a country town. How could there be enough space to stretch a leg out, or extend a foot? What's more, Brightstrider, and his brother behind him, had pressing matters on their minds [namely, how to make life unpleasant for Second Jin's wife when she returned]. So they came by in a rush.
>
> Brightstrider himself, leading the way, was tripped up. He lay on his face 'like a dog eating shit'. Brighthard, following close behind, helped his brother back to his feet. The little cobbler, in the confusion caused by fear, swallowed his pig's bristles. He yanked the hemp threads from the sides of his mouth and rolled his eyes, giving a whimper as he did so.
>
> Brighthard took no notice of any of this—why should he have done?—but delivered a dexterous kick to the cobbler's pack. It landed beside a latrine under the piles of a plank bridge. In the same motion he bestowed a number of crisp and resonant smacks to the little cobbler's ears. He walloped him so brutally that the latter's five senses seemed to be on fire and smoke gushing out of all seven orifices.
>
> Once his pain had calmed down, he contemplated the two of them moving off into the distance. All he could do was to make his way down to retrieve his pack. He examined the pair of shoes, which had tumbled into the latrine. Panic seized him once more. The shoes were so rotten they had split open. The only luck-bringing course of action was to sneak off. He forthwith hoisted his pack and fled.
>
> From this time onwards the little cobbler had nothing more to do with Prosperton, where he had once lived and made his living. We shall say no more about him. (RHC 17)

A human existence has been turned topsy-turvy by a concatenation of hazard, malice, and stupidity. The disappearance of the shoes will also turn out to be one of the causes leading to the death of the young widow.[13] Absurdity intertwines with tragedy.

Brotherly Love

Brightstrider is meanwhile retailing the story of why Second Jin's wife had decamped to Shanghai, and why Third Jin, the youngest brother, was living in a shack on top of a cowshed:

> One night [said Brightstrider], Second Jin and his missus were sleeping together, heads far apart. Around midnight, Second Jin woke up and heard some slight noises in the bed. He groped about for the feet at the side of his own pillow ... and found there were too many.
>
> "Whose foot is this?" he asked his wife.
>
> "Mine," she answered.
>
> He found another foot and again asked whose it was.
>
> "Mine," she said as before.
>
> He groped about and found yet a further foot.
>
> "Whose is it?" he demanded.
>
> "Mine," she responded once more.
>
> Second Jin was provoked by this.
>
> "You've grown too many legs," he said. "Just wait till I clear the matter up for you!"
>
> He hurriedly struck a light and had a look.
>
> —There, stripped stark naked, was none other than his own little younger brother. So they spent the night, until it was late, all twisting around together (and one might even say that it must have been quite a pretty sight, with all of them absolutely bare).
>
> Next day, though, Second Jin asked his wife's uncle to come over, but he couldn't resolve the problem. So I reported the case, on his behalf, to our rural district director, the Honorable Fortunatus Qian. Fortunatus told the wife's uncle to take the lead in driving the youngest brother out of the house, and this latter realized that he had no option but to remove himself from Second Jin's place. (So from this time on all he could do, night after night, was to engage in 'bovine practices'.)[14]
>
> Once this had been achieved, the Honorable Fortunatus wanted a thank-you present from Second Jin. Not only did Second Jin fail to stump up a single cash, he said words to the effect that the Honorable Fortunatus had driven his wife away. He wailed, and made such a commotion, that Fortunatus became most annoyed, and wanted to have him taken to the branch police station. Luckily I was able to intercede

on his behalf, but the Honorable Fortunatus is furious—even now. (RHC 16)

Brightstrider, Lilliputian tyrant that he is, is therefore planning to collaborate with the rural district director to give Second Jin's wife a little "exemplary severity" on her return, so as to "frighten her till she farts and pisses herself." Then they will drive her back to Shanghai to assuage their hatred.

Fortunately for Second Jin's wife, she has a resourceful ally in old Mrs. Huang, who comes armed with soap, sugar-cane, and two packets of silver wrapped in red paper to plead her cause:

When she saw the Honorable Fortunatus and Brightstrider sitting there [in Fortunatus's house], old Mrs. Huang went up to them, smiling in greeting:
"What good fortune! Both of you gentlemen are here. My aged self has come on behalf of Second Jin's wife to offer you an apology. When she came home today, she went ashore at her mother's house, not daring to come to town to encounter you two gentlemen.... She is ashamed before you two gentlemen for what happened last year. Please, with your own great good fortune and great capacities, have some regard for my poor face."
So saying, she placed the soap and the sugar-cane on one side, and continued:
"These trifles are tokens of the filial respect that Second Jin's wife feels towards you two gentlemen. Here, too, are some small presents that she offers you two gentlemen so that you may buy a bowl of wine to drink. I beg you to accept them."
Old Mrs. Huang fished out the two red-paper packets and laid them on the table.
"What are we to make of this?" observed the Honorable Fortunatus. "The money she earned by service as a maid was scraped together at the cost of great exertions. There's blood in every cash. Who could be so unfeeling as to covet it? As for that business last year, Second Jin was simply lacking in proper conduct. Now it's been talked over, let the matter rest there. Let her keep the two paper packets. We'll retain the articles as a favor from her."
Having delivered himself of these sentiments, he weighed the two red-paper packets in his hands, and returned them to old Mrs. Huang. She, for her part, put them back on the table and would not take them.
Fortunatus turned his head and winked at a maid-servant, who took the red-paper packets and stuffed them into old Mrs. Huang's bosom,

saying as she did so, "That's it, then! The master's dealt with your case and is much obliged to you. Let's go to the kitchen and chat."

So all that old Mrs. Huang could do was to keep the packets.

Fortunatus looked at Brightstrider.

"Was I right to say what I did?" he asked. "How could it be proper for two old gentlemen like you and me to take the money of underlings? These articles are of no great acount, so we can share them. I'd say they cost her from three to four dollars to buy them.... Brightstrider, you go and tell the bailiffs Toto Jin and his brother that my orders are not to make things difficult for Second Jin's wife if they meet her."

(The power of soap and sugar-cane is far from trivial.)

Brightstrider was vexed at this (having missed out on a packet of silver), but how could he venture to disobey? He took his leave on hearing these words. At this point, old Mrs. Huang re-emerged from the kitchen, proffered her thanks, and went straight off home.... Fortunatus's maid-servant meanwhile shoved certain objects into her master's pocket. (RHC 19)

Thus the rural district director has snaffled both packets of silver for himself, while engaging in an elaborate charade of humanitarian sentiment. The fraudulent nature of the established moral order, and its moral bankruptcy, are underlined by Mrs. Huang as she recounts the success of her mission to the Jin family afterwards:

"How would you say that the hearts of people function in the world today? They are nothing more than magnets for money. Which one of them doesn't dream of 'turning a somersault through the hole of a copper coin'?[15] Their mouths are full of words like 'fellow-feeling' [*ren*], 'public spirit' [*yi*], 'The Way' [*dao*], and 'charismatic virtue' [*de*], but their minds, if they are men, are fixed upon theft, or, if they are women, on whoring. What sort of worthy old gentlemen are they? Even we underlings are not as bad as they are." (RHC 20)

The moral currency of the old system has become a counterfeit philosophical coinage.

The Imperial Infant

Second Jin's wife has brought back a baby from Shanghai, not her own but one to foster. It is soon common knowledge—thanks to Mrs. Huang's indiscreet gossip—that the child's mother is the secondary wife of the son of the President, Yuan Shikai.

This episode may be in the nature of a private joke, as one of the book's prefaces is written by Yuan Hanyun, the son of the President, who praises it for its realism and its "style of keeping [moral] accounts."[16] It is also a comical pantomime that displays the credulity of the villagers and their leaders.

Fortunatus, Brightstrider Qin, Teacher Quartus Wang, and Big Jin (as the baby's foster 'senior uncle') hold 'a conference before the Throne' to consider how to handle this alarming situation:

> "It is no trifling matter," averred Fortunatus. "A president is an emperor. An emperor's sons are 'dragon's seed'. How can it be proper for them to be privily concealed among the common people? If a rural district produces a metropolitan graduate who comes top of the list, or even a provincial graduate, this is still enough to remove the vital energy of its [limited quota of] good luck, and cause the fields to be wasted and the land barren. How can we ensure that the nurturing of this dragon's seed in your family does not make it hard for this place to pass its days in peace?" (RHC 23)

Big Jin fetches the baby, followed by an excited rabble of curious country folk. Fortunatus, Brightstrider, and Quartus subject it to examination.

> "He has a far from commonplace face," they pronounced. "He must in fact be dragon's seed. Regrettably, we have never in our born days seen the emperor's dragon countenance. So it is impossible to tell if the child really resembles a dragon or not."
>
> ... Jade Ego, who was Fortunatus's son, lavished unceasing praise on the infant, saying: "Very similar! The real dragon face has two sweeping moustaches, but apart from that there's not the slightest difference in features or posture."
>
> "What nonsense you're babbling!" Fortunatus scolded Jade Ego, "You can hardly mean to say that you've seen the dragon countenance?..."
>
> "When's the day I don't see it?" Jade Ego returned. "If you don't believe me, father, fish a coin out of your pocket, and make the comparison...."
>
> Fortunatus got the point. He fished out a ... commemorative dollar with a man's likeness on it.[17]

... He made a side by side comparison, and never stopped nodding his head. An instant later the entire crowd had pulled out silver dollars so as to make the same comparison. Some of them likewise declared, "Alike!" But others said, "The nose is too small." In no time there was a confused babble.

Quartus Wang told Second Jin to have the baby make an obeisance to Fortunatus as its stepfather, but the latter shook his head.

"There's not one dragon's seed that isn't a star constellation descended from the heavens," he declared. "If I become his stepfather, that will take at least ten years off my life."

Having said this, he observed very mildly to Wang and to Qin: "Wouldn't it be better for *us* to pay *him* an obeisance? Elder brother Quartus, you're a qualified examination candidate. Old Brightstrider here has advanced as far as the first traditional examination degree, while I am an Imperial Academy Student.[18] We've had our little share of good fortune.... If he has luck and takes us up with him, then we shall ride along on the dragon's tail in the future. But, if a lack of good fortune results from his having used up his allotted share of good luck too soon, then he will have no good reason to feel resentment against us."

The other two agreed, and Fortunatus said to Second Jin and Big Jin: "This baby is a lucky star from heaven, with a certain amount of good fortune. Since he has come here, we must ask him to protect the peaceful well-being of this place. For those of us who bear the responsibility of being rural directors, safeguarding the tranquillity of the common people of this place is of the utmost importance.... We must perform the appropriate ceremonies. You hold him, and stand exactly in the center. Wait for me to offer him incense, and each one of us will perform this ritual."

... Quartus Wang hurredly lit some incense and candles, and laid out a cushion. The Honorable Fortunatus made his obeisances first, kneeling down before the baby three times and making nine kowtows. Brightstrider, Quartus, and Jade Ego followed in the same fashion. Second Jin and old Mrs. Huang's son Honestus bumped their heads noisily in a somewhat confused manner. The entire concourse of spectators, men and women alike, saluted the infant with their hands folded, then stood to one side, laughing happily. Brighthard also came and performed three heel-squats.

Big Jin told Second Jin to take over the baby, and dragged his wife out to perform repeated obeisances. As he did so he prayed silently that, if he had to act as the child's senior uncle, this would not mean any deduction from his good fortune, or, in other words, a shortening of his own life. (RHC 25)

This ridiculous deference by the deluded rustics continues for some weeks. The infant is named 'Dragon Official' and a strip of paper is pasted up at the roadside outside the baby's house, which reads 'August, august is Heaven, and august, august is Earth!' This has the useful effect of stopping it from crying at night.

In due course the excitement dies down.

The City God Marries Again

Ping Jinya has a gift for evoking what the poet Elizabeth Bishop once called "the surrealism of everyday life." Nowhere is this better displayed than in the story of Gold Pearl Chen, the only daughter of Elderluck Chen.

When Gold Pearl was young it had been arranged that she would marry Little Lotus Wang. He grows up to be a wood joiner, however, while she works in a high-class brothel in Shanghai under a madame called Boss Jiaxing. She has not the least desire to return to Prosperton to marry her fiancé. Her father, who is more than seventy, makes a special trip to the city to plead with her to change her mind. After a whispered consultation with the madame, she agrees, much to her father's delight. He feels that he will not have fulfilled his obligations to her without seeing her married. After three days of marriage, however, she takes advantage of her husband's absence at a teahouse to slip away back to her brothel. This leads to a row between Little Lotus and Elderluck. The joiner accuses the old man of having been an accomplice in a deliberate swindle, and of causing him heavy financial losses. The old man, however, argues back:

> "My daughter absconded from *your* house. I cannot be concerned with this. I have married off my daughter. The water has been spilt. Alive, she is one of you Wangs. Dead, she's a Wang ghost.... If you want a favor of me, let me on the contrary ask you, When are you going to give her back to *me*?" (RHC 27)

Fortunatus then intervenes to rule that the husband and his father-in-law are to go back to Shanghai, at the husband's expense. Faced with the possible loss of one of her most valued girls, Boss Jiaxing whisks up a soufflé scenario of make-believe.

One evening, Juventus Huo, who has been the go-between for the marriage, turns up, his face awash with tears. He informs Little Lotus that his wife has died. A boat has just arrived from Shanghai with her coffin on board. Little Lotus and Elderluck make their way down mournfully to the river-bank. There they find that next to the vessel carrying the coffin is moored a larger and more splendid one, glittering with lanterns and inhabited by beautiful women. Elderluck tells Little Lotus that this is Boss Jiaxing's boat, and leads him on board to be introduced to her. Hardly has this been done than the young man bursts into tears.

"What are you sniveling about?" asked the lady suddenly. "Whenever did your wife die? Who says she is dead?... Ai! Your wife has simply become an immortal. She really has had all the luck! I should have loved to have gone with her, but there's no such good fortune for me.

"Your wife was my foster-daughter. I called her 'Second Missie'. I adored her in the course of our daily lives as if she were my sweetheart. If she was cold, I would stoke up the fire. If she was hot, I would fan her. Once she was sick for seven days. During that time I ate nothing at all. What sort of an illness do you think it was she suffered from? Until the moment she died she remained in good spirits, and spoke to me in coherent sentences.

"Less than two miles from here, where we are in Prosperton, is a village called Southdark,[19] and within it is a temple to the City God.[20] The idol inside it is called His Worship Zhang. He has been particularly concerned to search through the districts roundabout for women of beautiful appearance, but throughout the last three years he has been unable to find anyone to his taste.

"On the eleventh of this month, Second Missie was waiting at the ferry crossing early in the morning. There was a fine misty rain falling at the time, and she could only dimly see an official boat that was passing by. A mandarin was in the cabin, wearing a silk hat and holding a folding fan. He gave her a smile, at which a chill shiver ran through her body, and she broke into a cold sweat. From this time on, it seemed to her as if her souls had passed out of her.

"On the twentieth her sickness worsened, and she began to talk to me in a mandarin accent: 'I am Second Missie. I am going to be the secondary wife of His Worship Zhang, the city god of such and such a place. He has ordered you to fashion an idol of Second Missie, array it in full bridal regalia, with a phoenix cap and a ceremonial collar, and have it taken to be married at the temple, selecting a day for the nuptials to be completed. If this is not done, he will also grab you away!'

"I was terrified, and promised her that I would do this, whereupon she died, smiling. As her death approached, she gave me another order: 'I am your foster-daughter. When I have died, you must on no account make it known in the countryside. I most definitely do not want to see *their* faces. *You* must dress my corpse for burial once my eyes and my mouth have been closed.'

"Her vital force was cut off that evening, ... but once I had prepared her corpse for interment, I had another dream. A hazy vision of Second Missie, decked in her bridal finery, stood before me and told me to hasten to have her married.... When I awoke, to my surprise I was dripping with cold perspiration. The pattern of causes and effects in this case is really extraordinary....You should now take over her coffin for burial, and for this purpose I am herewith giving you three hundred dollars...."

Little Lotus had been suspended between belief and disbelief. Once he saw the bundle of banknotes, he had no more doubts. He nodded his head unceasingly, indicating his desire to accept it and to buy a separate plot of grave-land where it could be buried and lie at peace.

The madame bestowed a further two hundred dollars on Elderluck, remarking as she did so: "These are for you, old man, to provide for you in your old age." Never in his life had Elderluck laid his hands on a sum measured in hundreds of dollars. His heart was a hundred thousand times more elated on receiving this stack of banknotes than it had been when his daughter had come home. He thanked the lady profusely at once, whereupon she presented him with another hundred dollars, with instructions to share them between the rural district director and the bailiffs. A further fifty dollars followed for the director of the city god's temple....

The next morning Little Lotus found a way of temporarily depositing his late wife's coffin on a bank by the edge of a field. He covered it over with a shock of rice-straw, and with this reckoned the matter was done with. (RHC 29–30)

The sentiments of the poor are as insincere as the pretenses of the rich.

On the appointed day, sumptuous preparations are made for the nuptials at Southdark Temple. There are decorations, lanterns, a

wine feast, a band, and bridal maids and a best man. A throng of
'religious devotees' gathers to see the god take a concubine.

> [The local notables] instructed Tigerlike Zhao, the village head, to tell
> the temple director to remove the idol of the existing wife of the city
> god, which was in an alcove in the inner hall, and to have her lodged in
> the Hall of the Trinity of Heaven, Earth, and Water at the rear of the
> village, lest she feel pangs of jealousy and stir up trouble. (It was lucky
> they remembered not to treat her with disdain.)
>
> "The Hall of the Trinity has too strong a male-bright vital energy,"
> said Tigerlike. "Wouldn't it be better to deposit her in the temple of
> the Goddess of Mercy?"
>
> At this everyone said, "Quite so!" (RCH 32)

The bride then arrives on a boat to the strains of music:

> The crowd of those in charge, headed by Elderluck and Little Lotus, ...
> saw an idol ... indistinguishable from a living person, its whole body ar-
> rayed in a mass of flowery, brocaded finery. Although the well-fleshed
> face was modeled in clay, it was as subtle and becoming as if it had been
> alive. Though the body was carved out of wood, it was exceedingly
> graceful. If one looked at it from a distance, the eyebrows, the eyes, the
> mouth, and the nose were seductively natural. One also felt that it had
> a kind of bashful expression, as if it were unwilling to raise its head. It
> was the living likeness of a bride 'whose melon has not yet been bro-
> ken.'[21]
>
> "This idol," said Boss Jiaxing, "has been carved according to her pho-
> tograph, and bears a marked resemblance to her when she was alive.
> She has, in addition, an entire trousseau—bed-curtains, bedding—it's all
> there as it should be." (RHC 32)

The madame's political influence is demonstrated when policemen
and a representative of the county magistrate turn up to lead the
ceremony. All present kowtow before the idol and his bride. But
the farce is only beginning.

> That evening, after the semi-civilized wedding[22] between His Worship
> the City God Zhang and Miss Gold Pearl Chen, the two of them sat in
> the bridal chamber and—if one looked at them from far away—it
> seemed as if they were exchanging countless ineffable secrets and all
> sorts of mutual sympathies.
>
> A commotion then arose among the guests offering their congratula-
> tions.

"It is not to be wondered at," said one, "that so lovely a figure of a woman should have caught the eye of His Worship Zhang. But what a pity she was given to the little carpenter for him to deduct his percentage first.[23] Unavoidably there's a flaw in the white jade."

"His Worship Zhang has embraced the philosophy of wife-sharing," remarked another. "One can hardly accept that he would concede the right of priority to anyone else. He wouldn't even bat an eyelid if you performed the great ritual of the Duke of Zhou [that is, sex] with his wife before his face every day."...

Everyone was convulsed with laughter. It was no different from the usual lewd horseplay at a wedding. The hubbub continued until the moon was waning....

The director of the temple and his staff could not contain themselves for delight. They reckoned that they might just as well—as in the case of a real marriage—get the pair of ceramic figurines to 'play at subtle emptiness' [that is, sex]. They began by spreading the new bridal coverlets out nicely so as to make a restful nuptial bower for the newlywed couple, ... and the two of them passed the night together without saying a word....

Just as the dawn was breaking the next day, one of the temple servants rubbed the sleep out of his eyes and groped his way into His Worship's wedding-chamber to offer his morning salutations, and to steal a glimpse of the bride. Her powdered cheeks had a faint blush to them, like cherry-apples in their spring sleep.

Moved by an impulse of make-believe, he murmured in a low voice: "It's daytime. Get up!"

All at once he saw the bride give a yawn. Her starlike eyes glittered with a slight smile.

"It must be my defective eyesight," the servant muttered to himself.

When he approached closer to have a look, however, the bride gave a roar ... and so terrified him that his three spiritual souls vanished up to heaven and his six physical souls departed into the earth below. He passed out.

The idol thereupon climbed off the bed in an unhurried fashion, helped the temple servant back onto his feet, slapped his chest a few times, pinched his upper lip, and brought his gaggle of panic-stricken souls back from the devils' gate. When the servant opened his eyes for a closer look, was it Miss Gold Pearl, the idol, the new bride?! No! it was that vagrant and layabout from Paxville village, Jin the Third!...

The previous evening Little Jin had sauntered into Southdark village to look at the excitement. He had waited till the depths of the night before slipping into the kitchens, where he saw any amount of fish, meat,

wine, and rice scattered about in profusion. His gluttonous nature had
asserted itself, and he had gobbled down the lot. Who would have
imagined that then, having drunk so much wine that he had lost control
of his body, he would have groped his way into His Worship Zhang's
bridal chamber?

He had glanced about him to make sure that no one else was there,
and since the nuptial couch was spread with multi-colored finery, he
had bundled the idol of His Worship Zhang underneath the bed, rolled
the statue of his bride over to one side, and dropped off to sleep there
himself, mumbling as he did so, "Shcuse me if she keepsh me company."...

When the temple servant had regained his composure, he wanted to
summon the temple director to seize Little Jin and have him flogged,
but the latter apologized.

"My good sir," he said, "be more relaxed about it. If there's a row,
you won't escape being caught up in it. What sort of care were you
taking of His Worship's new bride, they will ask, to let her be given to a
stranger to sleep with on the first night? Hmm? How do you think
you'll be punished for that?"

The servant weakened. Little Jin thereupon tidied everything up for
him, and gave him a beguiling smile.

"Look there, now!" he said. "Though I slept with the bride in the
same bed, and under the same quilt, not a hair on her body's out of
place."

The temple servant spat at him, but Little Jin was already out of the
temple gate and slouching along in his devil-may-care manner away toward Prosperton. (RHC 33–35)

In this welter of idiocy almost the only sane figure appears to be Jin
the Third, that embodiment of anarchic disorder filled with animal
energy, and the resourcefulness and guilt-free amorality of the dis-
possessed. He is less taken in by nonsense than anyone, though
happy to peddle nonsense of his own if survival or profit require it.
Perhaps significantly, the country people refer to him as "a spirit
who wanders by day and by night." (RHC 35)

He triggers disasters. Thus on one occasion the two young men
Bullatus You[24] and Jade Ego Qian are run into in the street by a
woman who is fleeing in the opposite direction. She loses one of
her embroidered shoes but pays no attention to this and vanishes
into the distance. The two youths are puzzled but proceed to the

Temple of Accumulated Good Actions where Lapillus Hu, the local
street storyteller, explains what has happened:

> Little Jin, that spirit that roams abroad by day (and a lost soul), was sit-
> ting in Toto Jin's tea-house when he spied a woman going into the
> temple. Since a long while had passed without her coming out again, he
> went in to have a look for her, but even after some time he could find
> no trace of her.
>
> He did not believe she was capable of vanishing into the ground, so
> he used his ears to detect her whereabouts. They led him to the room
> of the monk Nebulosus, from which there was emanating the sound of
> female laughter. And that laughter seemed to have a certain amount of
> panting in it.
>
> He rushed forthwith to Tertius Sun's opium den, putting on the ex-
> pression of someone who has just laid his hands on something precious.
>
> "I've just seen Master Nebulosus with my own eyes," he reported to
> them. "In the Temple of Accumulated Good Actions! Digging up a
> crock of stolen loot at the back of the building. The Master and a disci-
> ple are sharing out the booty in his room. At this very moment. I saw it.
> Clear as clear could be. Roll after roll of snowy-white dollars! Coming
> in, going out. If you come with me at once, we can have ourselves a
> share!"
>
> The mob uttered a bellow and stumbled out after him through the
> door. What a pity that at that time Monk Nebulosus's Buddha's Tooth[25]
> had not been fully exposed to the woman. Luckily for her, she had
> quick eyes and quick feet. She all but flew out of danger. They punched
> and kicked Nebulosus for a while, then cleaned out everything in his
> room. It was both a matter for laughter and not. (RHC 46–47)

Little Jin may be a mischief maker, but one of his functions is to
strip away pretense in the process. Boss Jiaxing's mendacity, on the
other hand, has a magnificence of invention that compels admiration.

Monk Business

In contrast, the theme of the story of how the Buddhist temple
collapses as an institution is ineptness in deception. The tale of how
the bald-pates (*guangtou*) have fled clean away (*taoguang*) is recounted to Bullatus by Toto Ding, the teahouse proprietor:

"Moonseal is the monk in charge of the Temple of Accumulated Good Actions.... There's not one person in town who doesn't say he's a good man.... He's accepted three disciples, Nebulosus, Fumosus, and Undosus. Since Undosus has taken up opium and spends every day learning his lessons in the den, and Fumosus died two years ago.... Nebulosus has wanted to take over as monk in charge. He has made a pretense of moral behavior, and his wooden fish[26] has the misfortune of being beaten by him from early morning through the rest of the day. Once dusk has fallen he retires to the meditation room to meditate or to gabble through the sutras.

"It happened one night that an old lady who was burning incense peered at him through a crack in the door. He was sitting on a prayer-mat ... with strings of rosary beads in one hand, and turning a folding paper scroll back and forth with the other, examining it intently. She could hear him exclaiming 'Goddess of Mercy!', bubbling with excitement.

"The old lady was certain this folding book must be a copy of the *Eminent King Sutra*,[27] and might be a powerful spell against troubles. She waited till he had gone out, then slipped in to filch it, after which she made off with it. She gave it to her husband to have a look, saying that the old monk had presented it to her. When her husband examined it more closely he found that it consisted of pictures of men and women without clothes on. When they were folded up they could be transformed into any number of entertaining postures...He became so enraged that he half died in consequence, and addressed the foulest abuse to his wife." (RHC 81–82)

After other misdemeanors, such as being found to be wearing women's clothes—and inside out, at that—under his robe while officiating at a ceremony to deliver souls from purgatory, Nebulosus is caught in his room with Big Auntie, a moneylender. Moonseal almost dies of chagrin at this scandal, and officers are sent out from the county magistrate's office to arrest the miscreant monk. Toto recounts what follows:

What sort of a bucket of goods d'you think this Big Auntie was? She'd have the nerve to lick the blood off a knife-blade! Yesterday morning the county magistrate despatched a water-police boat to apprehend this monk.... Moonseal would have preferred to have kept himself out of the matter but he felt he could not abandon his disciple. So he went with Nebulosus to the tribunal.

When the case opened that evening, who'd have imagined that the accused would be none other than Moonseal! Nebulosus appeared as a witness. So who d'you think the plaintiff was?—None other than Big Auntie Wang!

What's more, she didn't submit a written plaint. She went to the court in person, where she set forth her grievance with tears and shouting. She actually asserted that the old monk, Moonseal, had forcibly raped her.

She was, she said, over forty years of age, and still a virgin. She'd been having her monthly period at the time, and demanded that the court inspect the injury, which—she declared—had been inflicted by Moonseal in the course of raping her....

When that pitiable old monk knelt down in court, he was so scared he was trembling.

"You've abandoned the family all your life," said the magistrate. "Why should you forcibly rape someone's virgin daughter?"

"I'm seventy years old," said Moonseal, looking for mercy. "I'm not capable of raping anyone, never mind forcibly. The charge is false...."

The court ordered the plaintiff to be cross-examined, and Big Auntie came up, a pink handkerchief pressed against her lips. She gave her buttocks a wiggle and a twist, then knelt down with a pretense of every sort of bashfulness. When the magistrate questioned her, she sobbed elegantly for a while, then set her mouth and declared:

"I resent it! The old monk should not have forcibly raped me! I want to die right here!"

"What relationship does the old monk have to you?" the magistrate asked Nebulosus.

"He's my master," Nebulosus replied.

"Do you clearly affirm that your master forcibly raped this woman?" pursued the magistrate.... "Did you see it yourself?"

"I was standing behind when it happened," said Nebulosus. "How could I have failed to see it?"

"Why didn't you pull them apart?"

"He is my master," said Nebulosus. "He is of a senior generation. I wouldn't dare to pull him."

"You are talking nonsense," said the official, ... and he turned to interrogate Big Auntie:

"How old are you this year? How many years have you been married? When, and where, did he forcibly rape you? And why didn't you cry out?"

"I am forty-eight this year," answered Big Auntie. "And I'm a virgin. After my husband died, I have never been married. Sometimes this hateful old monk forcibly raped me in the daytime, and sometimes at

night. Sometimes he came to my house to do it. At other times he summoned me to the temple to be raped.... When he was forcibly raping
me he also made me put the tip of my tongue into his mouth. With the
tip of my tongue submerged in this way, I couldn't cry out.... May the
Great Lord of Azure Heaven state my plaint on my behalf, his servant!"

"You scoundrelly baggage!" said the magistrate.... "I can see that you
are not a proper sort of woman [*zhèngdàng-de fùrén*]."

"I make loans at interest on the security of the borrower's seal," said
Big Auntie. "So I am indeed a moneylender [*zhèngdàng-rén*]."

"I am asking you," said the official, banging on the table, "why you
have colluded with this little monk to denounce the old monk
falsely?..."

"The only reason I hate the old monk," said Big Auntie, "is that he
borrowed ten dollars from me and, before the full month was up, hastily returned them to me. This was detestable."

"Why, when he hurries to repay you the money he borrowed," asked
the official, "do you on the contrary hate him?"

"I rely on my copper coins to sweat from their holes on my behalf....
If he returns them quickly, the interest I earn from them is so much the
less.... Why shouldn't I hate him?"

The court thereupon clapped Big Auntie Wang and Nebulosus into
prison, and let the old monk go. (RHC 82–83)

Alas for poor Moonseal. When he gets back he finds that Undosus
has absconded with everything he can carry, and the younger
monks have scattered far and wide. Bullatus draws the moral: "In
this world, those who hurt others hurt themselves. All too often
the carpenters who make the penal neck-collars for others have to
wear them themselves." While Toto and Bullatus exchange these
commonplaces of traditional wisdom, there is a sense that everything is crumbling.

Murder by Slander

Rural life is not just comically absurd. It is cruel. 'Spider' shows
how the old religion of the family, the obsession with 'face' and the
fear of being mocked in public, the folly of traditional medicine,
and the damage done by malicious or simply unthinking gossip,
could kill people. When his characters express conventional ideas,
like the belief in ghosts, or the cohabitation of the souls of spouses

after their deaths, he either ridicules them or contrives that the story shows them to be invalid.

All these elements can be found in the tragedy of the widow of young Qin, the deceased only son of Brightstrider:

After Little Jin had spent the night at the City God's temple, he had gone to Prosperton, where he had messed about for most of the day. Then, as evening was closing in, he had gone to the Temple of Accumulated Good Actions and caught the monk Nebulosus in fornication. While doing so, he had appropriated a set of bedding coverlets, which he had sold to meet his expenses. After downing three cups of sorghum wine, he had then set off along the road to Paxville village.

Dusk had already fallen. The moon was darkened over. Stars were few and far between. A west wind was blowing through the stalks of the rushes, as if a ghost were crying, and the leaves were tossing on the trees along the banks. If one looked at them from a hundred yards away, they seemed to be skulls—coming in pursuit. (But how could they have scared a night-wandering spirit like Little Jin? They must have had some other purpose in arranging this desolate scene.) Wouldn't ordinary people have been quaking in fear if confronted with these things? But Little Jin, thanks to his being more than a little intoxicated, was not frightened in the least.

When he came closer to the village he heard an uncanny wailing, ... sometimes breaking off and then resuming again. He pushed his felt cap back off his brow, gave it a pat, and exclaimed:

"I've lived now for twenty-six years but never set eyes on a demon. It's hard to believe that the wife of the City God is coming back with me tonight! In the world of the living, the sexually depraved women are always running away with other men, but who would have thought the City God's wife would also be following the fashion? Hmm! I'm not afraid. Not me, Little Brother. Come and let me give you something pretty to look at!"

As he said this, he urinated at the side of the road.

The sound of crying came nearer and became more insistent.... A solitary owl joined in with several hoots—*koo-ah! koo-ah!*... He passed beside a grave-plot overshadowed by shrubbery, and had the feeling that the crying was coming from this tomb.... He bolted past it and crawled up, panting, into his cowshed, where he fell asleep.

When he awoke, it was late at night. Suddenly, on a gust of the west wind, came the sound of wailing.... He became irritated.

"That crying demon," he said to himself, "is dead set on keeping me company tonight, and transfixing me with its sobbing. But there's no enmity between the two of us, no grievance. So I should like to ask it to explain!"

He jumped down from the cowshed roof and carefully tracked the sound to its source.... Peering through a crack in a window he could just make out a young woman facing a single oil lamp, and sobbing. Her hair was disheveled, her eyes without life.... In front of her, on the table, was her late husband's soul-tablet. (RHC 52–54)

She is the widow of Little Strider, Brightstrider's son.

There is a contrast here between Little Jin, who has to some extent escaped from the social system and the widow who is enmeshed in it. Her tragedy is the consequence of the slightest of matters—a hazy fear of social disapproval, a fever that her husband caught when walking home at night in an unhappy state of mind caused by this fear of hers....

On the second day of the fourth month of the previous year, the town had celebrated the festival of greeting the gods.[28] Little Strider and his wife had gone to his mother-in-law's house, where they had eaten in the best of spirits around the single table. Little Strider's wife had wanted him to spend the night at her mother's house but had also been frightened that there might be mocking talk among the idle gossips.[29] ...

"Why don't you let me stay this evening?" said Little Strider. "If you don't, it will be the first time since we were married that we've slept in separate beds.... If you are lonely, you can share a bed with your mother; but if I go back home, I haven't got a mother. All I'll be able to do is to go to sleep hugging a pillow.... If I go back, not only will I find no pleasure in coming here tomorrow, but I'll never be happy to come here—*ever*. What's more, when you come home, I won't let you sleep in the same bed with me."

Little Strider's wife gave his hand a squeeze.

"What's so bad about us keeping apart for one night?" she said. "There's only one small bed in this house. If we keep you overnight, people are certain to make fun of us.... And what do you mean by saying that, when I come home, you won't sleep with me? Fine! Let's each go our own way, like the proverbial bowl-riveters from Jiangxi.[30] You are not going to get the better of me with pressure like that!"

With this she gave him a determined stare. Little Strider grabbed hold of the hair on his wife's temples.

"Well, then!" he exclaimed. "Won't you see me off for the length of a field?"

"Feelings should be kept for the heart," said his wife. "If we do anything in public, other people are certain to laugh at us.... I'm not going to see you off." (RHC 54–55)

Public opinion disapproved of married couples being too overtly fond of each other, and she may also have feared that people might think her husband had too insatiable a desire for sex. But his psychological bullying, prompted by his sexual urges, and her determination to stand up for herself and to observe the proprieties for both their sakes, combine with the puritanism of public opinion—often a hypocritical puritanism—to cause disaster. Those who are sincere, and honestly attempt to observe the old values, as Little Strider's wife does, inexorably suffer as a result.

She lodged that night in her mother's house, but when it was close to midnight, Little Strider suddenly came back in.

"What are you up to?" she said. "You've come back."

Little Strider smiled and said: "When did I ever leave? I stuck myself under your bed. Let's sleep together!"

His wife looked for her mother, but she had disappeared somewhere. So she silently indicated her assent to his sleeping there....

All at once she saw her mother coming out from behind the back of the bed. She felt her face becoming mortified with shame, and hurriedly told Little Strider to get up and let her mother lie down. Little Strider went under the bed.

"You're quite heartless!" he said. "I was beautifully snug in the bedclothes when you forced me back. Now, *you'll never see my face again*. You and I will part forever."...

"What are you saying?!" she called out to him, but he returned not a word. Just as she was about to haul him out, she woke up, and found it had been a dream. (RHC 55–56)

Dreams are the means, in China, by which one talks with the dead and to supernatural beings. Little Strider has in fact caught a fever after walking home through the dark. The traditional doctor summoned to attend him tells his father:

"Your son is suffering from a deficiency created by the dark-female principle, which has brought in noxious influences. It will first of all be necessary to externalize these noxious somatic influences, and next to reduce the sexual appetite so as to nourish the vital seminal essence. It would be best to tell your daughter-in-law to avoid the sick man completely." (RHC 56)

Brightstrider therefore tells her, "If you want to remain here, your love for him will be precisely the means of harming him," since his desires must not be aroused. She returns to her mother's, and shortly afterwards he dies.

This medical gobbledygook sets her father-in-law against her:

> From the time that Little Strider passed away, every word that Brightstrider uttered was "My daughter-in-law killed him!" If he felt like cursing her, he would. If he felt like beating her, he did so. Every day he remembered his son and abused her as an obscene baggage begotten on a whore.... She wept until her face was worn away and the bones stood out, and seemed to feel nothing when Brightstrider cursed and flogged her. (RHC 57)

He refuses to provide her with money to buy the food and paper ingots needed to sacrifice to her dead husband's soul. "You killed him!" he declares. "It's no use your giving him sacrifices or wailing for him. The best thing for you to do would be to die, so I no longer think of him.... Why don't you hurry up and die?" He denies her the only socially honorable role left to her, that of the faithful widow caring for her parents-in-law. She nonetheless gets the sacrificial materials from her mother, and calls up his soul: "How can I now, with my bitter fate, come to keep you company?... Come quickly, and lead me away with you!" His image appears before her and though he wipes away her tears, he speaks coldly: "In the world of the living there are sentiments of love. For those who come *here*, though, each must go his or her own way." "If I come to where you are, in the world of the shades," she cries, "how can you abandon me?" Marriages endure—or were thought to endure—forever, even beyond the grave. Little Strider gives a chilling laugh and dismisses this time-honored consolation:

> "You are in the bright world. Yet, in the black depths of this night, you have unfeelingly forced me to return. If you were to come to where I am now, what feelings between husbands and wives betrothed since infancy are there to be spoken of? One sentence sums up what happens in

the world of the living: 'The husband deceives the wife, the wife the husband.' Where are the mutual affections that do not change though the heavens grow waste and the world becomes old?... These phrases are all to fool people.

"I have now become a ghost. I will not permit you to engage in further deceit. In the world of the living there is love. In the world of the dead, none. Come to your senses! You and I will each of us go our own way." (RHC 58–59)

Little Strider has spurned the predestined affinities of love, traditionally believed to underlie all marriages. She faints and crashes to the ground. Not only her personal world has collapsed. Her metaphysical world is in ruins.

The author comments that the vision she has just experienced "was caused by her feelings of attachment, an illusion that arose from her mind." (RHC 60) He does not himself believe in ghosts, but using the illusion of the *revenant* of Little Strider enables him to indicate that the old pieties are gone, or remain only as a cover for hypocrisy. She should not remained chained to a dead love forever.

In the meantime Brighthard's wife, the young widow's aunt-in-law, is spreading a false story. The widow, she says, is having an affair with Big Jin. Her assertions gain a certain plausibility from the handkerchief she has found in Big Jin's house—the one, the reader knows, that the widow used to wrap the shoes in—and from the frequent visits that the widow makes to Big Jin's house, to ask what has happened to the shoes. The bereaved woman denies Brightstrider's insinuations, and tells him to go and ask the cobbler himself.

"Humph!" he said with a cold laugh. "I've no intention of asking the little cobbler anything. The 'shoes', I fear, have already been 'worn out' by Big Jin.[31] What a nice business you're up to, destroying my family's reputation!... I am sorry to say that everyone in Paxville, indeed in Prosperton, knows what is going on.... You have sliced bare, slice by slice, the flesh of the cheeks on my face!.... Speak! Speak! Aren't you having an affair with Big Jin? Must you persist in telling falsehoods to the faces of decent people?!... Your husband is weeping in the world of the shades. Can you hear him?... Our household is reckoned to be the

leader in this village. It is not to be compared to a family of farmers!...
Hurry up and do me the favor of taking yourself back to your own family." (RHC 62–63)

Since Brightstrider does not have the proofs that would permit him
to throw her out, he sets about creating some. His brother
Brighthard waits in the dark outside the window of the widow's
room armed with a knife in order to catch Big Jin and slice off his
pigtail. What ensues is another twist of capricious chance.

It so happens this particular night that Jade Ego, the son of Fortunatus, is playing mahjong at Second Jin's house—the house next
door—and comes out to relieve himself. Brighthard thinks he is Big
Jin, though it is too dark for him to be certain. He cuts off his pigtail and vanishes into the shadows. Brightstrider now has his
'proof'. He has Fortunatus, in his capacity as the rural district director, assemble an informal court at a teahouse the next morning.
Big Jin is hauled in by the bailiff and his pigtail inspected. It is
found to be sound. One of the old gentlemen on the bench thereupon rebukes the Bright brothers:

> "What you have said is not true. His queue is well and truly on the top
> of his head. This business is a complete nonsense.... If you can bring in
> someone whose pigtail has been freshly severed, then we can discuss it
> further." (RHC 73)

The 'court' breaks up in confusion.

These events have left Jade Ego in a hazardous position. He has
been playing mahjong, of which his father disapproves. He has lost
his pigtail, which will arouse paternal fury. He therefore stays under cover, away from home, and entrusts his friend Bullatus You
with concocting some plausible falsehoods to save him.

Bullatus is an artist at lying. He sets to work on Fortunatus in a
way that allows the reader to delight in his suasive untruthfulness;
and also, since the reader is better informed than the rural district
director, to relish the dramatic irony that reveals the threadbare nature of the pieties by which the local ruling class professes to live.
The conversation highlights another of the author's convictions,

namely that the complexities of actual events are almost always too tortuous to be grasped by general reasoning alone.

> "Did you recognize whose pigtail it was, uncle?" asked Bullatus.
>
> "A pigtail doesn't have eyebrows or eyes," said Fortunatus. "How could I have recognized whose it was? Taking all things into consideration, even if Brighthard did cut off the wrong one, the person who lost it was certainly not a good man.[32] It's likely that he did have relations with this woman. Thus he had no concern for the blood and hair he received from his father and mother.... If it was cut off for no good reason, why has he been unwilling to raise an outcry against it?... To sum it up in a word, it must have been that of someone who was committing adultery....
>
> "I saw that pigtail yesterday evening. In all likelihood this adulterer is a dissolute youth of depraved ways and corrupted virtue. His father and mother cannot have given him any familial instruction ... and ought to be subjected to the law, together with their son." (RHC 74–75)

Bullatus sets to work to undermine these convictions. He notes that "in all affairs there are unfathomable illusions. One cannot tell when they will go outside common principles and regularly occurring circumstances. More than ever before, the world of the present day is one where people's hearts are treacherous and deceitful.... To speak plainly, hearing of something is not as good as seeing it, and theoretical considerations are not as useful as actual experience." He then gives Fortunatus a censored version of the events of the evening when the queue was severed. But he does not name names and he omits all mention of mahjong.

He next undermines Brightstrider:

> "He had that pigtail cut off because he wanted cast-iron proofs that his daughter-in-law was having an adulterous liaison. His initial suspicion fell on Big Jin, but when he realized that the cutting of the pigtail showed his error, he felt he had to make the best of a bad job, and maintained that, no matter whose pigtail this was, it had to be that of a person committing adultery with his daughter-in-law.... Because of his rage over one pigtail, he was only too happy to befoul someone else's name."

Fortunatus has been maneuvered in the right direction psychologically. Bullatus therefore transforms the loser of the pigtail into a moral hero:

"Suppose, by way of hypothesis, that Brighthard had cut off Big Jin's pigtail. This morning Brighstrider's daughter-in-law would have been plunged into the depths of the sea of grievances. It is good fortune that the other man's was cut off in error, leaving Brightstrider no way of demonstrating her culpability. In a profound and mysterious way this saved his daughter-in-law's reputation, and her life.... It was not Brighthard who cut it off but [the deity] the Jade-Blue Elder[33] making use of Brighthard's hand." (RHC 77)

When Fortunatus asks if the young man affected has taken so generous a view of the matter, Bullatus assures him that the young man exulted, declaring, "although our hair and skin are received from our fathers and mothers, and we should not dare to damage them, yet we must be of some benefit to others.... We have no choice but to act like the men of old who would have plucked out a hair without regrets so as to confer some advantage on the world." (RHC 77) Pressed by Fortunatus to reveal who this paragon is, Bullatus tells him that it is Jade Ego, Fortunatus's son. Thus social reality, whether loathsome or flattering, is created by those skilled in the propaganda of everyday life, and both versions are approximately equally false.[34]

As Bullatus takes his leave of Fortunatus he meets a crowd and follows it. They all come to an old and broken-down house. This is the scene that meets his eyes:

> In a little chamber was a young woman of barely twenty years of age, yet she was so shrunken that her bones were like sticks of firewood. She was leaning against a bed and concentrating on vomiting. She had vomited so frequently that her eyes had rolled up, leaving only the whites visible. Her whole face was covered with the streaked courses of her tears.
>
> At her side stood an old woman, wiping the tears away with one hand and holding a bowl of soapy water with the other. Her one concern was to get the young woman to drink it. She kept pressing her: "Drink it, my child!"
>
> The young woman shook her head.
>
> "I can't get it down, Mother. Even my guts want to spew it forth. Your child is dead, Mother.... Let me well and truly die. I'm sorry, Mother, that you brought me up to no purpose, as far as my twenty-first year...."

She stopped speaking and had another fit of vomiting. A bout of panting followed and continued until she lost consciousness.

Bullatus was about to go, unable to bear this tragic sight, when he heard someone say that the young woman was the daughter-in-law of Brightstrider Qin.... Her husband's family had sent her home the previous evening, alleging an illicit love-affair.... The mother had herself gone out to boil up a bowl of noodles for her to eat. Who would have thought that she would have taken advantage of her mother's being off her guard to swallow down the red heads of two boxes of phosphorus matches? This red phosphorus was unrivaled for its toxicity.

"All women who have illicit love-affairs," said another, "seek death in this way in order to frighten people. I've seen any number of such cases. Have a look at her, all of you.... If she suffers death, I'll forfeit my own life."

This callous dismissal of the widow has hardly passed the speaker's lips when Bullatus sees that

the young woman's cheeks had gone a scorched black color. She was spitting blue smoke from her mouth. Her jawbone had locked. Her eyes seemed to be on fire. She was thrashing all over the bed. After a while of this, she bit the corners of the coverlet. Having done this for some time, her legs straightened out and the sound of her breathing stopped, but the blue smoke continued to come up and out of her mouth like a ribbon. (RHC 78–79)

She is dead.

The absurd has become the macabre. The more so for creating a suffering that has no meaning.

The Pleasing Prospect[35]

Ping Jinya has a vision of a lost rural paradise in which people once lived in harmony with nature and themselves. He refers to this explicitly in the so-called 'wedge' or introduction to his book; and there runs through his pages a sense of the contrast between the beauty of the countryside, whether gentle or severe, and the economic desperation and the predatory viciousness of the humans struggling to live in it. This contrast is made more poignant by those evanescent moments when his characters feel a psychological freedom or a humanity untouched by mercenary calculation.

He describes the land of Jiangnan at its most alluring:

For several tens of miles around Prosperton the creeks crossed and re-crossed each other. Here was nothing but a domain of waters, level and beautiful. The countryfolk raised fish and tended ducks, planted water-chestnuts and grew water-lilies, as their main sources of income. The year round, almost all their clothes, their food, and their houses depended on these waters that gleamed in the springtime and flowed by rippling in the autumn.

In Clearcreek village, less than two miles from the town, the inhabi-tants made the water their homestead and the waterbirds their compan-ions. In the dawn they would be singing beside the curving bays where they raised their fish. As the dusk fell they would make themselves tipsy in the crab-sheds. Their was a world of eyots girt with reeds and shorelines of rushes, and for them to sit in a flat-bottomed boat was the pleasure of a lord.

The village had a mere seventy or eighty households. They were in two settlements encircled by the waters, ... veiled by the mists at dawn, and at nightfall by the vapors rising off the lake. Seen from far away, this little village seemed to be like a mirage....

As the sun was going down, every family would spread out their nets to dry. The fish-scales would reflect the light and sparkle like a multi-tude of stars.... Once the sun had set, and the chickens and the dogs had fallen silent, and the weary birds returned to their nests in the thickets, it seemed like the fabled fairyland where the springs flow among the peach-laden trees. (RHC 88)

Of these ordinary people Ping says that "even though they had no reserves of grain in their storage jars, and their houses were as bare as musical chimestones, they would still be whistling and singing, and be content with themselves." (RHC 89)

That evening there had been a heavy fall of snow. It had piled up across the countryside like hill-slopes of silver, or an ocean of white jades. Cir-rus[36] [the sixteen-year-old nephew of the landlored Prosper] ... walked out along the lakeshore in the early hours of the morning. He saw ... a man from Jiangbei,[37] clad only in unpadded trousers and with the upper half of his body stripped bare, extending one arm into the water and groping about for the fish that lived in the fissures of the stone em-bankment. After a long time spent doing this, he pulled out an earth-wife carp, a fish with a large mouth and fine scales....[38]

After the man had been ferreting about like this for a considerable while, his arm became numb with the cold and slowly lost all sensation.

At this point he plunged it into a caldron of water that was steaming away on the stern of his boat in order to warm it up again. This done, he reinserted it into the water to grope about for another fish. (RHC 122)

Survival in this world turns on fine margins of skill, strength, resources, and luck. Ping Jinya describes the lives of some migrants from Jiangbei who husk rice for Prosper:

A powerful man could husk three to four mortars of rice a day. A woman could husk only two. Each mortarful earned 120 cash. On three of the boats in the group there were numerous males who could together bring in more than a thousand cash a day, and they had no trouble in making a living. On the last boat, however, there were only a husband and wife, together with the husband's old father who was incapable of doing any husking.

There was also a girl of some fifteen or sixten years of age lodging on this boat, but she had no great physical vitality, and was unable to husk one mortarful of rice a day to a fully white condition. As may be calculated, the four of them could get from 500 to 600 cash a day, and, as you can imagine, this hardly paid for their food. For this reason the three of them grumbled on from one day to the next in a half-starved and half-fed condition, every one of them eager to drive out the girl....

She had come to Jiangnan with her own parents on their boat to look for a living. In the autumn, though, her father had died quite unexpectedly in an epidemic. The mother and the girl, having no money, had borrowed 30,000 cash from a neighboring boat that was in the business of selling sugar, in order to pay for the funeral.... The girl's mother had then suddenly run away with a man on another boat—no one knew where to—leaving the girl alone on her parents' boat, which was then seized by the creditors as forfeited property.

As she had no place of her own to go to, she had then lodged on this other boat, because the old man had taken a fancy to the idea of taking her home as a wife for his second son.... When a letter came out of the blue to say that this son had died, she became a useless excrescence, and one costing at least three meals a day.... They longed to drive her out, since ... one fewer pair of lips would mean one more pint of rice a day for them. (RHC 106)

This background helps to explain the behavior of Prosper. He is insistent on getting his money's worth at all times. On one occasion he catches his servant Little Third eating some eggs to which he has no right, and when Little Third looks sulky, he scolds him:

"You cur! Pouting, and getting angry and annoyed, are you?! You're not thinking! You are being employed by someone else. Do you want to enjoy the happiness of being your own master?" (RHC 96)

This threat of sacking forces the servant to put a swift smile on his face. The author comments that "everyone in this world has to eat, and so there's not a single person in it fit to be reckoned a hero. If you want to be a hero, first learn some way of not having to eat." (RHC 96)

Prosper's main obsession is collecting his rents. When he complains how difficult it is to extract money from his tenants, Teacher Li, who acts as his secretary, echoes this sentiment with what appears to the reader as a grotesque parody of the old moral-meteorological religion:[39]

> "The hearts of those who farm the fields are of the blackest dye. They treat the land as if it were their own property. They'd like to be given every last one of the landowners' fields that the latters' ancestors bequeathed to them.
>
> "Because people's hearts are so lacking in a sense of what is fair, the Lord of Heaven has to inflict floods on them, and droughts, and famines, together with insect pests that destroy the rice. Even after receiving this retribution they still do not come to their senses. Once the harvest has ripened in the fields, they hurriedly sell the rice, and get drunk, and gamble. There's no thought in their minds of paying the rental rice." (RHC 102)

Prosper comments that he would like to make such behavior by his tenants a capital offense, and then he tells his nephew that they are going by boat to pay a visit to rent-prompter Qin, to stop him being so lax. The contrast between the smiling face of nature and the local children's spontaneous games, on the one hand, and the harsh economic realities, on the other, is again the theme:

> Cirrus pushed his head out of the cabin window and gazed all around Clear Lake. On both its banks lay an even covering of lightly flecked snow, glittering in unstained whiteness. In the clumps of reeds, broken stalks bent their heads at the touch of the snow, trembling in the wind. When the yellow sparrows came flying in to perch there, the snowflakes splashed about on all sides, like pearls being scattered.
> Cirrus felt that his spirit was in harmony with all of this, and that his

mind was ranging far and wide. Surveying this world covered with its ceramic glaze, all he could do was to fix his thoughts upon it in an absent-minded concentration....

When rent-prompter Qin saw his financial boss arrive, ... he promised he would make every effort to press for payment. In the cases of those who obstinately refused, he would tell the rent-pressing officials to get their black ropes flying and tie up the defaulters until they paid. While he sat in the back of the boat, he could not refrain from making his rent calculations.

Cirrus could see the colors of the country as they passed by.... The last shreds of the sun's light sank from his sight, leaving the gloomy mists hanging over a land already half dark. Waste vegetation and dried stalks of weeds moved past outside the porthole....

After reaching Clearcreek village ... the boat went by the bank where the fishponds had been. Cirrus noted that the water pumps, which had been there the previous day, had now been removed. The ponds had been drained, and boys were leaping about in them trying to catch the little crabs and whelks in the slime. The sides of the ponds were slippery and covered in patches of snow, so that if one were not careful one could lose one's footing and slither down to the bottom. The boys were heedless of this and spurred each other on to bravery. Where one rushed in, the others followed him, leaping about in simple-minded delight. (RHC 103)

Later, Cirrus makes another trip to Qin's village, this time only with the boatman Felix. They laugh at the mischief of the children on the bank, particularly that of a seven-year-old who slips some icicles into a pan in which an old woman is roasting popcorn for a younger child. Then the sense of real evil haunting this countryside under its visual beauty and human innocence resurfaces. Felix tells Cirrus the story of a large mansion that they can see is being dismantled:

"Under the former Qing dynasty, that family had limitless resources, and at least three or four thousand *mu* of good riceland.[40] But the owner had a heart and thoughts black beyond all measure. He was too exacting in his financial calculations, too cruel in his levying of rents. His only concern was to cheat his farmers, and he regarded their lives as worth less than an ant's.

"When he was collecting rents in the wintertime, the official runners would seize the tenants and inflict more unofficial tortures and beatings than you could count. They would squeeze a man into two osier baskets bound tightly together with hemp cords, then throw it this way and that across the snowy ground. After they had tossed him about for a while, they would let him out and spit mouthfuls of water into his face until he had revived. They they would throw him about again.

"After being tossed about three times in this way, even if your sinews were of bronze and your bones of iron, the first would have become spongy and the latter soft, and your entire body like a meat-filled dumpling. You can imagine how cruel it was!

"The owner would stand on the terrace above, wearing fox-furs and nursing a hand-warmer between his hands. He would urge his children to have a good giggle as they watched. His name for this torture was 'Lions Sporting with a Brocaded Ball'.

"If it so happened that a tenant could not endure this treatment, and died, and the family of the deceased was standing around weeping, the master's children would rain down several handfuls of silver dollars from above. The aggrieved relatives, seeing that the man was dead, and that they could not afford a lawsuit, could only pick up these snowy-white objects from the ground, and take care of the burial.

"Not a hundred years have passed, but it has fallen into the decay you can see." (RHC 124–25)

Cirrus learns that the owner had no children who survived him, and that the villagers believe the mansion to be haunted. "Such," he comments, "is the supernatural speed of retribution in the world below." (RHC 125)

Rural Idiocy

Almost every aspect of country life is riddled through with absurdity. The episodes that follow illustrate this in a variety of ways.

At times the mockery is gentle. When Cirrus visits a teahouse and orders a pot of 'strong' tea, he is given what looks like boiled water. He lifts the teapot lid:

The teapot was stuffed full of tea leaves. It was only when he turned his head to look at a huge heap of 'revived-soul tea leaves' drying on the window will that he suddenly understood. The leaves could be re-infused and then dried out like this in a never-ending cycle. No wonder they became as blandly flavored as the social relations of the proper gentleman![41]

It was lucky, he mused to himself, that they had brewed 'strong' tea for him. Had they brewed weak tea, he could not imagine how they could have made it any weaker. (RHC 126–27)

Sometimes the humor is sharper. Seated in his teahouse, Cirrus watches the real-life theater that is played out in the traditional Chinese pharmacy across the road under its proud sign SAVING THE WORLD THROUGH THE BLUE-GREEN MEDICINE BAG:

He saw a man come running in a great hurry with a prescription which he gave to the clerk, shouting as he did so: "Show some speed! Some speed! The sick man's on the point of death!"

"Why all the hurry?" said the clerk. "It will be just as effective if he has it when he's dead. If it's so important, why didn't you come in yesterday?"

The first man did not argue. He stood at the counter, waiting. The clerk made a point of weighing everything out with meticulous deliberation. Suddenly the customer picked up a worm-borer[42] from among the ingredients and gave it to the clerk to inspect.

"Look at this! Just look at this!" he said. "Is it proper to sell a worm-borer for money?!"

"That," said the clerk, "is a ginger caterpillar.[43] A most important medicament."

"How can a ginger caterpillar be alive?" asked the customer.[44]

"It has eaten some of our medicine resembling the cinnabar pills of the immortals," said the clerk. "So of course it's alive."

... At this moment another clerk—from the accounts office—came over to have a look.

"This," he pronounced, "is an In-Winter-an-Insect In-Summer-a-Grass.[45] What do you understand of such things? If a sick man has died in the winter he has only to swallow this down to live."

The customer nodded, and replaced it in its wrapper....

The two clerks waited until he had gone some distance, then they took an In-Winter-an-Insect In-Summer-a-Grass and a[n actual] ginger caterpillar [of the proper size] from a drawer, examined them, and dumped them in the street without showing the least sign of compassion. (RHC 127)

At times the humor verges on savagery. Cirrus watches a dispute between two choleric old rustics being arbitrated in a teahouse by a village headman called Master Fifth:

"Tell me, tell me," said Master Fifth, "what is it that you two are quarreling about?"

The first old yokel pointed at the second.

"One of his family's water buffaloes walked into our family's graveyard and ate the grass there. Is that hateful, or isn't it?"

At this point the second old yokel slipped a red-paper packet of money under the table and into Master Fifth's left hand. As soon as he was aware of it, Master Fifth remarked:

"The essence of it is then that a buffalo would not be capable of recognizing your family's graveyard. On the other hand...."

The first yokel, in his turn, shoved a red-paper packet into Master Fifth's right hand.

"On the other hand," Master Fifth continued, "it behooves one to be circumspect when looking after a buffalo. Mmm! On the other hand...."

The second yokel stuffed in another packet.

"On the other hand," Master Fifth resumed, "it only consumed a modicum of herbage. What real harm can that be supposed to have done? On the other hand...."

The first yokel slipped in an extra packet in his turn.

"On the other hand," Master Fifth pursued, "the trampling on the graves must be deemed, per contra, a matter of serious import. Nonetheless...."

The second yokel contributed yet one more packet.

"Nonetheless," Master Fifth continued, "it would have been correct to have lashed up a bamboo palisade along the margin of the site of the graves. Under these circumstances the buffalo would not have been able to effect an entrance. On the other hand, of course...."

The first yokel slipped him an additional packet.

"On the other hand, of course," Master Fifth went on, "bearing in mind the consideration that they have *already* been subjected to trampling, it would be right that...."

The second yokel slipped him yet another packet.

"It would be right that attention be paid to preventing this," said Master Fifth, "on any *subsequent* occasion. Notwithstanding...."

The first yokel had slipped him three red-paper packets of money, and these were all that he possessed. He could only gaze at Master Fifth with a piteous look in his eyes. The second yokel, however, pressed two further packets into Master Fifth's hands. The latter now spoke with decision, 'as if cutting off the head of a nail or slicing through iron'.

"That's it, then!" he said. "There's to be no trampling *next time*. What are you two quarreling about?" (RHC 128–29)

When Cirrus later tells tax-prompter Qin about this dexterous dialectical auctioning of justice, the tax-prompter observes that Master Fifth is a village head of "upright character and free of any selfishness." The reader no doubt wonders what other village heads of lesser probity must be like, but Cirrus merely responds enigmatically, "One would expect no less."

Fraud, sadism, and financial gouging are all tinged with an element of the ludicrous, even when they are also repellent. Jade Ego and Cirrus see a 'dumb' beggar soliciting money from a teahouse proprietor, making abusive gestures when he gets nothing, and then going across the road to pester the staff of a cake shop:

> For all of his reputed business sense the cake shop's owner was unable to get rid of the fellow. But his apprentice had already realized that the beggar would be coming across to demand money, and had quickly picked up a copper coin with a pair of iron chopsticks and thrust it into an oven until it was red-hot. He now pulled it out and called on the dumb man to come over.
>
> When the dumb man saw there was a coin gripped between the chopsticks he spread out his hands to receive it. The iron chopsticks opened and the little coin dropped onto his palms with a *schh!*
>
> The dumb man's body doubled up with pain.
>
> "Uh! Yuh!" he bawled. "It bloody hurts!"
>
> "The pain won't kill you," laughed the apprentice. "We've got you into hot water, all right, haven't we, Mr. *Dumb* Man?!"
>
> The beggar blew on his hand and advanced to hit the apprentice, but the owner of the cake shop gave him a flying kick that sent him into the middle of the street. When the proprietor of the teahouse saw what was going on, he also took advantage of the situation to rush over and pummel the beggar. The latter realized he could not fend off two people and could only slink away. (RHC 167–68)

A more sinister con artist is the moneylender whom the two young men watch stalking his victims in a gambling house:

> At the table next to them was a man so thin that his veins and bones stood out, and his face all but resembled a skull. His legs were virtually like those of a crane.... As he sat there, he gave a dry cough, and his eyes flashed an evil light in the direction of a young man in the gambling den. The young man reacted as if he had been struck by lightning, held fast in the rays from those two eyes. He bowed to the ground and called out: "Fourth Uncle!"

Fourth Uncle slowly opened a small pocket in his waistcoat, from which he extracted a little notebook. He gave it a glance, stretched out his left hand, and flexed his fingers in turn. Then he closed his eyes and knotted his brows.

"Forty dollars and eighty cents," he said.

The young man gave a panic-stricken start and answered: "I borrowed *one* dollar off you, *four* days ago. How could the sum be so enormous?"

"It only needs interest on one dollar over four days," said Fourth Uncle. "You are being charged according to the formula *Plus fifty per cent at night, doubling up at dawn, with one dime extra for each meeting face to face, and ten per cent on top for each adding up of the total.* You may re-examine it yourself to see if I am even a trifle in error."

"You do the calculations and I will listen," said the young man. "I do not understand your method of calculating."

"...On the first night the capital plus the interest came to $1.50," said Fourth Uncle. "On the morning of the second day, this changed to $3.00. With the 50% addition at night, the total was $4.50. On the third day, the sum changed to $9.00, and the nighttime addition of 50% interest raised it to $13.50. Today is the fourth day. This morning increased it to $27.00, and the nighttime 50% has brought it to $40.50.

"This covers only the capital and the interest. We have also to add in the face-to-face meetings at a dime each. On the morning of the second day, weren't you at Toto Quan's teahouse, where I had a glimpse of you? We have therefore now to add on 30 cents [for three meetings, including those for the arranging of the loan and the present occasion], making $40.80, which is not an excessive sum. I would suggest that you give it to me. If you don't return it to me today, it will increase greatly. Our meeting at this moment in time has in itself required the addition of 10%, or $4.08 [for adding up], bringing the total to $44.88...."

When the young man heard this, his tongue stuck out and he could not retract it.

"If the present occasion is not convenient for you," said Fourth Uncle, "you can repay me in a few days, but once a full ten days have passed, I shall have to come to your firm's premises to collect it. By that time the total will have become enormous, and I shall have to use the means of obtaining rights of constraint over a debtor's property." (RHC 165–66)

The terrified young man runs off without uttering another word.

There are other humorous episodes with other targets. In one such, an old-style teacher is trying to give a vivid quality to his explanation of a passage in the *Analects* (which he has misinterpreted). He pretends to be the chief character in the story, who rides on horseback,[46] and seats himself astride a school bench. Full of enthusiasm for this charade, he wallops the rump of his 'horse' with a ruler. By mistake he hits his other hand, makes his finger bleed, and grimaces with pain. Cirrus watches him silently in bemused contempt. He reflects that he has called him 'Teacher' because he studied with him, but this teaching was like the performance of ritual or the intoning of scriptures by a Buddhist monk or Daoist priest, whose object was merely to delude the donors of vegetarian banquets into feeding them. (RHC 116, and see also 97–98) Traditional learning has become meaningless.

Mocking the frauds practised by others could have dangerous consequences. Jade Ego, Bullatus, Cirrus, and Albedo are returning from a mildly flirtatious outing to a nunnery when they meet a young woman who offers to remove the worms that cause tooth decay, tell fortunes, and 'blend a bowl of water'.[47] Bullatus asks what this last might mean.

"A simple way of making contact with the dead," the young woman answered, "and of talking with the ghosts of deceased family members."

"Is it accurate?" asked Bullatus. "How many cash for one blending?...."

"One hundred," she said. "And if it doesn't reach the target, there's no need to pay."

Bullatus thereupon pretended to look very solemn, and told her to 'blend a bowl of water'. He borrowed a bowl from one of the peasant families [standing watching], filled it with water, and placed it in front of her. She drank a little and rinsed out her mouth.

"Are you inquiring about someone of the senior or of the same generation?" she asked. "Is the deceased a man or a woman?"

"A dead woman," said Bullatus, "and she may be reckoned to be of my own generation."

"And what were her married and maiden surnames?"

Bullatus was stumped [*daile dai*], but seeing a poplar tree [*yang*] by the house across the way, he improvised.

"Her married name was Stump [Dai]," he said, "and her maiden name was Poplar [Yang]."

"How long did she live for?" continued the young woman. "In what month, and on what day, did she die?"

Bullatus made up some more fibs, and—when he had finished speaking—assumed a heart-broken expression, with his two pitiful eyes fixed on the young woman. She closed her own eyes and concentrated for a moment, giving three or four yawns in succession. Suddenly her eyeballs popped from their sockets. She burst into a wailing and a sobbing that struck a dazed fear into all of those present....

"Ai!" she cried. "My dear husband! You've left me in such a grievous state! You, there, in the sunlit world, are like the dew on the lotus leaf ... more happy than can be told. Who would have thought that I, after so short a span of life, would be suffering such torment in the realm of shadows?"

As she spoke, she brushed her tears away, and there really were one or two falling. The crowd was guffawing. Bullatus was making a show of joining in the tears, but he was laughing inside till his guts split....[48]

Once the young woman had noticed that they were taking advantage of her, she wiped her tears away and stopped crying, just as if it had been a business deal, and the money and the goods had now been exchanged.

Jade Ego and Cirrus were laughing till their stomachs ached.

"That's enough!" Jade Ego exclaimed. "But why do you sell your tears so cheap? I wouldn't grudge paying you if you cried for us a second time." (RHC 45)

This gibe nearly costs Jade Ego dear some months later. The young woman comes across him after his queue has been lopped off and lures him onto her boat for 'a cup of tea'. After forcing herself onto his lap, in order to arouse his lusts, she discusses her performances with a certain candor:

"Some people use raw ginger, ground up and rubbed into the corners of the eyes, to force out the tears. I've no need to fake them in this fashion. Although my mental and emotional capacity is small, it seems to be linked to the open sea and an all but endless supply of tears that couldn't be exhausted in a lifetime.... One item of business needs eight to ten tears, and I only have to be careful not to overdo it." (RHC 150)

Her food and clothing, she observes, are "the transmutations of my tears and sniveling." (RHC 151) Then her resentment shows itself:

"Sometimes I meet smooth-spoken young men who try to find people to make fun of," she added, "and laugh at them for all they're worth.

The more I think about such people, the harder I find them to endure. I sob my throat out. They wait till I've finished crying but still don't think the matter's done with. They want to force me to give a laugh before they'll hand over any money. I'm sorry to say that for me producing this sort of laugh is much harder than crying. But—since the cash is in their hands—if I don't give a laugh, I've wept in vain. There's nothing for it but to make a pretense, give a false laugh, get the money, and make off—with a couple of tears still in my mouth." (RHC 152)

She clearly has Bullatus and Jade Ego in mind.

She has no difficulty in seducing Jade Ego, and the young man goes off to sleep in the cabin of her boat afterwards. When he wakes up in the morning, he finds he has been kidnapped, and the boat is being poled along by her two brothers. He smashes his way out through a porthole, leaps to the bank wearing only a cotton shirt, and rushes to a nearby monastery. He is pursued by one of the brothers, who accuses him of interfering sexually with his sister. Fortunately the local monk is an old friend of Jade Ego's and drives the man off.

When he talks the matter over with Cirrus later they agree that it was probably a kidnap for ransom since they had not even bothered to take his wallet. When Jade Ego has to explain to Cirrus's girlfriend what he was doing overnight he says he was playing mahjong [*maque*, which also means 'sparrow']. When she is out of earshot, Cirrus unleashes a volley of sexual double entendres at his friend:

"It's not very polite to me, your old pal, to concoct such lies. Let me ask you, what sort of sparrow session did you play last night?!... I'd guess you were definitely a big loser. Your sparrow got into the bivalve clam just in the nick of time, and he's already turned to water. Poor sparrow!... Now he's all but numb [*mamu*], and incapable of sensitive feeling."

"Stop making fun of me," said Jade Ego. "That sparrow of mine almost fell into their nets, to be cooked and carved as a dainty morsel to help them swallow their wine."

"Tomorrow, then," said Cirrus, "we can give you a new courtesy name—'Mr. Under-the-Pants Narrow-Miss', and that will stop you forgetting about it." (RHC 157)

This obscene quickfire repartee was much admired in young men, but there is also a serious point. Jade Ego had been in real danger.

The Awakening Lioness

Bullatus is a young man more than half in love with his own wit. At times he can be offensive. When a man eating dumplings at a table next to him in a restaurant unintentionally splatters him with a spot of gravy on his forehead, Bullatus contemptuously declines the man's courteous offer to wipe it clean, observing that the diner has still six more dumplings to eat, and he will wait and wipe all the spots off at once. (RHC 169) Sometimes, though, his tricks are used in a good cause. He saves Big Jin from the wrath of the Bright brothers by scaring the brothers away from Paxville. He does this by hiring two outsiders to dress up as official runners and move around the village at night, ostensibly searching for the criminals guilty of "coercing the loss of a a person' life and forcibly cutting off a pigtail." (RHC 187)

His insensitivity is at its least pleasant in his treatment of his father, Aquilonius, a hardworking, self-made man who runs a shop for miscellaneous goods and farms an acre or so of land. Modern education, provided by Aquilonius's own efforts for his son, has opened a psychological gap between them:

> Aquilonius and his wife used to carry manure across the bridge every day, making more than ten round trips before night fell. At that time Bullatus was still a youngster, and going to the primary school at the county capital. When he had come home for the Mid-Autumn Festival, he had been wearing a brand-new uniform and a pair of white leather shoes, sticking out his chest and puffing up his tummy. To cross the bridge he had to go along a narrow plank, but had persisted in practising his military march-step. *One, two! One, two!* He had not been prepared to meet his mother coming toward him, carrying a tub of manure.
>
> As soon as she had caught sight of her son returning, her eyebrows had risen and her eyes had begun to sparkle. She had hurriedly put the tub of manure down at one side to let him pass, but, through inadvertence, a drop of liquid ordure had splashed onto one of his white leather shoes....
>
> Bullatus had arrived home with his two little cheeks swelling. He

had paid no attention to his father, and when his father had questioned him he had burst into tears. His father ... had scooped a lump of lime out of a white-washed shed, crouched down, and rubbed the spot on the white leather shoe until it was white again....

Now that Bullatus ... had graduated from the teachers' training college, ... not only did his father treat him as if *he* were the father, but as if he were some remote ancestor. He had only to say the word and his father would do what he asked. The father ate two bowls of rice porridge a day. His son had a bowl of pork noodles each morning, and insisted on sauce on top of that. The father kept a smile on his face, but felt pain in his heart. (RHC 48)

Other events intensify this suffering. On one occasion Bullatus invites his high-class friend Albedo round for a meal, without regard for his father's limited economic means:

He ordered the apprentice who worked in the shop to go round to Third Matron's wine house next door to fetch a catty of wine, a bowl of fried eggs, and a saucer of boiled shrimps.

Aquilonius kept up a flow of banter, but did a mental calculation. —That was one of the two piglets he was rearing in a pen gone. His heart hurt.

Bullatus and Albedo became merry with wine, and started to play at guess-fingers; but the sound that Aquilonius heard in his ears seemed to be that of a piglet, squealing.

A while later, when both of them had eaten, Bullatus further told the apprentice to fetch two portions of bream soup. This added new pain to the pain already afflicting Aquilonius. He reflected that he would not be able to keep either of his piglets.... He gave a cold, silent choke and went away into an inner room to brush away his tears. (RHC 49)

The same evening Bullatus also entertains Jade Ego at home. The two of them swap scholars' jokes that Aquilonius is too little educated to grasp; and the last of the jokes is in fact aimed at making fun of him to his face. Bullatus is "both ashamed and amused by this." (RHC 50–52) Filial obedience and respect are all but dead in him—and social pressures to make him filial are too slight to have much effect.

Bullatus's supreme act of deception is that which he plays on Leonina, whose name in Chinese—'Awakening Lioness'—symbol-

izes the New China. This episode makes a mockery of *both* the old
and the new ways of conducting the affairs of life.

Tigerlike Zhao, the village headman of Southdark, is a charitable
man but given to social climbing. He wants Leonina, his only child,
to be the headmistress of a primary school. Since she is unlikely to
get such a position in the ordinary way, he founds a school for her
himself in Southdark. The premises are the front parts of the City
God's temple, the God being permitted to retain the rear third.
The pupils have to come to school between the lines of the infernal
lictors with their scowling black faces and red beards. The former
religious plaque HAVE YOU COME?—meaning 'come to judgment'—
has been inadequately covered by the new sign saying SCHOOL
ROOM. The question mark is still showing, so it reads SCHOOL
ROOM?

Fortunatus declaims the formal opening speech before a crowd
of worthies and parents, but the absurdity of his would-be gran-
diloquent phrases undermines his good intent:

> "It is my aspiration, speaking in my capacity as Director of this Rural
> District, that you will all of you be coming in perpetuity to be grounded
> here at this cheap and gratuitous place for studying free of charge! It is
> likewise my hope that there will appear a second, and indeed a third,
> Mr. Zhao with thick enough wits to be willing to provide funds for the
> engagement of teachers, to help provide for this cheap and gratuituous
> place for you to be grounded at." (RHC 215)

He tells the pupils they must think of the headmistress as their
mother and the male teachers as their fath.... He stops himself at
this point, having noticed that one of the elderly male teachers has
gone red with embarrassment. He harrumphs himself out of this
difficulty, but a barefoot mother can be seen dragging her child
away and muttering:

> "Who would want to be grounded at this cheap and gratuitous place?! I
> showed every respect for your social reputation in sending my boy here
> to study. Now you're insisting on treating him as *your* child, and he's
> going to have to call you 'parents'. A person has only one father and one
> mother. Whose parents do you think you are? Look at your faces in the
> mirror! See if there's any likeness or not!" (RHC 216)

This misunderstanding of a metaphor symbolizes the uneasiness of the coexistence between the fragments of nascent, ill-assimilated, modernity and the residues of tradition.

Leonina herself is not present at this occasion, as she is still finishing her training course. When she arrives to see how the school is doing, she is shocked. The out-of-date pedants hired by her father are "stuffing for coffins," and have "completely buried the natural inner liveliness of the children." He would have done better, she tells him, to have thrown his money into Southdark Creek. "In that case you'd at least have had some ripples to look at, and not damaged other people's children." (RHC 217)

Leonina has her own problems, though. A massively outsize and domineering young lady, she has no boyfriend. When her girlfriends at the training college fix up a blind date for her, the young man flees in terror the moment he sets eyes on her. After this

> Leonina returned to the college in a fury, and devised a clever stratagem. Taking advantage of the large numbers gathered for a sports meeting, she made thirty-six mandarin-duck name-card cases, and into each one put a photograph of herself, five or six name cards, and a ring. Then she scattered them all over the sportsground like the seeds of love. (RHC 220)

She harvests one hundred and sixty-five-and-a-half love letters, the 'half' being a picture postcard. Nineteen of these letters are from Albedo, the son of Quartus Wang. He has become 'drunk on freedom' after reading books by the late-Qing reformer Liang Qichao, and has rejected the girl to whom his father betrothed him as a child. He has no liking for the traditional "soft and pliant women with willow waists, elegant and slender." (RHC 219) He admires Leonina's picture, which strikes him as "strong, heroic, and masterful." They agree by correspondence to marry, sight unseen, once he has acquired some teaching qualifications. Shortly after this, the elderly pedants are sacked, and Bullatus and Albedo given appointments by Tigerlike to take their places, though they cannot assume these jobs at once.

Bullatus is to teach music, so he travels up to Shanghai to get his organ mended. He also agrees to collect some name cards that Albedo has had printed there. He is waiting in the boat to start on the return journey when it shudders as someone else gets on.

> "Walk a little more lightly, if you please!" sang out the boatman, "or the boat will turn over!"
>
> Whoever it was that had come aboard replied in a voice like a [deep] bell: "Your boat's not made of papier-mâché! What's wrong with people standing on it?" (RHC 224)

Then he sees her. She is "neither male nor female, and as fat as a bull. Her dumpy thighs were plumper than a pair of lampshades.... Her feet slapped freely as she galumphed along. She was dressed entirely in pink silk, both her blouse and her trousers, and a short gown that fell to the level of her knees. Her hair was as disheveled as a sparrow's nest. Her face was square, her ears huge. Her mouth gaped, and her nose was of a giant size. She was holding a parasol of plain-weave silk, and clasping an English book." When, somewhat later, Bullatus is hunting for his cigarette holder, and empties his pockets out in the search, he also takes out Albedo's name cards. Her eyes, "like flashes of lightning," fix on them at once.

She thinks he is Albedo. She starts to chat to him in an affectionate, bantering manner. He, on the other hand, has no idea who she is, or what has happened. Out of an impulse for casual mischief-making, he plays along, but she rebukes him. "Your heart's not in it!" she says. He is "a man with a mouth but no heart." Why, he can't even remember her name! Bullatus adroitly contrives to get a glimpse of her name card. When he sees it, he goes bright scarlet. My future employer! he thinks. And I've been lying to her. Then he reflects that since the job has certainly gone, he might as well go on impersonating his friend.

He implores her to marry him at once. "I really can't wait," he vows. "You must perform an act of goodness. As soon as we're back home, have the ceremony performed. Why pick a day? Saving a human life surpasses building seven tiers of Buddhas!" Then he launches into an encomium of "stolen, unmarried love" as the only "true love." Marriage is the tomb of love. Why should they even be concerned with these formalities? He will not spare himself in helping her to enjoy "all the flavors." "It is so hard to endure," he concludes. "Each night is like a year. Keeping myself pure is like being beheaded." These totally insincere avowals so stir her up that the moment she is home she instructs her father to have a go-between arrange the marriage—with Albedo—as fast as possible. In the meantime, Bullatus has slipped away, "laughing silently in the darkness of his heart." (RHC 224–31)

The ceremony is described as a "civilized" one, but it abounds in comedy, both intended and unintended. Bullatus has sent a number of congratulatory calligraphic scrolls, most of them under the forged signatures of his friends, all making fun of the immensity of Leonina and the scrawny frame of Albedo. One, which sends Jade Ego into roars of laughter, will serve as an example of this rubbish (RHC 233):

> With a cry of Oyo! the lioness pounces
> Upon the brocade ball's stalk!
> With a squeaking of "Goody!" the rat licks the oil
> Out of the bowl of the lamp.

Jade Ego and Cirrus drag Bullatus from his father's shop, where he has been hiding himself, and scare the full story out of him. Then they start to tease him. Since he has already acted the play of *The Twins*, they say, he ought to continue with *An Error in the Flowery Field of Love*. "Change your clothes," Jade Ego urges him, "and sit in the bridal chamber waiting for the newly wed bride to arrive. Then you can—!" But Bullatus, now distraught, begs them to think of a plan that will let him escape. Manic cheerfulness, counsels Jade Ego. That's the only way. "No one will be able to take you seriously." (RHC 236–37)

Firecrackers go off. The band plays. Quartus Wang and Fortunatus, as the go-betweens, negotiate over the final demands made by the modern-minded Leonina. They agree that there will be no kneeling, but a sedan-chair will be used. Two extra bearers, in addition to the usual two, are needed to lift this chair with Leonina in it. She enters the hall followed by thirty or so of the school's pupils in white uniforms and black caps topped with white kerchiefs "as if they were following a *funeral* cortège"—another indication of how awkwardly the old style and old symbols consort with the new. The teacher in charge draws them up in two lines "like temple arhats" and bellows: "Atten-*shun*!! Standa-*teeze*!" The spectators, looking at their bare feet and tousled hair, mutter: "Wherever did they drum up these little performers from?" (RHC 238)

Leonina descends, "thrusts out her chest and sways majestically, like a movable screen of human flesh," while the chair bearers rub their swollen shoulders.

> She not only had no collar on her neck but had scooped out a space there to show a snowy-white undershirt and two breasts that faced each other like northern and southern summits. Her headful of wild hair was secured by a satin ribbon. A pair of spectacles with black lenses perched on her nose. The pink scarf on her head fell down to her shoulders and was topped by a massive paper flower. She was shod with yellow shoes. (RHC 239)

She and Albedo have still not seen each other face to face. At last, after bowing to their guests, they turn to look at each other.

> Leonina felt a violent pang of dismay. Involuntarily she uttered a subdued "Yow!" She closed her eyes and called to mind the image of Bullatus that she had stored in her brain. It was, in her estimation, quite different from the bridegroom now standing before her. (RHC 240–41)

The masterful modern young lady has lost control of the situation. Chance, or predestined affinity, still rules modern marriage as it did the traditional kind. She can only "allow herself to be ordered about." (RHC 241) She soon pulls herself together, however, and summons Fortunatus.

> "Who is this bridegroom?" she asked abruptly.
> The question flummoxed Fortunatus. For a short while he was unable to answer.
> "That man," pursued Leonina. "Is *he* the real Albedo?"
> Fortunatus could only laugh at this.
> "Really and truly," he said. "The authentic article."
> "Did he *use* to be known as 'Albedo'?" Leonina went on.
> "Since the day of his birth," replied Fortunatus.
> "*How many* Albedos are there in Prosperton?" demanded Leonina.
> "Altogether."

"I only know of this one," replied Fortunatus.

"Did *this* Albedo graduate from the teachers' training college in the county capital, and does he serve as a teacher in our school?" asked Leonina.

"Right on both counts," said Fortunatus.

Leonina nodded.

"That clarifies the matter, then," she said. "My apologies, Senior Uncle." (RHC 240)

The moment has come for the time-honored custom of lewd horseplay at a wedding. Bullatus improvises obscene doggerel verses. Cirrus, who has been peeking through a hole in the wall, gives a blow by blow account of the first tête-à-tête between the newly wed couple:

"Miss Leonina takes off her sunglasses, and she subjects Albedo to a thorough scrutiny, just as if she were a professor of physiognomy. Having looked him over for a while, she interrogates him with a severe expression on her face.

"Albedo gets flustered. He digs out a photo and some name cards from a book box, and also a ring that looks like some sort of token, and ceremoniously hands them over to her for examination.

"Our bride acknowledges them, but she's far from being wholly convinced. She takes out a brush and some ink, and demands that he write a few characters for her. Then it looks as if she is checking up on his handwriting.

"After that they talk for a while. Then I hear them chuckling with laughter. A singular farce, I think you would agree?" (RHC 243)

When the couple summon Bullatus to appear before them, he first puts on a 'skullcap' made from a pomelo casing, holds an unripe banana in his hand as a 'pipe', and conducts himself as if he were an elderly official, using pompous language and 'lighting' his pipe from a bridal candle and pretending to puff on it. This sends Albedo into paroxysms of laughter, and Bullatus takes his chance to sit down next to the bride, whose handkerchief he steals. Leonina, who has recognized him, picks him up bodily and dumps him on the bed, where he lies gabbling and pretending to be drunk. When the teacher in charge of the children comes to take his leave, Bullatus tells him: "Not so fast, teacher! You'll be needed here tonight [in the bedroom] to call out *One! Two! Three!*" (RHC 246) When Fortunatus also calls by to bid farewell, and Leonina has thanked him, the rural district director replies: "My task is finished, and was no pain at all. The pain that you two are going to suffer is only just beginning." (RHC 247) There is general merriment.

The first-night encounter also has its comedy. Albedo is bashful and Leonina has to take the initiative, observing: "If you don't come to be my teacher, this marriage business is not going to get off to an amazingly quick start." (RHC 248) In the end they agree to pretend to be tigers, and matters come to an appropriate conclusion when Albedo asks her, "Where's your tiger's lair?" and she replies, "Just give me your tiger's tail!" (RHC 249)

Next morning Bullatus calls by, waving the stolen handkerchief, and starts to tease Albedo, who finally exclaims:

> "Shut your mouth, you chatterbox! You not only left me in a mess yesterday, you've messed me up in all sorts of ways. You knew what you were doing. Why don't you examine your conscience?"
>
> "I can examine my conscience without any sense of shame," said Bullatus. "... Let me turn the question round. Did *you* know what *you* were doing? In that experience of yours last night [you'll have seen that] not one hair of your lioness's fur was rubbed up the wrong way.... As for my chance encounter with her on a certain day, it was supernatural beings who sent me on that mission. For the sake of your face, old friend, I abandoned the body nurtured by my father and mother, and took over your body. For your sake, I adopted the most diplomatic style of talking, and injected her full of [psychological] morphine, so stimulating her to attain that happiness that you now enjoy.
>
> "If I hadn't done this, I fear the two of you would have proceeded in opposite directions as before, each of you leading a lonesome life. It was like cultivating a plant. You only put in the seed. Again and again I watered it for you, and fertilized it, until the fruit was ripe and you could enjoy it.
>
> "...If you hadn't mentioned the subject, I would have said nothing. Since you raised it, the two of you ought by rights to invite me to a banquet!" (RHC 250–51)

Bullatus's tongue-in-cheek self-justification, which contains of course a modicum of truth in addition to its cargo of humbug, sums up Ping Jinya's sense of the contingent as a driving force in human existence.

Things Fall Apart[49]

The rains pour down. The land is flooded and people are drowned. Prosper's grain reserves are looted. He and his wife flee.

> Cirrus took his shoes off and went outside to gaze at the light that spread across the empty expanse of waters that reached to the horizon. He could distinguish neither fields nor cottages, nor the dikes between the fields. The villagers' wailing and moaning were unbearable to listen to. Boatload after boatload of refugees were out looting everywhere. It was, in simple truth, a world that had fallen apart. (RHC 256)

He goes to Albedo's house and finds Leonina there, reading a newspaper—the final absurdity. He asks her what the news is:

> "A lot of news," she replied. "In Shanghai a Pekinese dog has been crushed to death by a motorcar. There's a wife who murdered her husband in Tianjin. They've not caught her yet. Heavy snow's fallen in Harbin. There's been an earthquake in Japan. The value of the German mark has plunged...."
> "Anything in it about the enormous flood here?" asked Cirrus.
> "There's no enormous flood," said Leonina. "I don't know of any such thing, not having been out of doors for the last five days.... The weather's been uncommonly oppressive. The best thing would be for the rain to keep falling for ten days, and clear the water vapor out of the air. That will make it much more fresh and pleasant." (RHC 257)

At this juncture Albedo enters and observes that there are ten feet of water outside, that their school has been destroyed by the country people, and one of the teachers kidnapped. The county government has authorized soldiers to kill people on the spot if necessary, to maintain order. "If the school's been destroyed," says Leonina, "then don't be concerned about it. I wonder how my family is? My old cat gave birth to two kittens last month.... I wonder if they've been drowned?" The detachment of the young, modern, local elite elite from the realities of local life could hardly be more heavily underlined.

Cirrus and Bullatus agree to leave for a stay in Shanghai. They meet Big Jin and Second Jin on the boat, and the brothers tell them that Jin the Third has joined forces with Brightstrider and Brighthard to loot their house, using the pretext that the baby Dragon Official had taken all the luck away from the area. The Jins have fled with the baby, as they are now dependent on the remittances sent for its upkeep. They, too, are headed for the great city.

What are we to make of this once popular but now forgotten work?[50] First of all, perhaps, that the history of what is actually widely read is often significantly different from the history of what is later defined as 'literature'. Both can be significant for the historian of the emotions, but the first is likely to be a surer guide to the temper of particular epochs than the second. Second, and more important, that the patterns of meaning in human existence that we found on the whole confidently asserted in the *Flowers* and *The Bell of Poesy* a century or so earlier are no longer believable, at least for the urban readership that presumably formed Ping Jinya's audience in the 1930s. Their disintegration at the level at which life is lived—not the theoretical level, though they had collapesed there, too—is consciously explored by the author in a multitude of different situations; and the absurd and accidental—and cruel—nature of much of human existence is evoked, not only by his descriptions but also by the structure of his plots which are often contorted beyond the bounds of reasonable suspension of disbelief (as with Leonina's marriage) in order to convey his underlying vision. He has, moreover, nothing specific to offer as a counterweight to absurdity and accident and cruelty except a certain implicit humanism and sense of decency. Third, that in so far as this sort of spiritual anomie was widespread at this time, it may be plausibly thought to have been too difficult for most people to endure indefinitely, especially in the increasingly hard circumstances of the Pacific War (1937–45) and the Second Civil War between the Nationalists and the Communists (1946–49). There was a need for a solution—even a false one—that would provide a new, hopeful, and livable story.

CHAPTER FOUR

The Magic of Moral Power

THE CONQUEST of China by Communism, in all senses
of the word 'conquest' and not just the military victory
over the Nationalists on the mainland in 1949, was a complex
process that has been discussed in many books and can be given
many interpretations. Here the analysis is limited to exploring the
new elements of emotional life introduced and spread by the Chinese Communists, and above all the new 'story' in which they lived
themselves and tried to persuade others to live.

The imaginary domain in which these themes will be examined
is a novel by Hao Ran, *The Children of the Western Sands*, published in 1974.[1] It is a masterpiece of propaganda: inspirational, lit
by make-believe stage-lighting, awash with revolutionary romanticism. Compared to the best non-Chinese examples of this genre—
such as *The Bronze Bust* by the Albanian writer Dritëro Agolli
(1970)—it appears as something of a wish-fulfilling fantasy. But
Hao Ran is a virtuoso of pace, suspense, and highly colored description. His narrative carries the reader along like a canoeist down
a series of rapids, not always having the time to be fully aware of
the ideological scenery through which he or she is being taken: the
joy and duty of morally justified hatred; the never-ending nature of
the revolutionary struggle against class enemies, national enemies,
and backward thought; the inevitable victory of those with superior
moral power; and the inspiration of building at breakneck speed a
technically advanced society based on self-sacrifice and a rejection
of any ambitions for oneself or for one's family.

It shows how the new story of Communism put an end to the

torments of absurdity, and tapped deep sources of idealism in doing so. Those who peddled it then betrayed their own vision with a cynical hypocrisy that has had few precedents in history. It is possible for the sensitive reader, especially with the advantages of hindsight, to intuit this betrayal, even as he or she reads, in the falsity of the book's brilliance—but brilliance nonetheless.

The Children of the Western Sands is set in the Paracel Islands, the 'Western Sands' of the title. This is an archipelago between Vietnam and the Philippines and claimed by several countries besides China, because of the oil that is thought to be there. Part I, entitled "Correct Attitudes," describes the period of war against the Japanese. The struggle of the fishing people against their boss, whose sobriquet is 'Shark's Teeth', is interwoven with the fight led by the partisans under Communist leadership against the invaders. Part II, called "Exceptional Ambitions," describes the Western Sands under Communism. The first subsection tells of the Great Leap Forward in 1958, and the second tells of the later part of the Cultural Revolution, around 1972. The underlying structure is a linear sequence of social developments; and it is set up to show how human character changes in a fashion that reflects, in one way or another, these changing circumstances.

New Birth

The opening chapter evokes the romance of birth. It is a dark night and a storm is raging. On a fishing boat, a woman is in danger as she labors in the last moments of a pregnancy. The midwife, old Mrs. Fu, tells the woman's husband, Cheng Liang, that she can save mother or child, but not both. He pleads with her to save both, and launches into an impassioned speech:

> "Her mother fell ill, and there was no cash for a doctor.... Her father did not have the money to pay the rent for his boat. He was beaten by the Boss of the Fishermen until he spat fresh blood from his mouth. As he was about to breathe his last, he drew my father by the hand and ... gave his daughter in betrothal to me.... For fifteen years now, among

the births and deaths in the winds and the waves of these Western Sands in the southern seas, she has not enjoyed one day of happiness with me. How could I toss her away like this? We have had two girls.... The eldest died of hunger. The second fell in the sea and was drowned.... How can I not want this baby? Midwife Fu ... think of something for me!" (XSEN I. 3)

But the midwife is helpless. Standing on his boat, facing the sea and the sky, Cheng Liang bursts into a rhetorical address to the unborn child:

"Baby! Little baby! Why won't you be born? Do you look with distaste on our poverty? Yes, we are poor, with no patch of heaven above our heads, not one board of our own beneath our feet. Our ragged clothes do not cover our bodies. But child! Your father is strong. Your mother works perseveringly. The great sea is kind to us. The Western Sands give us their hidden treasures. We shall hazard our own lives to bring you up.... Do you fear the darkness of the world? Yes, it is dark. There are sharks in the sea, plunging through the evil surges. There are wolves on the land, doing cruel and wicked things. Poor people are in deep water and blazing fire. But the present time is not the same as your grandfather's day. The risen tide is reaching the point of return. When the dark night is past, the daylight comes. Poor people will lift their heads then, and straighten their backs. The ways of the world will be greatly changed. *Baby, little baby, you are the root of the generations of us fisherfolk to come.* The more the rich cheat us and oppress us, the more we shall continue to live with our chests thrust proudly forward ... and continue for generation after generation!" (XSEN I.4)

Ideology works its magic on nature:

This voice sounded like thunder. It flashed like lightning. It shook the fishing boat. It pierced the great ocean.

> *Fierce winds, you have lost heart!*
> *Huge waves, you have lowered your heads!*
> *People in the boat, brush away your tears and lift your heads!*

Was it in answer to the father's call, or the urging of kinsmen? As the sun broke through the mists, and cleared away the dark rains, at that instant when the wind-beaten waves rested a brief space for breath, the Cheng family's baby cried *wa-la*—the birth had taken place! (XSEN I.4)

These passages should not be read casually. They express the Maoist vision with exemplary clarity: a secular Zoroastrianism illumined
by the hope of a secular redemption. The human drama is is a
never-ending war between the evil, those people who devour others, and the good, those who assist others to have life and to have it
more abundantly. Outside this drama, Nature has no meaning,
coming into human consciousness only as an expressive background,
a contrastive counterpoint or an appropriate response—just as in
The Book of Songs, now almost three millennia old.

We return to the sharpening conflict. When Shark's Teeth hears
of the birth, he interrogates his sidekick, One-Eyed Crab, about it:

> "Dead baby or live one?"
>
> "Alive."
>
> "Fuck it, man! Didn't I tell you no live ones were to be allowed?"
>
> "Big crowd at the boat just then, Sir. The midwife was one of their
> lot, too. There was no way I could easily interfere...."
>
> "There will be difficulties—for us—if it stays alive."
>
> "No, sir. Not a chance. It's a girl."
>
> "A *girl*! They drowned her?"
>
> "They're too poor. I don't think they'll be able to keep a girl alive."
> (XSEN I.6)

Shark's Teeth, it appears, needs to find a wet-nurse for a Japanese
army interpreter, which is why he does not want any live births in
his workforce just at present. One-Eyed Crab goes to see Cheng
and offers him some "gifts from the boss": a sack of rice and two
chickens. His wife, he adds, is to "come up to the mansion" in
three days. Cheng rejects this bribery and drives the Crab off his
boat. His friends criticize him. Such bravery might have been worth
risking for a boy, but it's foolish to pick a quarrel like this just over
a girl. He disagrees:

> "The greatest of all losses is to abandon future generations.... Why have
> so many people despised girls since ancient times right down to the pre-
> sent? Moneylenders and depraved bosses think like this. Should we
> poor people, with our darkened understanding, think the same way?...
> We cannot go on like this! From this generation onward we must
> change this Heaven and this Earth around, smash this tradition! The
> sons of poor fishing folk are jewels. The daughters of poor fishing folk

are jewels, too. We rely on them to carry on our people. We rely on their spirit of struggle to bury this man-eating world!" (XSEN I.12–13)

And he names his daughter A-bao, 'Jewel'. As Hao Ran develops his story, he evokes in her and around her a new complex of stereotypes relating to the body and the personality: a kiddy-directed sentimentality, the toughening of physical solitude, an antisensual healthiness, a revolutionary asceticism.

Some time after her birth, we see the idyll of parenthood, gently but firmly tempered with the communist work ethic. The family is out at sea:

A-bao was placed in the cabin, next to the doorway. Her cushion was ragged fishing-nets. Her head was pillowed on her father's torn cotton shirt. How sweetly she slept!

The sea wind blended the strong smell of the fish with the pure cool of the sea, and blew gently through the inside of the cabin. Shining on the thousand layers of the jade-blue waves, the sun lit up ten thousand flecks of silver light whose reflections flashed inside the walls.

The heavy white sails, the grumbling surges, the rhythmic sound of the fishtail oar, the irregular tread of busy feet as people hauled in the nets—to their accompaniment A-bao dreamed dreams of honeyed sweetness.

When her mother went to the cabin to look at A-bao, she could not stop herself from clapping her hands softly and calling to her husband: "A-liang! come quickly and have a look. A-bao has smiled!"

Cheng Liang did not so much as glance over his shoulder but called the woman impatiently: "Hurry! Hurry up and help me haul the nets on board!"

Concerting their strengths, man and wife together dragged the heavy, fine-meshed nets onto their boat. Each netful of fish, flashing blue-silver, crowding thickly against each other, leaping and jumping, was piled into the fish hold. One little saffron-colored fish leapt into the cabin and—with a flick of its tail—sent a droplet of water to splash like a pearl on A-bao's plump and rosy cheeks.

A-bao's spirits stirred a moment. She opened a pair of dark and shining eyes, and looked in surprise all about her. When she saw her father and mother, she smiled again. She unclenched two little roly-poly hands and, looking toward her parents, began to say *Ah! Ah! Ah!*...

Her father smiled and rubbed the drops of sweat from her brow. Her mother smiled and stuffed a nipple between A-bao's lips. Today was a prosperous day.... Just after noon, the boat was already laden full

... and it was time to put the helm about and sail home with the wind astern. "Today," said Cheng Liang, "the great sea has given its rewards to our A-bao." (XSEN I.16–17)

This is an evocation, in more modern terms, and with a transposition to the sea, of the traditional delight in the plump babies and bulging ears of grain that used to feature in the colored posters pasted up at the New Year in almost every Chinese peasant home, and delight in human multiplication and the abundant provision of nourishment.

The minions of the fishing boss now kidnap Cheng's wife and try to kill A-bao by setting fire to the fishing boat while she is sleeping in it. Her father hears the baby's screams and rescues her just in time. Meanwhile, her mother is lying bound, gagged, and hooded in Shark's Teeth's private jail. His plan is simple. He wants to persuade her, or force her, to act as a wet-nurse for the child of his Japanese friend, the army interpreter. This will repay a favor he owes the man and have the additional advantage of discrediting Cheng Liang in the eyes of the fishermen, among whom he has been spreading pro-Communist propaganda. The theft of a mother's body's milk is the ultimate form of exploitation, being the theft of life itself.

The boss begins by having Mrs. Cheng unbound and trying bribery. She contemptuously retorts that "neither gold nor silver can be turned into mother's milk." Then he says he will release her if she suckles the Japanese baby for four days. She snaps back:

"Shameless, shameless man! This milk of mine is to feed the future generations of the poor. Not one drop is for running-dogs or traitors, still less for the wolves come from abroad. If you think you can force me, you are dreaming." (XSEN I.27)

At this point Shark's Teeth ceases to be amiable. "If you don't do what I tell you," he says, "you will never escape from this house, and neither your husband nor your baby will survive." Mrs. Cheng knocks the tray of jewels, used to tempt her, out of the hands of the serving-woman holding it and attacks the fishing boss with a stool. He runs from the room in terror, yelling at his servants to tie her up again. Ritual convention requires that evil be shown as gutless when faced with a principled resolve.

The boss then has her given to a junior Japanese officer to take to the interpreter. On the way there, by boat, she leaps overboard and begins to swim for the shore. The Japanese soldiers kill her in the water with a hail of bullets. The author comments:

> This resolutely pure woman from a southern-seas fishing family, unwilling to enter the foreign-style house of the Japanese devils, sank with her heart at ease to the depths of the seas of the Ancestral Land, *becoming one with its rocks and shoals* (XSEN I.35)

The literal meaning of the phrase he uses in the last clause is 'to co-exist with'.

Mrs. Cheng's determination to risk death rather than defilement puts her in the tradition of the 'heroic women' whom late-traditional Confucian piety celebrated with countless memorial arches in the countryside, and hagiographical biographies in the local gazetteers. But there are differences. She does not deliberately seek suicide, which was the time-honored course when rape was threatened. Nor is her motivation to preserve her own bodily 'purity'. It is a patriotic concern for the next generation. Nor is she going to an afterworld. The most common view in late-traditional China was that wives and their husbands were reunited after death 'under the ground', but there were alternative scenarios. One of these, though it was not taken as being the norm, was that the virtuous dead continued to dwell in the groves and rivers around their homes as a sort of benevolent *genii loci*. It is from this earlier idea of post-mortem geospiritual absorption that Hao Ran has drawn his solution to the problem of finding a meaningful fate for the individual after death that meets the requirements of being both patriotic and free from 'superstition'.

The Island

Cheng himself now flees with A-bao to a small island called 'Gold-and-Silver Island', and joins the Communist guerrillas there.[2]

They are led by an old man known as 'Grandpa Wei', a name that means 'guardian'. This island also serves as a symbolic parent, and parental body, because it is a source of nourishment:

> When his mother was pregnant with him, they had come to catch fish in the Western Sands Isles.
> His father had planted in the ground a coconut he had brought from Hainan.
> Amid eager expectations, Cheng Liang had been born on the little island; and here the coconut had put forth its sprouts.
> Thereafter, fishing folk traveling north and south could touch the shore and taste the fresh nuts, whose fame spread far and wide....
> Cheng also went to see the well of fresh-tasting water [dug by his great-grandfather].
> The well was like a mirror full of light, firmly inset in the soil of the little island. It supported the blue sky and the white clouds. It reflected the green branches and their red blossoms. *It kept within itself the kindly mirrored faces of generation after generation of the sons and daughters of China.* (XSEN I.57–58)

This well is a symbol of Chinese culture, an ever-renewed source of sustenance, drawn up from unseen depths. Like the Western Sands, it inspires in Cheng a sort of terrestrial filial piety, because it feeds him in a terrestrial way:

> For more than thirty years, Cheng Liang had ... constantly been eating the fruits from its trees and drinking from the springs below its soils. This had enabled him, his body brimming with strength, to go down to the sea to catch turtles, sea cucumbers, and fish. How could he not be grateful to the spring of fresh water? (XSEN I.58)

The island responds like a living being to the events of the human world. When Grandpa Wei goes down to confront the Japanese, planning to fool them into thinking there is no drinkable water on the island:

> The rolling breakers on the great sea sounded like drums booming!
> The shaking of the tips of the island's trees seemed like flags being hauled up!
> From the beach came the wolf-like and dog-like cries of the invaders! (XSEN I.140)

Eventually, suspected by the Japanese of misleading them, Wei is shot and left dying:

> The clouds did not move. The birds did not fly. No tree stirred. Stillness was complete. (XSEN I.141)

As he passes away, Wei gasps out his last injunctions. The coming generations must do all that he has been unable to do. Then, and only then:

> The wind came up.
>> The tide swelled.
>> The disordered clouds rolled along.
>> The seabirds soared.
>> The thickets shook.
>> The southern seas of our Ancestral Land, the Western Sands of the southern seas, the mighty tumbling breakers, lifted up their dirge of heroic grief! (XSEN I.142)

A-bao and a friend ask what has happened to Wei, and her father answers:

> "He has kept safe for us this rich and lovely island.... He will be with us forever. Remember! Grandpa lives where you planted your coconut trees [at his graveside]...."
> The light from the clouds burned and flamed. Brighter it burned, and redder.
> The impetuous sea, the stern islands, the raging forests, all that was hidden beneath the waters, perched on the land, or flying through the air, all—all—seemed to be covered by one immense red banner. (XSEN I.147–48)

In this magical world, the human being and his fate are sensed as being mystically interwoven with their environment. When Wei protects the well, he is protecting China, both actually and physically. Traitors, who are in league with outsiders, are described as having no 'predestined affinity' with it. One would be startled, in the context of this way of thinking, to meet with some line like Burns's "How can ye chant, ye little birds, And I sae weary, fu' of care?"—some presentiment of Nature's ultimate indifference.

The Star of Salvation

Cheng Liang has a dream:

> He'd seen too many armies. One wore this uniform, a second wore another; one had one name, another had another. There were Chinese armies and foreign armies, all of them guns commanded by the rich to beat the poor. He had never seen an army belonging to the poor.
>
> [He] had heard it be said that there *was* a poor people's army. That was when he was in a little tavern on the shore, whispered by some folks who had been to Canton and pushed into the hinterland.... Such talk delighted him to an uncommon degree and he made a point of remembering it. He elaborated it further in accordance with his own desires, as one might weave a fabric out of threads, or congeal a candle out of drops of wax. And thereupon there appeared before his eyes a tumultuous, many-colored tapestry of clouds, and a bright dazzling lantern rose before his mind. From that time on, he dared to have doubts about the way of this world, and to anticipate that it would change, to live and walk a road that went against the life of this world, and to hope for the swift arrival of the tempest that would 'overturn Heaven and reverse the Earth'. (XSEN I.46)

But his efforts to find the Red Army are at first in vain.

When Cheng first comes to Gold-and-Silver Island, the old man Wei is a mystery to him. He never talks about himself, but only about Chinese history, the war against Japan, and "the Great Star of Salvation of the poor people of the whole country—Chairman Mao!" (XSEN I.65) He also teaches certain basic lessons:

> "We must not simply avenge our personal enmities and hates, we must take into consideration all the unavenged hatreds of poor people throughout the world.... If we do not completely overturn the old society of today, the great collective enmities and hatreds of us poor people cannot be avenged, and our sons and grandsons will be oppressed as they have been before." (XSEN I.67)

He asks why so many revolutionaries in the past have failed, why so much blood has seemingly been spilt in vain. And he answers: "They did not have a proletarian political party, or Marxism-Leninism." At this point, "Cheng Liang's feelings reached the summit of a lofty mountain, and his eyes suddenly lit up." His heart leaps with a wish to "liberate all of mankind" and to "create a new world."

That night he is so restless that he cannot sleep, but wanders about. He stumbles on a group of men with rifles sitting in the old man's hut discussing matters. They are the local branch of the Red Army, and they tell him, to his delight, that approval has come through from above for him to be admitted. Hao Ran goes on:

> They had no lamp.
> An ever-bright lamp had been lit, brighter than any other lamp.
> They uttered no phrase.
> The voice of the heart of class brothers touches the hearing more surely than any phrase. (XSEN I.73)

And, "for the first time he really and truly knew that his life had a goal, that his life had a meaning." (XSEN I.75)

He rows a sampan laden with munitions for two days and nights without stopping. To the two soldiers accompanying him and who beg him to take a rest he replies:

> "Consider a moment, comrades.... You have taken part in our revolutionary struggle for a good many years.... I have wasted my many months and days to no purpose. So now I must turn each day into two days of revolution, so as to make up for the waste!" (XSEN I.112)

Here is the myth of what might be called 'revolutionary superperformance'.

He comes off best in a battle of wits with a Japanese patrol boat, and his consciousness is changed:

> Cheng Liang was very familiar with this sailing route ... but he had never looked at the scenery with such delight as on this occasion.... In the past he had been a fisherman ... but now he was appreciating and judging everything through the eyes of a soldier who has been through a life-and-death struggle with the class enemy and the national enemy. Only a soldier who has resolved to safeguard his ancestral land at the sacrifice of his life can grasp the true beauty of each blade of grass, each tree, each mountain, and each stream of the ancestral land. (XSEN I.118)

He has found a story in which to live.

Revolutionary Successors

The Communist's body has to be the servant of a revolutionary and patriotic will. To little A-bao, growing up among dedicated soldiers, this is almost second nature, and soon she is giving them lessons. On one such occasion, the guerrillas have to lie in wait to ambush a Japanese munitions ship. This means no fires, which would give away their presence, and hence no cooking of food. (Chinese regard raw food, apart from fruits, as barely edible.) Days go by, and those waiting get hungry:

> One of the soldiers said: "We grown-ups can bear it, but what about the little one?"...
> Grandpa Wei wanted to say something, but he swallowed down his words and looked at Cheng Liang.
> Cheng Liang gritted his teeth and said: "No. No. Don't cook even a little food. The orders of higher levels—discipline—must be observed."
> "What are we going to do," said a soldier, "if the little one starves?"...
> Cheng Liang gave a dismissive wave of his hand: "No cooking of rice, even if she is starving...."
> Grandpa Wei nodded.
> "A-bao," he said, "if we're going to give the wolves a thrashing, thrash the Japanese devils, we've got to take a bit of suffering, bear a bit of hunger. Can you manage?"
> A-bao turned her jet-black eyes first on one person, then on another.
> "I'm not the least bit hungry," she said crisply. "Even if I am, still don't cook rice."
> No one laughed when they heard this sincere and moving answer. They all nodded gravely in her direction.
> By afternoon even the grown-ups' stomachs were rumbling with hunger. Little A-bao snuggled in her father's arms, blinking her eyes but not uttering a sound.
> None of the soldiers could bear to look at the child. (XSEN I.87)

This physical self-discipline is reinforced by a new style of child-rearing that creates a new sort of human personality. Although Cheng Liang is a devoted single parent, he believes that his daughter "will rely on all of us to be brought up, and when she is grown up will belong to all of us." "A-bao," he tells Grandpa Wei, "is everybody's. Everyone will be concerned with A-bao." By slowly withdrawing from his earlier physical closeness to her, he produces a more independent and self-sufficient character. She is trained for an inner solitude:

> In the past, A-bao had been Cheng Liang's shadow. Wherever he went, she went. If he didn't see her for a moment, he would call her anxiously and search busily, not relaxing until she was in his arms. But now, when A-bao followed him, he would say: "Go and play by yourself!"
>
> Once they went out to sea to catch fish. As soon as Grandpa Wei noticed that A-bao was not in the boat, he wanted to go back onto the shore and call her.
>
> Cheng Liang blocked him: "Let her stay on the island and wait for us."
>
> "Leaving her all by herself—" said Wei, "is that right?"
>
> "It's testing her!" said Cheng.
>
> There came a day when, around noon, Grandpa Wei saw Cheng Liang take a torn mosquito-net out of a bundle, patch it, and then hang it in a separate place in his grass hut. He asked him what he was doing.
>
> "Letting A-bao *sleep by herself*," was the answer.
>
> "If she wakes up, won't she be unable to find you?" asked Wei.
>
> "It's testing her!" said Cheng.
>
> This change in Cheng Liang produced many changes in A-bao. (XSEN I.97)

Chinese parents always used to have their small children sleep beside them in the same bed, and many still do.

The motive for Cheng's new physical remoteness is soon explained. He has been steeling her so she will not miss him when he leaves to fight the Japanese. He tells Wei:

> "Ever since I resolved to enter the Party, I gave myself and my descendants to the Party. What's more, the child can't be forever sticking to my side. We are fighting for our land on their behalf. We must make sure that they grow up able to fight for it. In this way I can fulfill my duty as a father, and will not have toiled bitterly in vain. (XSEN I.100)

So the older A-bao—now living under Communism—approaches life as an endless moral obstacle course, whose purpose is a continuous self-toughening. She decides, for example, to go out in a small boat with some other girls *because* a storm is coming up. When the somewhat weak-natured but kindly Brigade leader tries to stop her, she retorts that if courage is to be developed, the danger has to be real. Of course the author sees to it that they return safely.

The age-old Chinese love of food is scorned by the true revolutionary. "Eating," says A-bao, "is a minor matter." In her mature years, when there is a water shortage during a battle (against the South Vietnamese), she commands others to drink while refusing to do so herself. Cheng Liang, bringing relief supplies, puts his daughter *last* on the list for help, knowing that *she* will hold out where no one else can. She does so—even as she faints and begins to spit blood. When her husband, no weakling himself, sees the condition she is in and gently reminds her, "your body is an important prerequisite for the struggle. You must get it strong and powerful," she goes one better. "For victory in this struggle," she says, "I am prepared to give my body and my life." (XSEN II.243)

The Dragon from the Sea

The partisans fighting the Japanese have an orphan in their charge, a boy called A-hai or 'Sea', who is as sturdy as "the iron anchor from a great ship." He has survived the wrecking of his family's ship by the Japanese, kept afloat by the gourd tied to his belt and tossing for many hours on the waters before being flung ashore. His first encounter with A-bao, by now perhaps seven, is the nearest the first part of the book comes to a hint of sexuality. She is having a nap in a grass hut when he arrives:

> A-hai entered the hut, swallowing down the words that rose to his lips.
> A mosquito-net hung over the bed, and a plump child was asleep there, with a little pigtail bound on her head.
> A-hai came up softly and pushed his head in through the curtain....
> Little A-bao slept sweetly, unaware that someone was looking at her.
> Little A-bao slept on one side, her plump little cheek pressed against the pillow. Her little lips hung awry, with a single drop of saliva on them.
> She had fallen asleep while playing. A bunch of wild flowers was placed at one side, and a branch of red coral was still gripped in her hand.

When A-hai saw her, he thought to himself: "What a fine little sister. Why doesn't she get up and play with me?—I've come to play with you! Shall I wake her? No, I can't...."

A-hai sat at her side, waiting. He waited for a while. Then for a bit longer. But A-bao didn't wake up, which he found too vexing.

He took a small bag from his back, opened it, and out of a pile of much-loved playthings selected two tiger-striped shells and put them before A-bao's eyes.... He further drew out his little wooden pistol, played with it for a moment, then pulled out the red coral from A-bao's hand and pushed the little pistol in its place. Last of all, he thought of the sweets in his pocket. He was just about to take them out when he heard the sound of movement inside the curtain, so he stopped.

Little A-bao was startled awake. Her two large black eyes flashed all of a sudden.

She saw the shells by her pillow ... and the little pistol in her hand.

She also saw a head sticking in from the outside that was not the old man's, nor an 'uncle's', nor her father's....

She scrambled fiercely into an upright position ... and asked in amazement: "Who are you who've come to our island?" (XSEN I.106–7)

The scene is done with restraint, in spite of its sentimentality, but the Freudian symbolism is evident: the moist, half-open lips, the torn-out red coral, and the thrust-in pistol. Perhaps this sort of kiddy romance was to some extent a substitute for the overt adult sexuality that was taboo during this period. Children's bodies were the only bodies in which adult eyes could take a public and permissible pleasure.

When we meet A-bao in the first section of part two, almost grown up, the author's emphasis is on a healthy attractiveness:

Her jet-black hair was worn in a long, coarse plait. Her round face was of a ruddy, youthful delicacy, her large eyes bright and vivacious. She wore a flower-patterned shirt with short sleeves, and loose-fitting dark-blue trousers. On her lapel was the badge of the Communist Youth League. (XSEN II.5)

The nearest Hao Ran comes to a hint of adult sexuality is in the following episode, which ends with a brisk return to ideological propriety. A-bao is poling her sampan along the shore one day when she finds a crowd waiting anxiously by a reef. They tell her "a naval comrade" has dived in to find the cause of a recent wreck, but has been under the water a worryingly long time.

> A-bao took off the bamboo hat from her head, removed the singlet that covered her chest, curved her body with her legs together, and plunged into the water with a neat sound. A flower-like whirlpool appeared on the clear blue surface of the sea, then swiftly subsided, leaving the ripples floating like veins in marble. Her empty sampan tossed about uncontrolled. In the waves, the shaft of the oar stirred time and again, and banged against the gunwales....
>
> A-bao sank down to the seafloor and swam this way and that, groping.
>
> A large, fat fish brushed across her back, then fled, startled.
>
> A bunch of long, soft seaweed floated past, rubbing against her chest.
>
> Suddenly her hand encountered a sturdy, pillar-like arm, and at the same time her own arm was gripped by a firm hand.
>
> Pulled by that hand, her head broke clear of the surface....
>
> Following the sailor, who had risen through the water at the same time as she had, she scrambled back onto the little tossing sampan. She took a breath of air, wiped the water from her face with her hands, looked up, and was all at once struck dumb.
>
> "It's you, A-bao!" cried the sailor.
>
> "Elder brother Hailong [A-hai's real name—'Dragon from the Sea']!" A-bao could not prevent herself from exclaiming....
>
> "What have you come to do here?"
>
> "Build up the Western Sands," she said. "What about you?"
>
> "To defend them!" (XSEN II.53–54)

On the surface the meeting of childhood friends is wholly proper. But it is unlikely that it is only the European mind that finds the undressing, the dive, the whirlpool, the jerking oar, and the underwater caressing suggesting rather more than they speak of openly. The old Shanghai slang for sexual penetration was 'entering the fishpool'.

On another occasion, Hailong and A-bao stroll together through a moonlit night, on their way to a Party meeting and talking about—what else?—the problem of imperialism. Some time later, when A-bao's closest female friend, Yajuan, says that young men and women should not sing together, because her mother has told her to keep men at a certain distance, A-bao disagrees:

"That's a remnant of old feudal thought. We can't bring it into our pure Western Sands. We mustn't follow their way of thinking or acting. We must do the opposite!" (XSEN II.117)

Internal restraints in the psyche of the new Communist personality are assumed to be so effective that traditional sexual caution appears—by a paradox—to be provocatively dirty. Physical proximity between those of the opposite sex becomes permissible in proportion to the establishment of a kind of inner psychological distance.

Of course, A-bao and Captain Hailong eventually marry.

The Poetry of the Plan—and the Temptation of a Career

Developing a new economy is a source of almost romantic excitement. Even when his hair is grey, and he wears spectacles and carries a briefcase, Party Secretary Cheng Liang feels the same enthusiastic urgency as he did when young. Here he is in his office:

He gathered his concentration together and looked at the plan ... holding in his hand a red pencil that had already been worn away until it was extremely short.

This was a long-range plan he had devised himself for building a new, socialist Western Sands. On the fresh colors of the map were drawn the wide sea frontiers of the Western Sands, and within them any number of islands like jewels, while around them, each one linked to the next, were the fishing grounds, stored full of riches.

The red pencil in his hand rose and fell: tall buildings and new houses rose from the level ground.

The red pencil in his hand moved along: a thousand boats and ten thousand sails moved forward.

The red pencil in his hand drew circles: the People's Militia were busy at their arms drill....

Cheng lifted off his spectacles and looked at the small alarm clock on the table.

"Is it already past midday?" he said. "Time passes really quickly!"

"Of course it's gone fast," said A-bao. "In the year when you'd just brought the comrades of the Work Committee to the Western Sands to set up the organization, I was starting primary school. Now I've finished lower middle-school."

> Cheng Liang rolled his plan up carefully and remarked with feeling: "Time does go swiftly, and we have done too little."
>
> "Changes in our Western Sands have been very great all the same," said A-bao. "On Yongxing Island ... there wasn't even a grass hut at first. Now there's an organization office and a new fishing village." (XSEN II.5–6)

Advanced technology is useful, but there is a fear of becoming dependent on specialists. When engines are put in fishing-boats, for example, everyone has to learn how to use them, "so as to be able to maintain the initiative." Wishful Maoist economics is frequently invoked. A new boat costs "only sweat," (XSEN II.107) and machinery will never put people out of jobs, since expanding production will provide new employment and there may even be a shortage of labor power. (XSEN II.112)

The new society is structured on the two-class system—cadres (mostly members of the Party) and the masses—and the plan carried out through this structure. The cadres meet first and decide what is to be done; then they go out to manipulate the others. Thus, after one such meeting,

> "Good!" said A-bao, closing her notebook. "Everyone here will go to the small groups among the masses, to arouse the masses, and carry out matters according to the plan!"
>
> The Party and Youth League members, and the [other] cadres were, each one of them, inspired. Out the meeting-room they went like 'dragons soaring and tigers bounding', hurrying to the cabins and onto the decks to plunge themselves into the midst of the masses. (XSEN II.214–15)

It is a directed community, where initiative and decision lie in the hands of a small group, and enthusiasm for the Party's line is meant to be obligatory.

In fact, almost every family is trying to find some way of getting its children out of the commune and into a city for special training and a career. A-bao, however, causes a sensation by quitting a college in Guangzhou (Canton) and coming home. She explains to her father:

"After I'd been at the school for a few months, it gradually became clear to me that what they were pouring into my brain was not knowledge and thoughts that would serve to build up the Western Sands and protect them.... I saw that some of my fellow students who had been through this conditioning desired nothing but to grab higher education and become engineers. Some of them who couldn't pass their examinations even sniveled, or used their parents and friends to find a job in the city, using every stratagem to avoid returning to a fishing village to catch fish.... I felt that if this sort of attitude and these actions were to spread among young people, it would be exactly what you used to call stepping irresolutely along the narrow old road!" (XSEN II.38)

She intends to "study through actual practice." Her schoolmates, she says, were startled when they heard of her decision, and the teachers arranged a Youth League meeting to criticize her, but she "withstood the pressure entirely." After Cheng Liang has read the letter she has brought from the headmaster, full of toadying phrases, he says he supports her position:

"A-bao, ... I have the duty to support every action that leads the revolution upwards. I have no right to be a laggard." (XSEN II.40)

She says that she has now understood him more deeply than ever before, and that he is really "without selfish feelings," in other words, without ambitions for her to have a career. He answers:

"You are much more advanced than we are. Your father must learn well from you, you of the new generation!... *Among comrades there can be no old and no young.* We must learn, humbly and earnestly, from anyone who acts in accordance with Chairman Mao's leadership.... We, in this family, ought to keep to this new rule, too, don't you agree?" (XSEN II.41)

There is a dream here, probably impossible in a Chinese context, but still a dream, of transcending the old hierarchy based on age, and the definition of the good life in terms of individual and family success.

The Magic of Moral Power

Except for a few crafty exceptions who manage to conceal their true nature, fully blown class enemies (as opposed to selfish back-sliders) and national enemies appear physically repulsive. They are frequently described as devils or animals. The morality play of Communist existence is, to a considerable extent, acted out in terms of a body language in which appearance, expressing an inward power of character, has an immediate effect on the course of events. Here is how a Chinese fishing-boat, steered and inspired by A-bao, cows a South Vietnamese frigate trying to reinforce Vietnamese claims to the archipelago:

> The enemy vessel seemed like a wild beast. It loomed up, clearer and clearer, rushing with a grunting-chugging sound toward the fishing-boat from the [Chinese] Sunward Brigade.
> Its large guns stuck out their necks.
> Its signal lights winked unceasingly.
> Scrawny soldiers of different sizes stood about limply, or sat deject-edly on deck.
> There were a few officers, with their caps set awry, and with evil glances, holding rifles in their hands, while cigarettes dangled from their mouths....
> An officer on the enemy vessel, who was wearing a hat that did not fully cover his scabby head, was somewhat surprised when he saw that the fishing-boat did not give way. He blinked his eyes and gave the or-der: "Let them begin by feeling our authority. Straight ahead! Straight ahead!"...
> The enemy vessel and the fishing-boat came closer and closer to-gether. They were about to collide.
> The soldiers dodged backwards in panic.
> The officers hid themselves—even more quickly and further away.
> "Cap'n! Cap'n!" said a little officer, almost unable to speak. "This won't do, won't do! We're going to meet head on!"
> Without any concern for doing it in the proper form, or putting on a proper act, Scabby-head pettishly gave the hand signal to go astern.
> The fishing-boat forged past, straight ahead.
> Its motor sounded *putt-putt*.
> The water shouted as it swashed past.
> The red flag made a brisk flapping sound.

Some of the commune members even laughed at the enemy derisively.

A-bao stood, as tall as tall could be, in the wheelhouse, staring angrily at the foe. (XSEN II.207–9)

The Chinese sense of the theatricality inherent in the conduct of life probably makes, or made, this passage seem less ridiculous than it seems to a Westerner. Roles have power, if they are played with conviction.

Some days later, the battle resumes. This time there are two South Vietnamese warships:

The scabby-headed officer, who was in a rage from his shame, stood at the prow of one ship and purposely stuck out his stomach and blew up his cheeks, with his two hands placed on his hips. The soldiers who had turned tail, with their heads reeling, had all revived their spirits and, with beetling eyebrows and wide-open eyes, assumed an appearance of ferocity....

Several large guns rotated swiftly and trained their barrels on the Sunward boat. Several tens of rifles rose and together took aim at the fisherfolk in the Sunward boat. The fisherfolk scowled and treated them with cold disdain....

Scabby-head wiped away the beads of sweat dribbling down his face and stamped his foot, shouting: "Be quick and leave the seas around Western Sands Islands. If you don't, we shall not treat you kindly!"

Uncle Li put his fingers to his nose and replied: "The seas around the Western Sands are China's. Hurry up and beat it!"

Scabby-head went brown with anger, and suddenly pulled a pistol from his waist.... The soldiers ... pressed in cartridges and pushed down the bolts on their rifles.

A-bao, in the wheelhouse, had already seen that the enemy were outwardly strong but inwardly feeble.... She at once resolved to crush the morale of the foes....

Just at this instant Uncle Li, who was at the prow, gave a glare and took a pace fiercely forwards. With a ripping sound, he pulled open his clothes and stuck out his broad chest at the enemy. With a swishing sound, Yajuan and all the other Commune members surged forwards and all did the same as Uncle Li, facing the bayonets and rifles with no sign of weakness. Scabby-head could not help himself. He took a gulp of cold air. He brandished his pistol.

"If you don't retreat, we'll fire!"

> Uncle Li slapped his chest with a large hand. "Fire, you bastards! If any of you have the guts to do so, fire here!"
> Scabby-head's hand holding the revolver wobbled....
> A-bao gave a faint smile.... "If you are blinded by lust for gain and dare to disturb even one of our hairs, the entire Chinese people, the people of the entire world, will not forgive you! Not one of you need think of reaching old age!"
> Cold sweat covered Scabby-head's brow. His hands could not move. His lips could not speak. They had this final ace to play and would not throw in their hands. (XSEN II.225–28)

Willpower is superior to firepower, moral virtue to technological capacity.

Later there is a real naval battle between South Vietnamese warships and a frigate captained by Hailong. The vanquished Vietnamese are depicted as grotesque:

> The enemy ship broke out everywhere in flames.
> The enemy on the decks either died or crawled away.
> The junior officers expired on the spot.
> Scabby-head hung over the rails like a dried fish.
> The enemy soldiers still alive leapt into the sea at random like terrified itchy frogs. (XSEN II.314)

There are no honorable foes—a concept probably requiring a feudal background, something absent in China Proper for over a millennium, and in clear form for over two and a half millennia.

There Is No Individual Salvation

At the beginning of the book, Cheng's wife asks him wistfully if he thinks that they might ever earn enough to own their own boat, escape from the clutches of the fishing boss, and have no trouble paying taxes? He answers with great earnestness:

> "We could earn a little more, and have a slightly easier life. But there is no hope for the life that you long for. The troops of the Communist Party have not yet come. They have not yet changed the world from its very roots, and until that happens neither Chinese devils nor foreign devils will be willing to let us be genuinely fulfilled!" (XSEN I.18)

Evil is subdued but not eliminated by the coming of Communist rule. When A-bao asks Hailong if he thinks that the members of the former exploiting class have become obedient to the new order, he answers: "They can't. They absolutely can't. Chairman Mao has already warned us, reactionaries will never disappear of their own sweet will." (XSEN II.103) This is illustrated by the covert misdeeds of One-Eyed Crab, a deceptive evil much harder to detect than the wickedness of his now deceased boss, or that of the South Vietnamese. The author tells us that after the death of Shark's Teeth

> This traitor and local despot's henchman ... practised his evil ways in Qiongyai city for a few years. At the time of the Fishing Reform the masses pulled him out to be struggled against. During the campaign against counterrevolutionaries he was also investigated by the Public Security Bureau. The People's Government was generous to him and gave him a way out, so that he could begin a new life. But his depraved thoughts were not extinguished.... He continued to feel that the days when he had been a henchman and done foul things had been happy ones, and that his present life, when he had to support himself by his own efforts, was a pointless one. He hoped for times to change ... so that once again he would be able to act in tyrannical fashion. He therefore put on an appearance of sincerity in front of the masses, but once their backs were turned he was still full of mad hatred. (XSEN II.10)

The Crab therefore becomes an undercover agent for the South Vietnamese, and starts to subvert the commune where he lives. As to his fellow commune members, "the more they felt happy, the more he found it hard to bear." (XSEN II.23) He fans the discontent of the younger adults, so they rush off to the city, among them a much-needed mechanic, and local plans for the Great Leap Forward are undermined. The mechanic's father says it is natural for people to want to see their children advance, but the Brigade leader denounces the departure as 'freedomism'. A-bao persuades the young people to return, but arguments continue to rage. She denounces the Brigade leader and his wife for using backdoor influence to get their daughter into a city school. Their attitudes, she says, are causing the girl "to despise work and workers." And she asks the leader, "Isn't it the case that the root of your old [individualist] sickness is still not removed?" (XSEN II.45)

The Crab puts on a redoubled show of activism and obtains permission to work on Gold-and-Silver Island. His real motive is to be close to the nearby Coral Island that has been occupied by the South Vietnamese under the command of an officer called Big Melon. His secret plan is "to go out to sea fishing on the sailing ship fitted with the auxiliary motor, win over a few associates, find a suitable moment to kill the cadres on board, seize the militiamen's rifles, steer the boat to Coral Island, join up with the South Vietnamese traitors' army from Saigon, present them with the intelligence report that he had compiled ... and help the Chiang Kai-shek bandits counterattack the mainland." (XSEN II.163) This is only apparent to someone like A-bao, on whom advanced political thinking has conferred a power close to clairvoyance. When she interrogates the Crab as to why he has come, he says that he wants "to take this chance to reform my thinking" and that he will "work to the bone to make sure our brigade gets the winner's red banner!" This fills her with suspicion, and she tells the Brigade leader that the Crab should not have been allowed on Gold-and-Silver.

> "If I hadn't let him come and taste a little hardship," said He [the leader], "and had left him at home to enjoy the good luck of his leisure...."
>
> "Your way of looking at things is wrong," A-bao interrupted him. "It is *not* hardship to come to Gold-and-Silver Island for socialist construction. It is a sacred privilege, a glorious duty!"
>
> "He's put on quite a good show for several years," He protested, "and has excellent technical skills."
>
> "What's his heart like?" A-bao snapped back. "Is politics in command, or technique?"
>
> "He does not have a 'hat' as one of the four bad elements."[3]
>
> "Whether he has a 'hat' or not is a mere formality," answered A-bao. "You must look at his true nature.... There are no national divisions between class enemies." (XSEN II.155)

A meeting of cadres who discuss the matter condemn He as someone who has "in the last analysis not broken free of the fetters of the old thinking." He says bitterly: "I'm an incurable diehard, there's no need to wait for me." A-bao assures him: "One day you will finally be able to break through." Nor is there any magic, she adds, in her ability to see the Crab's bad character, "only eyes rubbed bright with Mao Zedong's thinking." (XSEN II.159)

Not long after this the Crab sets off at night in a sampan to meet up with a flotilla of motorboats prepared by Big Melon to attack Gold-and-Silver Island. He is able to do this because he has persuaded a former 'middle fisherman', Zheng An, to go out with him night after night on private fishing trips, and has so gained access to a boat in spite of the careful watch being kept on him. As a middle fisherman, Zheng once owned his own boat, and so is still tainted with 'selfishness':

> After he had joined the commune he had of his own accord announced his 'retirement' for reasons of old age.... He would not exert himself far away from home.... He had [therefore] had another reason for coming to Gold-and-Silver Island on this occasion. Work-points were higher for those who went far away from home; there were large bonuses and a subsidy for food.... If he could find some spare time to do a little personal fishing, he could get someone on one of the transport vessels ... to take some sea cucumbers or a few shellfish to Hainan for him, and make some money. (XSEN II.164)

It is these weaknesses of character that make it possible for the Crab to have this use of Zheng's boat. The author's moral is of course that even apparently slight defects in political correctness can be deadly. Zheng pays for his weakness, being left knocked out on the beach by the Crab as the latter departs alone.

When A-bao learns of the Crab's nighttime getaway, she leaps into the sea, fully dressed, and, holding her rifle above her head, swims after him, an extraordinary physical feat. In a symbolic reversal of her mother's death, she then rises out of the sea to kill. She scrambles on board the sampan. The terrified One-Eyed Crab argues with her that he is guiltless, but in vain. He leaps into the water. When his head comes up to breathe, she shoots him.

> The corpse of One-Eyed Crab was turned over again by the sea. Then it sank once more.

A-bao felt her heart give a jump at this moment, a tremendous jump.

It was a jump of excitement, a jump of joy.

She pressed her young face, her slightly flushed face, lovingly against the chamber of the rifle that was grasped in her hand.

The chamber of the rifle was warm too.

The waves leapt happily at her side. Was it because they wished to come on board the sampan to hug her, or to hold her hand affectionately? (XSEN II.181–82)

Hao Ran has the sinister gift of making killing beautiful.

There is also a deeper point. All failures in the realization of the Communist story can only be due to the workings of a hidden evil that must be perpetually, and ruthlessly, ferreted out. Like this.

The Ecstasy of Collectivity

The revolutionary's body is a component in a collective structure, or a collective machine. The absorption of the individual into the social is experienced as exhilarating, because it yields an increase in collective power that enables challenges to be overcome. When an exceptionally high tide threatens to engulf most of Gold-and-Silver Island, there is a race against time to shift the precious cement needed for the new pier onto the only piece of high ground. As 'collective property' it has to be defended at all costs. I have italicized key phrases in the quotations that follow:

A-bao stood in the wind and rain beside a pile of cement bags. Her heart seemed to be burning....

"Armed People's Militia!" she cried. "Follow me!"

As she shouted, she rushed into the angry tide. With a cry, the crowd of people followed her....

The tide was already up to their waists. They moved forward with difficulty.

The tide was already up to their chests....

"Let's go to their aid!" said Hailong to his sailors....

The surging waves knocked a militiaman over.

A-bao pulled him up.

The roaring wind blew another militiaman over.

Again, A-bao pulled him up.

The two lines met.

The tide tumbled over their shoulders, trying to drown them and roll them away.... The foam leapt over their heads.

"Comrades!" yelled A-bao, "*link arms!*"...

Commune members and sailors joined arms, one to the next, forming a line in which everyone helped everyone else push forwards.... At last they reached high ground.... A-bao wiped the sweat from her face and urged the others on:

"Comrades, we now face a severe test, which is also a precious opportunity for steeling ourselves. True gold does not fear the refining fire!..."

She made all the comrades *link their arms* and confront the still mounting winds, the still heavier rains, the still rising waves and tide, and the still greater test! (XSEN II.137–39)

In the final encounter between Scabby-head and Hailong's ship, the *Sturdy Pine*, the human body becomes an all-purpose mechanism that both serves machinery and transcends it, because of the will holding it in mastery. The electric steering-signal system on *Sturdy Pine*, and the main and the auxiliary steering, have all been disabled by enemy fire:

"Captain," said Chief Helmsman Liang Junfeng, "please order us to operate *a human-powered rudder*!"

He shouted this, then raced toward the afterdeck....

He took off the hatch-cover, and leapt into the aft steering cabin. He grabbed the clutch and gave it a powerful pull. The clutch had been smashed by a piece of shell, and could not be pulled by hand.

Two sailors leapt in after him and pulled with him. The clutch seemed as if it were cast solid into what was above it, and could not be budged by pulling. Liang Junfeng grabbed an iron hammer, swung it round, and struck fiercely.

The clutch was finally knocked free.

He gave a great shout: "Operate man-powered steering!"

Six sturdy young hands together held the wheel firm....

Seawater like torrential rain poured in uncontrollably through the hatchway, and into the man-powered steering cabin.

A band of sailors followed Liang Junfeng's plan and stood one next to the other along the deck, relaying orders from the bridge to the afterdeck.

"Increase speed!" commanded Hailong.

The chief navigator passed this command to the first sailor below the bridge, who passed it on in his turn. *This was using human beings to form a transmission line*, swiftly and accurately passing on commands....

The bandit sailors [the Vietnamese] were scared out of their wits.... The enemy ship shuddered and swayed. Slowly, and as if it were reluctant to do so, yet helpless to resist, it sank to the bottom of the sea!....

In the thick billowing smoke of the aft engine room, a strange and magnificent scene unrolled before people's eyes: the three sailors operating the man-powered steering were standing submerged to their waists in water, water that was awash with fresh blood. Liang Junfeng, that man usually of so few words, crouched in a daze over the wheel, crying out without stopping: "Follow the orders! Operate the wheel! Don't pay attention to me!" (XSEN II.312–13)

The glory of the revolutionary human being is to become the ultimate interchangeable part, both superior to and subordinate to the machine he or she serves.

The sacrifice of the revolutionary's life is also seen as having magical powers. As children, A-bao and Hailong planted coconuts at the grave of the martyred Grandpa Wei, the 'guardian'. When later they celebrate the destruction of Shark's Teeth, A-bao asks her father: "Will the coconut trees we planted bear fruit?" Her father answers, "Don't worry, A-bao. *They are cared for and cultivated by life and fresh blood. They are certain to bear fruit!*" (XSEN I.190) This is the guarantee conferred by sacrifice. The martyrs of the revolution will assure its eventual triumph.

The Children of the Western Sands does not preach values that are evil—often they are noble, or, as in the case of patriotism, at least pardonable. The tragedy of the book, or, more exactly, the tragedy of the system of thought that gave birth to it, is that its make-believe is a falsely simple view of the world, magical, unreal, and dogmatic; and that in practice it has been part of a system of mind bending used to cover the realities of a repressive regime that has ruined or distorted hundreds of millions of lives, killed millions, and put millions more into virtual slavery in labor camps.[4] The moral triumphalism that it so eloquently evokes has been only too easily used as an instrument of domination by a new ruling class. As so often, in the words of the bitter old Latin tag, *corruptio optimi pessima*—the corruption of the best is the worst.

This age now seems to be past or passing, but Chinese Communism did, during the time that it was a living faith and not just a discredited shell, provide the Chinese people with a story by which to live. With its current disintegration they face the loss not of one but of two systems of belief and life-orientation within a single century.

CHAPTER FIVE

The Punishment of Heaven

W E TEND TO assume that the meaning of modern history will be seen by those involved in it, and affected by it, in terms of one of a small range of more or less 'modern' frameworks, usually some type of economic or sociopolitical 'development'. In other words, that there is probably a 'unique intelligibility', or something close to it. It can happen, though, that premodern conceptions are capable of interpreting contemporary events in a way that can still carry conviction with those in the culture in which these conceptions have previously evolved. In other words, old stories can be adapted to encompass new events. The picture that emerges from this process can be disconcertingly different from what we might have anticipated.

This point is illustrated in the present chapter through the interpretation of the Communist revolution in China in traditional moral terms by a recent popular Taiwan novel, *The Bastard* by 'Sima Zhongyuan', that is, Wu Yanmei.[1] A recognizable, but bloodchilling, caricature of Mao himself even appears toward the end as one of the *dramatis personae*.[2] While, formally speaking, the views of the narrator must be taken as those of a fictional *persona*, there can be little doubt that they are close to those of the author himself. In a postface, he says that "even better than having this story in the libraries, would be to have it lodge in people's hearts. I believe that if everyone reads it, he or she will be able to make a dispassionate judgement, to pass through blood and fire, and take thought for the future of our nation." (NZ 270) It is a reasonable presumption that many of his readers must be, or have been, responsive to the conceptions expressed in these pages, but this view has not been subject to empirical testing.

The background to Sima Zhongyuan's interpretation is that of collective suprahuman reward and punishment. It was thought that Heaven-Nature (*Tian*) responded to the overall balance of good or evil behavior in a society, or part of a society, into which the fate of the individual was subsumed, irrespective of his or her personal qualities. This is a philosophical approach to the problem of divine or quasi-divine reward and retribution that can be found to some extent in the Middle East in archaic times (the relations of the Children of Isra'el with their deity being a case in point), but which has been largely absent in later Judeo-Christian cultures. Among the sins, late-traditional Chinese morality—in certain moods at least—found sexual depravity (*yin*) to be the worst. As the saying had it, 'of all evils, sexual filthiness is the foremost'. In Sima Zhongyuan's novel the Chinese Communist revolution is depicted—startling as it may seem at first sight—as the retribution sent down by Heaven upon the Chinese people to punish them for evil behavior motivated by, made possible by, or underpinned by, improper sexual lust. The author, who claims to be drawing on a true story, (NZ 270) shows resourcefulness in imagining the specific social and psychological mechanisms that give this conception a certain power, and plausibility, for his Taiwan readers. The baleful effects extend their influence across generations by many means, but principally through the malformation of the character of children and teenagers, especially those who are bastards.[3] These effects create a sort of secular karma, chains of moral cause-and-effect that work in the everyday world rather than through incarnational cycles.

The Bastard is painful to read, but not without insights, even if it can hardly be taken seriously as history. Thus the processes by which hatreds were engendered played a real part in the Communist movement. Its underlying message is that something is, or was, wrong with Chinese society. Most of its characters are repulsive, yet caught in circumstances in which it would not be easy for them to to act other than they do. The few possessing generosity, or a measure of principle, are swept away. What is implied to be wrong, though, is a lack of traditional values, not the absence of desirable new ones. In this respect Sima Zhongyuan picks up a line of thought adopted by the shrewder conservatives at the time of the 'Foreign Affairs Movement' in the second half of the nineteenth century. Officials such as Liu Xihong, Fang Junyi, and Wang Bing-xie, in their different ways, accepted that there was a crisis in China but prescribed the strengthening of tradition rather than its destruction.[4]

The book's vision is thus that the Communist revolution was both, on the one hand, evil and the outcome of evil, and yet, on the other, a merited punishment.

The Conceptual Pattern

The theme of retribution is established at the outset, but 'distanced' from what people in the past thought:

> If one leafs through the history of the northern plain, the years of fam-
> ine seem to follow one another almost without intermission. As the
> boys used to sing in the marketplaces:
>
> *Old Man Heaven, why can't you see—*
> *Nine years in ten there's nothing to eat?*
>
> In fact most of the disturbances caused by a shortage of food in Shan-
> dong, He'nan, Jiangsu, and Anhui were linked with the Yellow River's
> inclination regularly to play the devil.
> People believed in the absurd legend that, sleeping under the heart
> of the Yellow River, was a huge dragon, shackled there by God, and
> that the river flowed along its backbone. So long as the dragon slum-
> bered, the river was at peace, but when it woke up and moved—even so
> slightly—waggling its tail, perhaps, or shaking its head, then the river
> would gush forth. Down would come the floodwaters, breaking through
> the levees, bubbling and surging across hundreds of miles at a time,
> while the people and animals in the places they passed through would
> be swept along helter-skelter with them, and their homesteads left in
> ruins.
> Year after year, if the Yellow River breached its dikes at the time of
> peak water, the people wouldn't speak of this as a 'breach'. They cried
> in alarm that the dragon had turned over, or that it had shaken its tail.

> Clearly this huge dragon that existed in people's consciousness was an evil dragon of retribution, and, since God had chained it there, it must have been for the purpose of visiting affliction on the people. (NZ 7)

If we now shift to the end of the novel, we can find a summary of the pattern of retribution described in its pages in a speech made by Petite Jade (Xiaoyu) as her bastard son Patrimony (Duofu),[5] who has risen to become a local Communist cadre, is conducting a massacre in the Liu Family Hamlet, where he was born. What he is doing is motivated by revenge, but of course presented as a political campaign. She reflects on her history: deserted by her mother, betrayed by her nominal father who sold her to an old man called Liu as a sexual plaything, she has been the central figure of a long sequence of sexually motivated episodes thereafter, all of them spattered with the blood of the men who have had anything to do with her. She has gained a sometimes formidable but always unstable power by using her beauty to seduce men in positions of command, whether in the army, the underworld, or the revolution; and she has shown herself to be both a skilled organizer and cruel in the coldest of cold blood.

> Petite Jade stood there, in a countryside whose winds reeked [of carnage] and whose rain was awash with gore. She looked on from one side, and with no outward expression of feeling, at those from the Liu Family Hamlet whom her Patrimony had put to death.
>
> She hated herself for having been born in a whorehouse. She hated her mother for having been a bawd. She hated Hua, the music master who had been her 'father', but only in name. She hated the circumstances of her early life, and the tragedies, and the twists of fate, that had been her lot.
>
> She felt that only when all this had been washed away in other people's blood would matters stand a little better for her. She believed that Patrimony saw these things as she saw them herself. Wherever, some time in the future, a new Heaven and a new Earth might be found, there had—first of all—to be killing, before these could be looked into. At least, when these people's heads had been hacked off, they could no longer say words like 'whore' or 'bastard' any more, could they? (NZ 264)

But the villagers had lived in a different story; in other words they had experienced the 'same' events, but not understood them in the same way:

> The members of the Liu family had noticed Petite Jade's arrival at once.
> Though more than twenty years now intervened, the elder genera-
> tion could still call to mind what had happened then. As the people of
> the hamlet conceived of it, Petite Jade had lacked any sense of morality
> whatever. Old Liu had been stingy all his life. If a grain of hemp or of
> sesame had fallen on the table, he had always moistened one of his fin-
> gers and popped it into his mouth. When he'd brought back Petite Jade
> to be his [secondary] wife, though, he had made her offerings as if she'd
> been a bodhisattva. He'd seen to it that she lacked for nothing to wear,
> either on her body or her head, and for nothing to spend or make use
> of, either.
> But—not long after she'd arrived, she'd had a secret sexual liaison
> with Little Qin, the hired hand. From this the seed of sin, Little Third
> [Patrimony's baby name] had been begotten. This adulterous affair had
> been brought to light later, and Little Qin, gripped by a rage brought on
> one morning by the shame of this, had, among the dense mists, slashed
> at Derong and Xirong [Old Liu's sons by his first wife] in villainous
> fashion. They had lain there in the fields like bloody corpses.
> At first the villagers had wanted to burn the adulterer and the de-
> praved wife on a heap of firewood, but Old Liu had blocked this. He'd
> not only done nothing to hurt Petite Jade, but had given her several tens
> of silver dollars as travel money, and allowed her to take her child back
> to her home area in Xuzhou.
> Later they'd heard that she'd not in fact left, but had stayed on in
> the county capital, and struck up a relationship there with a captain of
> guards called Hua. Captain Hua had had designs of the foulest kind. He
> had waited until Little Qin had been released from jail, and then urged
> him to marry Petite Jade. This done, he had murdered Qin in secret
> and implicated Old Liu and his two sons as having committed the crime
> he had done himself. The case for this capital offence had dragged on
> until Old Liu had died in jail, his two lads having in the meantime fled
> to the back of beyond to save their lives. It could thus be concluded
> that the family had been wiped out and its members had vanished. (NZ
> 262)

Sima Zhongyuan seems to accept that Petite Jade had justified grievances against the old society, but to see her actions as even less justifiable. At the same time, though, he portrays her as almost helpless in the face of the forces both in the society around her and consuming her from within. Thus, when she is waiting for bandits to attack the Liu Family Hamlet, she meditates: "In the darkness before her eyes, fate branched out along hundreds and thousands of different tracks, and she did not know along which one she would be pushed." (NZ 34) When Old Liu's randy urges prompt him to buy a young girl to be his second wife, this is a breach of the moral rules governing the channeling of sexual desires. In the physical domain, moreover, he is not capable of satisfying her:

> There was ... much gossip among the members of his family.
> "Old Liu's really gone and committed a sin. He's got heirs. He's more than sixty. Buying a virgin to be his secondary wife is doing extreme damage to the intrinsic virtue of the Female Principle."[6] (NZ 24)

And in bed:

> He was like a handful of burning straw that flares brightly when lit, but doesn't even warm the walls of the stove. This made her feel that the act was without any relish. On the contrary, it became a penance. (NZ 27)

Starved of fulfillment, she lets herself be taken in the woodshed one night by Little Qin, the hired hand:

> The sparks were alight in every bone of her body. She was already gritting her teeth, steeling herself to do it, preparing herself to encounter an immense fire that would burn her physical being away.... She was so scorched by this young man that she began to shudder and shake. They rolled together in the wheat straw. She let him push her about as if he were raping her by violence.
> Hired hand Qin was coarse and untamed, as insatiable as a wild beast. It seemed as if he wanted to suck her blood dry, and gnaw her marrow to the last drop. Her sixteen-year-old existence was well and truly released into emotions that broiled her like meat over flames.
> Before this, she had hated Old Liu. Now her feelings of hatred had weakened. To tell the truth, Old Liu could not be reckoned to have treated her shabbily; and she felt she was going somewhat too far in paying him back like this. But she was impotent to resist this man on her body, and she had no desire to resist him. If they were to be unmarried lovers, that was fine. If it were to be an ill-fated liaison, that was fine, too. She would accept either. (NZ 47)

Patrimony is born from the pregnancy that results, and the future catalog of horrors engendered.

Probably the only character beyond reproach in traditional terms is Master Song, one of the elders of the hamlet. He is the mainstay of the resistance to the bandits, when Old Liu is selfishly unwilling to commit his two hired hands to the common defence. (NZ 33, 35–36, 42) When Patrimony, turned communist, is conducting his massacre, old Song denounces mother and son as being "smitten by the demon of madness," and doing things "that no human being would do." They are, he says, "beggars of the utmost evil." But, he continues, "even if you do sit at Court some day, Little Third, you will still be the embodiment of retribution, still an animal. Cut off my head. It will change nothing." Patrimony stabs Song, and tears out one of his eyes, which rolls about on the ground staring at him, as if mocking him with the words "Your mother is still a whore, and you—still a bastard." (NZ 264–65) Song's qualities of character have not done him any good service.

The Breaker Broken

Time: the last years of the Manchu dynasty.

Lascivus Hua[7] is a conscienceless, dissolute, jack-of-all-trades in the brothel quarter of Tongcheng (northern Xuzhou). He makes his living mainly by buying pretty girls from among those being sold by refugees from famine, and supplying them to the madames who run the whorehouses. Any girl who resists working as a provider of sexual services is gang-raped.

> "They just can't think straight, these wenches snatched from the gutter of death," he would comment afterwards, holding his birdcage in his hand. "It never occurs to them that people have paid good money for them, to have them brought to the brothel quarter, and treat them there as if they were female bodhisattvas, burning incense in front of them and lighting candles for them. It's like pissing on a moonless night—you can't even see the shadow of your cock!" (NZ 11)

When his friends tell him he's getting a good time free of charge, he disagrees. "The madames have no desire to feed these girls and get nothing back for it," he says, "and once they've been thoroughly deflowered, they become little darlings." Then he adds, with an unpleasant laugh: "Truth to tell, my sperm's already been squeezed dry by an orgasm-beast. [He means his *de facto* wife.] I'm just helping others make their living when I do this.—Obliged to exhaust myself in the public service on behalf of the madames." (NZ 11)

The author sums up Lascivus's character as "not up to being either really good or really bad," but declares that "his skill in insinuating his way through narrow openings was greater than that of a gecko in getting from one side of a wall to the other." (NZ) He is living with Goldshell, a former *fille de joie* whose reputation in her day was that the mere sight of her gave clients ejaculations, after which they had to go home and have their trousers washed. But his tastes also run to younger women, and Goldshell, in retaliation, starts to have young male lovers. Their sexual greed lights the powder train of later disasters.

Lascivus regards the natural catastrophes that provide him with his victims as "misfortunes decided upon by Old Man Heaven, and nothing for us to be aggrieved about.... Business is doing nicely in the brothel quarter." (NZ 10) He also pleads in self-excuse: "The rebel Huang Chao slaughtered eight million people. If your number was up, escaping him was none too easy. Here we're fish who live on the food that floats past us. If anything comes by, we gulp it down. That the world's in a mess is no concern of ours. If refugees are selling their sons and their daughters, and we find the price for them, well—that's a business deal, and nothing else." (NZ 14) His crony Hu the Seventh asks if he isn't afraid of retribution for the violent way he breaks in his young whores-to-be to their trade. "Don't talk nonsense," Lascivus retorts. "I've no sons. No daughters. Even my *de facto*'s a battered shoe.[8] A woman I picked up. What retribution of any effect could there be?" (NZ 12)

But in 1904, a year of the dragon, one of Goldshell's casual *amours* results in a daughter, the father an unknown 'dragon of retribution'. Goldshell runs away with another young man, leaving the girl, Petite Jade, with Lascivus. Seeing her as 'a tree from which

cash can be shaken', he cares for her well and teaches her his limited musical skills. At fourteen, she is even more beguiling than her
mother once was. "One frown, one smile, one gesture—and it was
automatic orgasm every time." (NZ 14)

His plan to sell her when she is about sixteen is endangered by
the arrival of the Beiyang Army in Tongcheng. An acquaintance tells
him, with earthy practicality, "if the cooking pot's bottom gets broken, there won't be any soup in it for you to drink." (NZ 15) To
safeguard his investment in Petite Jade's virginity, Lascivus dis-
guises her as a peasant lass, and makes off with her into the back
country to the northwest.

He uses the journey to destroy Petite Jade's opinion of her
mother. "She was a vile baggage," he observes. "Without a conscience. She abandoned you, not in the least concerned, and ran
away with a stranger. That shows you what sort of a place the
brothel quarter is, doesn't it? As your father, I couldn't bear to let
my own flesh and blood fall into that kind of a fiery pit!" (NZ 16)
He dangles before her the dream of a good marriage, and Petite
Jade thinks of him as her real father, which of course he is not.

The journey becomes physical, psychological, and financial torture:

> In these desolate and infertile places the generous attitude of the peo-
> ple made Lascivus, now old and weak, and ill, have pangs of remorse.
> He remembered how, in years past, the refugees from He'nan had
> come pouring into Tongcheng, and how he had treated them. Now he
> himself was adrift in these same areas. How were they treating him?....
> He could not help believing there was a god over his head. In ten years
> the wheel of fortune had spun round, but they were repaying a griev-
> ance with virtuous kindness. This made his days and nights even more
> uncomfortable. He was afraid a real retribution was about to fall on
> him. (NZ 17)

Fallen sick in a country inn, he dreams of demons issuing forth
from Hell to seize him, chains clanking in their hands.

In Jiaocheng, a small city near Taiyuan, the capital of Shanxi, his
money is running out, and he sells Petite Jade. The purchaser is

Old Liu, a wealthy but decrepit landowner who wants a secondary wife. But Lascivus's motive is not just money. He is eaten up by a "hate-filled desire for revenge on Goldshell." "Since that sex-crazed woman could run away, taking my property with her," he broods, "I can get my own back by selling the daughter she had by that stranger. I can clear away the pent-up feelings that have oppressed my heart these many years." (NZ 22)

Since Petite Jade screams and struggles, she has to be tied up and put on the back of a donkey to be transported to Liu Family Hamlet. As she is about to depart, Lascivus tells her the truth:

> "You shouldn't be calling *me* 'father'. You bastard daughter of an ageing whore, no one even knows the name of your real father. I have sold you off so you can settle the debt that your mother owes me.... If you hate me all the days of your life, I don't care a damn!" (NZ 22)

As he spits out these words, he collapses. The proceeds of the sale are used to provide him with a coffin.

Petite Jade now loathes both her parents.

Sons and Fathers

Old Liu's breath "reeked of onions and garlic, having a frowsty flavor. The skin hung loose on his body. His flesh had a pickled quality, so he looked like a dead toad dried in the sun." On the other hand he was "simple and straightforward. If she had not had to go to bed with him, she would not have in any way felt that he aroused disgust." (NZ 26) On one occasion, when he says that he wants to beget a son, so as to stop the gossip behind his back, she flirtatiously provokes intercourse, remarking to him "take care your plowshare doesn't get bent!" But Old Liu is gasping for breath in no more than a moment. He has become a 'clay ox', which dissolves in water. He is "scattering and sowing in every direction, but scattering more than sowing." (NZ 45) This time, however, "she did not dislike him as much as usual."

It is the lack of sensual gratification that drives her to have her covert affair with hired hand Qin. Sima Zhongyuan comments:

Old Liu, this local moneybags, ensconced in his rural redoubt, was—to tell the truth—of an extremely kindly nature. He was tolerant and honest, and without duplicity or trickery. If he'd been ten years or so younger, and if he'd been a little more lively between the bedclothes, she could have borne to have stuck with him, half-starved but half-satisfied. Who would have guessed that he was to be a 'wax lance that topples over'? No wonder this brought forth someone like hired hand Qin and an illicit liaison. (NZ 55)

Old Liu is delighted when a baby is born, and holds celebrations to proclaim it as his. The truth about Little Third's bastard origins only comes out because of another chain of karma.

Liu's two teenage sons by his first wife detest Petite Jade. She bears this in patience, hoping relations will improve. Once she has a son, however, the boys worry that they will lose part of their inheritance, especially if Old Liu raises her to the status of a principal wife. There is an internal family struggle.

Petite Jade keeps Qin at a distance, in order to avert suspicion. He becomes frenzied with unslaked lust. He even accuses her of "borrowing semen" from him in order to have a son and get her hands on some of the family property. His fellow hired hand, Old Hong, intensifies his inner turmoil by telling him the story of a local farmer who nailed up his sixteen-year-old daughter, once dearly beloved, in a coffin when she became pregnant because of a casual affair. He did not see how she could have "the face to go on living in the world when she was in such disgrace." (NZ 61)

Local gossip doubts if Old Liu really had it in him to sire a baby. Suspicion is thus sown in the minds of the young Liu brothers, and they hunt for proofs, with Qin as their prime suspect. Before they have found anything of substance, a quarrel breaks out. Qin and Hong are working in the fields, and the older worker is surprised to hear the younger singing obscene ditties. (This is because he cannot keep his mind off Petite Jade. *All karmic chains lead back to lust.*) Decorus (Derong), the elder boy, is turning into a bossy young master, and he thinks the work should be done in silence.

"You two! [he snaps] Are you working, or are you chattering? We engaged you to do long-term labor. The object of this was for you to come and help with the work. So, a bit less spittle flying about.—If that's all right with you!"

Hired hand Qin answers back:

> "Do you have so many rules you won't let us talk while we work? It's lucky the old man's still alive. My rice bowl would have been smashed long ago otherwise!"

Decorus snarls at Qin that if he doesn't do as he's been told, he can collect the wages owing to him, and "get the hell out." "Who would have thought that you'd have turned out so badly," Qin replies. He adds that since he has been told to go, he will indeed be off next morning to the county capital. He will sign on as a soldier, or if there are no vacancies, perhaps join the bandits instead. "And what," he concludes, "will you be able to do to me then?" The threat is blunt. Old Hong defuses the immediate dispute, but the rift remains. (NZ 69)

Old Liu now settles some land on 'his' son Little Third. Qin meditates bitterly:

> My son has a better fate than I do. By far. No sooner is he born than he gets a large slice of the hillside fields on Mount Xiaoliang. To think that when I came to Liu Family Hamlet it was to sell them my strength as a long-term worker, to drip my sweat into other men's fields! To think that if I wanted even one cash more, Old Liu would not be willing to concede it. It's a weird business, through and through. But this will not be the child's fate, even so. We shall have to take him with us [when we run away]. If I take Petite Jade, then of course I have to take him too. If I don't, and the cards are put on the table face upwards, the Lius will toss him alive into an unmarked grave, for the wild dogs to feed on." (NZ 72)

No opportunity presents itself for all three to make a getaway. Qin is now trapped. He is working in the fields one morning with Decorus and the younger brother, Hilaris (Xirong), when Decorus accuses him of the crime. Qin protests his innocence, but Decorus says:

> "Confess what you've done, if you don't want me to make it hot for you! I'm going to crush you flat, then tie you up, and send you into the hamlet. Then we'll see if you still dare deny it." (NZ 7)

A fight starts, and Qin has "no route of escape." In desperation he wounds both brothers with his sickle, but when he tries to flee the other villagers catch him without much trouble. He is beaten up to within an inch of his life. But Old Liu's happiness is shattered:

> He had spent a lot of money to buy a secondary wife, but she had committed adultery with one of the hired hands in his own household, and given birth to a bastard boy. He'd twice put his own prestige on the line to acknowledge the child as his. If any man in the world had a cause for grievance, surely he held first place. (NZ 79)

He will not permit murder, however, and sends mother and baby away with funds for travel, while directing that Qin be taken before the county court. These kindnesses later cost him his life and his sons their inheritance.

The Air-Drawn Dagger[9]

Petite Jade survives by singing at a hostelry in Jiaocheng. Here she meets with Captain Hua, commander of the city guards. Since they share a surname, and discover they come from the same place of origin, they agree to assume that they must be kin. Hua arranges better lodgings for her, and then moves in with her, but—on the surface—in a proper, elder-brotherly fashion:

> Every time he came face to face with her or exchanged a few words of domestic chit-chat, he felt an impulse that he could only with difficulty suppress. But, since he was putting on a show of propriety, he had to struggle to control it. His desire was to lay his plans deeply and in an unhurried fashion. Once his long-contrived trap had been spread before her, there would be no cause to fear that she would be able to escape by 'leaping off his palm'![10] (NZ 97)

When in his company, she feels "a heat as if she were near a coal fire, and hardly different from that she had felt with hired hand Qin." This is partly inherited from "the blood her mother had left her," and partly due to the influence of the brothel quarter where she was brought up. She has none of the traditional concepts of 'virtue'. When she sees Captain Hua sleeping with an erection under his trousers, she feels as if she has been "turned into a bundle of dry firewood that needs, not raging flames, but the merest spark" to set it alight. (NZ 98)

Decorus Liu, come to town, catches sight of her out shopping. "You stinking whore!" he shouts, "With no regard for your face!"[11] The other shoppers turn to stare at her with looks "like arrows," and she swears she will be revenged for this insult. Home again, she begs Hua to help her.

The Captain uses his influence to have Qin released from jail early. He then pays for a stylish marriage between the young farm-worker and Petite Jade. Hua earns social prestige for this generosity, and a grateful Qin says to his bride: "I can't imagine what virtue our ancestors must have accumulated in their previous lives for Old Man Heaven to have allowed you to come to Jiaocheng to meet this Captain who is an elder brother of yours!" (NZ 104) A cruel dramatic irony is hidden in this remark, but one that can only be appreciated when the reader is re-reading the book and knows what is to come.

When Decorus arrives in town with his kinsmen, intent on wiping out the insult provided by this conspicuous marriage, Hua over-awes him with a show of moral severity. But the next day Qin disappears. His corpse is later found in the countryside, swollen and beginning to stink. Hua tells Petite Jade to use her right as the dead man's widow to charge the Lius in the county court with murder.

Old Liu stoically takes the blame on himself, as the consequence of his having been "greedy for sex." He tells Decorus to flee to save his life. Master Song acutely observes that the Lius have been framed, but the other villagers see karmic cause-and-effect at work. Liu has been "an old bull wanting to nibble at tender young grass." (NZ 112)

Old Liu is flung into a prison that "exuded a sickening exhalation of moldy damp, and where every brick expressed a feeling of ill-fortuned desolation." As he awaits his trial here, he reflects that he is himself to blame for his misfortune, using the time-hallowed formula: 'All disasters are provoked, in their entirety, by us ourselves'. (NZ 115)

He dies before the judicial process comes to an end, and is post-humously convicted. Petite Jade now cohabits sexually with Hua, who proves "a dragon in the Sea of Desires." She puts the murdered Qin, who was less satisfactory in this respect, out of her thoughts. Hua, who is the actual killer, begins to be psychologically tortured by what he has done, and starts on an inexorable decline.

His unit is now transferred to Horse-Gate Pass as part of the war waged by the Governor of Shanxi, Yan Xishan, against opium smugglers.[12] In this soldiers' world, Petite Jade blossoms "like a flower beside a latrine trench." (NZ 125) She wears cosmetics, smokes, gambles, and flirts with the senior officers. She is not displeased that "all of them showed a greedy attitude toward her, like a den of dogs quarreling over a bone." (NZ 126) Hua worries that she may find out the truth about the murder, and she gradually acquires the upper hand over him, reversing their earlier roles.

The attitude of the two adults toward the child begins to shape the peculiar psychology of the future cadre:

> Even though Petite Jade had at her side the bastard with the baby-name of Little Third, she did not feel he was any great addition, or that his loss would be of any great moment. At an age as young as hers, all she had to do to get another kid was to bump sex organs with some stranger or acquaintance—just so long as he was a male—much as you can make a spark spurt out of flint by striking it against steel. This done, the man could die suddenly like Little Qin, or desert her—it was no great matter—she'd still have this little lump of flesh in her hand, steaming hot, and shaped like a sweet potato.—Wearing out her youth with its pissing and shitting, and bawling with a mouth the size of a gourd whenever it was a bit hungry, or had wet itself. A life that seemed to have formed a grudge against her in their previous existences, so that retribution was owing and was being exacted....
>
> "Cry! Since you know how to cry, you little demon of retribution," she would often say to it venemously. "Your father's dead, so bewail him!—Little mongrel that you are, depending on your mother to earn enough to fill your gut by opening her legs wide to accommodate the gentlemen ..." (NZ 128–29)

Captain Hua resents the child, even though he hopes that caring for him may help him to keep Petite Jade:

He'd struck the brat's father down. Now he was looking after him. Popular notions about the retribution imposed for each and every wicked deed were buried deep in his inner mind. One day, when this little whore's spawn had grown to manhood, might his own life not be delivered into its hands? This fear, whose origins lay in tradition, could emerge like a snake from the remote darkness and insinuate itself into his mind, so a chill sensation ran along his spine. (NZ 130)

He finds some relief in cursing the boy in front of its mother, with a half-veiled threat of violence toward her concealed in it, but she feigns indifference. She hires a local girl to care for Little Third, has a wet-nurse in to give him the breast, and buys him fashionable toys from south China.

Paying for Petite Jade's tastes is expensive. Hua wrings all the 'squeeze' he can from the merchants traveling through the pass (so they are paying indirectly for his sexual urges). One evening, when the rain is drizzling down, a former crony from his horse-trading days appears. This is Huckster Liu. He runs an opium-smuggling racket for a boss called Single-Quiff Liu, and is aware of Hua's problem. "Lucky in lust, eh?!" he ribs the captain. "Careful you don't bankrupt yourself!" (NZ 132) Hua accepts bribes from Huckster to let the smugglers move through his territory, and this evening a big deal is set up:

Rain fell through the black night. The Yellow River could be heard sobbing to itself. Before the eyes of Captain Hua danced visions of a financial killing.

In Huckster Liu's eyes this desolate northwest was a place where the heroic blackguards who had thrown the world into confusion had arisen. It was here, in this corner, that every such demonic monster had learned his destructive trade before gaining his evil fame across the entire country. In the eyes of those such as Single-Quiff and the Killer King, and the Big Bandit Overlord [*Da feiqiu* = Mao Laoda = Mao Zedong],[13] the former demon-kings like Li Zicheng, called the 'One-Eyed Dragon', and Zhang Xianzhong, known as the 'Eight Great Kings', bringers of chaos to their age, were their patriarchs.[14] Huckster Liu played the merest bit-part in all of this, but still cherished the desire to force his way through, and felt an almost blind impulse of reverence for these leaders, roving brigands who had sprung up in the northwest.

He knew every detail about their origins, conversant with the stories retailed about them, as if they were his own family's heirlooms. The seriousness with which he took these romantic fables showed his whole-hearted belief in a fate that had been determined long ago.

Captain Hua, for his part, was also bewitched by this belief in uncanny demons. His hands were stained with blood, his inner feelings as cold as iron or stone. He had long ago lost any fated affinity for what was 'correct', and so there was nothing for it but to submit to the lure of the 'depraved'. (NZ 134–35)

Though Hua is being drawn into crime to pay for Petite Jade, his relations with her are growing worse. He suggests that they should go back to Xuzhou and "build a peaceful nest there," to which she replies "in a minx's voice laden with resentment":

"So! You want me to warm up the tea, and boil the rice, so we can be ensconced in our wee nest? That's not for me. Outside there's a vast and alluring world. I'm not yet twenty. You want to stop my wings from beating before I've had the chance to soar a little and make my mark. You men! What honeyed tongues you have! Yet what more-than-a-little cold-blooded hearts!" (NZ 140)

She notes that he has not been telling her the truth about his connections with the underworld, and begins to think of him as a deceiver. She wonders if perhaps it was he who murdered Qin.

Her present existence with Captain Hua formed no part of any long-term plan. She intended to steer whichever way the wind might blow. If there was a high branch [a powerful person], why shouldn't she climb it? She was not going to be a fool. She was not the kind of person 'to follow one man till death'.[15] During the last two years she'd changed men three times. Whether she changed them frequently or not had long ago become a matter of indifference to her.

But Little Third, lying in his bamboo cradle, didn't grasp what was going through her mind when she said, "I've no idea which surname, out of all the surnames there are, is the one for you. Round here, everyone's your 'Daddy', but you've only got one ma." The little object thought she was singing him a lullaby. He actually opened his little lips and smiled—as if being a bastard was the most splendid thing in the world. (NZ 143)

Hua uses his criminal connections to try to browbeat Petite Jade into submission, but she is unimpressed. "I've already been to the

Hell of the Great Demons," she says. "In my own lifetime. What's left to frighten me?" (NZ 155) She allows herself to be seduced by Battalion Commander Wu, and this earns Hua promotion to the rank of major.

The Battalion Commander's secretary is asked to devise a personal name and a 'style' for Little Third. He comes up with the cruel pun of 'Duofù', which means 'a multiplicity of riches' when written, but has the same sound as 'Duofù', 'a multiplicity of fathers' when spoken. (NZ 163) The reference is to the way in which the officers who flirt with Petite Jade play games with him, promising him candy if he'll call them 'Daddy'.

The proposed 'style', or personal name for general use, is 'Guanfeng', which has the sense of 'Through Breeze' but suggests something like 'flapping up and down' in making love. The officers mock the child with doggerel like the following:

> Little Through Breeze!
> Poor wee bugger,
> Sleeping in the same bed—as your mother!
> Night after night with flapping covers
> Giving you the 'flu or the cold you've got,
> Your poor wee nose all dripping with snot!
> That's the disadvantage
> That you'll suffer
> When your daddies are such a lot! (NZ 16)

This life at the customs checkpoint ends when the battalion is ordered to attack the smugglers on their home territory. Major Hua does not want his own side to win, as this would destroy the source of his extra income. He therefore warns his underworld contacts of the campaign being prepared against them. Forewarned, the smugglers entice Battalion Commander Wu into a trap. At the height of the fighting, Hua deserts, taking most of his men with him. Wu, an overhasty soldier but a tough one, cuts his way out, but is later executed as punishment for incompetence, including his promotion of Hua. Sexual lust has claimed another life.

Hua plays only a minor part in the story after this. The bandits have no great use for him, and he drinks more and more heavily.

One day, in an alcoholic stupor, he tells Petite Jade that it was he who murdered Qin, and that he cannot endure seeing the dead father looking out at him through Patrimony's eyes.[16] Much later, when Petite Jade has become one of Mao Zedong's mistresses, she tells Mao the story. The ex-major is captured by the Communists and brought by the security guards to see her. They look at each other, saying nothing for a long time, "all feelings of gratitude extinct, and all emotions ended."

> "They told me [said Hua] that they wanted to set up a new network for smuggling opium. You've got here before me. Do you know anything about it?"
>
> "No," answered Petite Jade. "I gave up that line of business long ago."
>
> As she spoke to him she felt her spine suddenly go cold. She recalled the night when Mao had spoken to her. He must have told people to locate Hua in the far-off place he'd been living, and bring him back. So the anger she'd expressed against him was the reason they were going to finish him off. This captain from the Shanxi army, having rolled his way through more than ten years of a life of terrifying perils, had now to be reckoned as having been caught fast.
>
> Old Hua had all sorts of things he wanted to say to her, but a security guard tugged his arm and led him away. After a while the latter came back, smiling, and gave her a cup of wine to drink.
>
> "How is he?" she asked.
>
> "Buried," said one of them. "In the vegetable plot over there. Bet you the veggies grow well there next year, manured by the corpse."
>
> "What you're saying terrifies me," she said.
>
> "What's terrifying about it?" said another. "There are a lot of folks round thereabouts who were standing up once, and are buried now. You're new here. You find it unfamiliar. But you'll get used to it after a while, and feel nothing."
>
> Later, she reflected that ... if it were to be said that she had killed him, that would in no way be untrue.
>
> "That's right! What's terrifying about it?"
>
> She consoled herself with the phrase.
>
> "In a world so disordered as this one is, men's eyes are all bloodshot with their killing. Why shouldn't I, Petite Jade, dispatch a few who happen not to please me?" (NZ 253)

The author comments that "the affair of Old Hua was like the wind blowing across the grasses.—Over in an instant. Even before the next season's vegetables had grown, it made not the slightest difference to the world whether he was in it or not." (NZ 253)

The Heart of the Cadre

Huckster manages the opium-smuggling network headed by Single-Quiff. He is well aware that in this line of business his life is unlikely to have a happy ending, but he puts on a brave face:

> "Human life's so brief a span—a few decades—that when the time comes for your cadaver to lie stiff and your prick to run dry,[17] what does it matter if you 'leave behind a fragrant memory for a hundred generations, or a stench that lingers for ten thousand years'? The most realistic plan's to get something out of it for yourself.
>
> "So long as there are people in this world who want to smoke opium, we'll be there to supply it to them. Are you scared Yama, King of Hell, will condemn your crimes in the afterlife? Heh! Heh! We'll keep on selling and, when that day comes, who knows, maybe even Yama of the Ten Palaces will turn out to have become addicted, and without us he'll have to keep on drooling for it, and yawning!" (NZ 178)

Three months later he is caught and beheaded in public.

Petite Jade is having a sexual liaison with Single-Quiff. She persuades him, though not without difficulty, to let her take over Huckster's place and direct several hundred bandits. She rides on horseback and totes an ivory-handled revolver. On the surface she is mild-mannered, but her methods are "dark, cruel, and sinister." Bandits who disobey her are killed "as lightly as one might stretch out one's hand to squeeze a few ants to death." It was, says Sima Zhongyuan, "as if she felt an inexpressible resentful hatred against the human world, and had to use all sorts of different methods to inflict her revenge upon it." (NZ 182) For example:

> A woman was passing through an internal customs checkpoint, holding a child wrapped in a cloak. She said to the guards:
> "This little one is gravely ill, gentlemen. I'm taking him to be looked at by a doctor. My home's just nearby, in Fan Family Village...."

The guards at the checkpoint had already waved her through. Suddenly they heard their captain calling out for her to stop a moment.

A middle-aged couple had run up, panting and puffing, from behind the captain. They said that their boy had disappeared some days ago. They'd looked everywhere, but found no trace of him. They thought he must have been kidnapped.

The night before last, though, they had both had the same dream. They had seen their child, his body drenched in blood, crying, with his mouth wide open. When they had questioned him, he had not answered, but had stretched out his finger, pointing to a customs station. Then he had pointed to the yellow tiger's-head shoes on his feet. They had therefore come all this way to look for him.

The woman holding the sick child tried desperately to run away, but the captain blocked her.

"I'm sorry, auntie, but there are folks here who've lost their kid, and come to look for him. Is that child in your arms really yours?"

"Of course he's mine," she answered, her face going pale. Then, in what could have been either fear or anger, she added:

"There's no reason for me to be holding anyone else's child!"

"Don't be angry. If people have lost a child, they deserve every sympathy, don't you think? All you have to do is to let them take a look!"

"It's not that I won't let them look," said the woman, hugging the child all the more closely to her. "It's that he's got the measles. He mustn't be exposed to a draught!"

At this moment the woman who had lost her boy suddenly pointed to a yellow tiger-headed shoe peeking out from under the cloak.

"Dad! Look!" she cried out. "Isn't that the shoe I sewed with my own hand?"

She turned to the woman holding the child.

"All right," she said. "So it was you who kidnapped our Little Tiger. What were you going to do with him? If we'd come a moment later you could have been on the train and escaped. Give him back to me!"

"Why should I give my child to you?"

The two women began to strike at and tear at each other in front of the others. As they did so, the cloak was torn apart. They saw it was not a sick child at all.

It was a boy's corpse.

The captain seized the child from the woman's hands. He ran his own hand over it. By doing so he found that after the child had been kidnapped, its guts had been cut open, the stomach removed, and five kilograms of opium stuffed inside. Then the skin of the belly had been stitched up again.

The guards' hair stood on end when they saw the cruel method used by the Shaanxi bandits to slip opium past the control points.

When the woman who had been carrying the body was questioned under torture, she confessed that it had all been the idea of their new commander. But she had no idea that this person now was none other than Petite Jade. (NZ 182–84)

In the meantime Petite Jade has resolved that her own son will leave some sort of a name behind him, no matter if it is an evil one. She even contemplates that he might become another Zhang Xianzhong, or Li Zicheng. But her power collapses. Single-Quiff is murdered by his rival the Killer King at a banquet of 'reconciliation'. She has to find a new male protector. By now, though, Patrimony is old enough to grasp something of what is going on around him.

He was six, and reared among soldiers, smugglers, and brigands. He'd heard all too many accounts of beheading and killing, and his brain was full of robber kings.

Whatever he did in Old Hua's presence earned him a glare of disapproval, or a slap, and the words "Out of my way, y' little bastard!" He did not comprehend why the man he called 'Father' should be so cruel....

In contrast, the male visitors who always surrounded his mother were much kinder. They let him touch their blue-black pistols or their glittering daggers. They carried him on their shoulders to play with him. Sometimes they even bought him candy.

His mother treated him in a somewhat strange way. Usually, she was kind; but once night had fallen she turned strict. She wouldn't allow him to cry, nor to enter her room. He had to sleep by himself in the dark. Sometimes he'd wake up, and hear all sorts of sounds from the next room coming through the wall—derisive laughter, whisperings, the rattling of bed-curtain hooks, bed boards creaking against each other, panting, coarse-grained snoring, and the like.

At first he felt a kind of bleak feeling at having been abandoned in a corner, and a terror of the night, and of the blackness. Little by little he grew used to it. When the next day men came out of her room, men whose faces were now familiar to him, even the way they walked seemed feeble. They looked like sweet potatoes boiled to a pulp. But his mother's face would be as bright as it had been before, just as if nothing had happened. (NZ 199)

The neighborhood children mock him with ditties about his mother's lovers. These take a grip on his memory. His resentment surges up. He clenches his fists and makes faces at them, raging with his teeth bared. All he meets with is more mocking laughter. He fights with them, and gets his nose bruised and his eyes puffy. "He learned to hate." (NZ 201) He also listens to storytellers, and he dreams at night of "swordsmen whose mouths spit blue light." He imagines that he is himself one of them, and beheading the youngsters who torment him.

An aged accountant is asked to teach him, but he cannot get the boy even to memorize the multiplication table. "Nothing makes its way into that little head of yours," he complains, "except killing and arson.... If I didn't work for your mother, I'd take hold of your ear and chuck you into the cesspit." (NZ 203) He confides to his collegues that "that little bastard Patrimony looks like a halfwit on the outside, but his insides are full of devilry. Hmm! He'll be a venomous centipede later. Just watch how he'll bite people!" (NZ 204) When Petite Jade gets wind of this talk, she sacks the old man.

The men in her life move around her "like a running-horse lantern."[18] Several of them meet bloody ends. Then Mao Zedong's forces move into Shaanxi and take over the drug-smuggling network from the local bandit leader. The profits are used to finance the purchase of guns and ammunition.

It is around this time that Petite Jade meets Ignotus Ye,[19] a good-looking young man just under thirty who presents himself as the owner of a local coal mine. His interest is in smuggling opium, however, and in buying arms, businesses in which Petite Jade and her associates, such as Hua and a certain Guan the Eighth, are well versed. She spreads her spider's web of sensuality, and is soon living with him.

The excellence of Ye's intelligence system arouses Guan's suspicions. Hua agrees:

> "This Ye—who's to be certain that even his name isn't bogus? He's cut from the same cloth as the Reds who've set half the sky ablaze in the south. Types such as these are sharp-witted and venomous.... When

they went south along the Putao River [the Hutuo/Putao-he, running from Shanxi into Hebei], and into desolate and out-of-the-way areas where there are swamps between the mountains, even so the numbers in their gang kept growing."

"How come you know this so well?" asked Guan.

"When I worked in the Shanxi Army," said Hua, "old Yan Xishan took strict precautions against them. He used to liken them to rats who gnaw the walls away.... It's hard even to see their shadows."[20]

"So, then, Ye belongs to this lot," said Guan. "But they're 'red' and we're 'black', not at all on the same road."

"Who says we're not on the same road? Since they're 'red', that means they're also 'black' as well. The 'red' is other people's blood, the 'black' is their own inner feelings. Killing people and making off with their goods, kidnapping and demanding ransoms, smuggling opium, stirring up the people to make trouble—they do all these things, don't they?" (NZ 228)

Their suspicions are confirmed by an old criminal associate from Jiaocheng who implies that Ye holds a high rank. Guan muses that the Communists are not like other bandits. They have "an indescribably evil quality" and "a mystery and terror that causes men to shudder." They have become "a snake insinuating itself into people's hearts." (NZ 230)

Ye tells the thirteen-year-old Patrimony to accompany the smugglers as an apprentice. He wants him out of the way while he pursues his affair with the boy's mother, and also hopes, perhaps, that Patrimony will pick up skills that will be useful to him later. But the adults find the teenager hard to handle:

His nature was very odd. He never showed any surface emotion toward anything that happened, but in his heart he was oppressed by a causeless, limitless, hatred. He resented the way Old Hua had mocked him and maltreated him. He resented those strange men who appeared like the horses on a running-horse lamp, and took possession of his mother, leaving him neglected on one side. He felt hate at the story his mother had told him about Liu Family Hamlet. He swore that the day would come when he would butcher the people there, and get back Old Liu's property—that property of which he should have had his share. His mother, Petite Jade, had been his only support for more than ten years, but the other children had abused her as a trouser-dropper. That filled him with mortification and rage. So he had come to find all women

odious who, like his mother, let their trousers drop. In his mind he
hacked them with his sword, and sliced them up into a mound of fragments of flesh. (NZ 232)

Patrimony's eyes have a "stern, and darkly cold" quality. He does
not socialize with his older colleagues in the smuggling ring. He will
not gossip, and he dislikes being touched. Yet he is a shrewd judge
of character:

> Patrimony was somewhat headstrong. He felt little respect for the older
> and more experienced drug runners. When they boasted of how quick-
> witted they were, of how they had their ways of fighting the defence
> forces, or of how they'd escaped from prison, or side-stepped danger,
> he would squint at them with a disdainful look, summing this up as no
> more than lying designed to boost their courage. (NZ 233)

His evaluation is proved correct, and he is lucky to escape, with
one companion, when Guan the Eighth is arrested and executed.
He joins up with his mother, and they go to one of the areas where
the Communists are assembling their forces. Petite Jade formally
joins the Party, and Patrimony become a 'Little Red Devil'. Having
the backing of Ignotus, they both do well.

The character of the future cadre is almost molded. We have no
need to look in detail at how Petite Jade attracts Mao's sexual attention, or how Mao then contrives Ignotus's death so as to be free
of his competition, but it is important to record how she draws a
lesson for her son from this last episode. One chilly morning, as she
leaves Mao's bed, she reflects as follows:

> It was of no great moment that, using her ample endowments as a
> woman, she had climbed up Boss Mao, that chieftain of demons. This
> was no more than being a ghost that came in the night and then went in
> the night. She could only be concerned at the present moment with
> training her son Patrimony so that he would learn how to protect him-
> self in this gang.—How to be opaque and ruthless. Ignotus Ye was the
> most immediate example. Why had he failed to realize that merely by
> being involved with a woman he could lose his life? That showed he was
> still not smart enough. If one wanted to establish oneself in this gang,
> not the slightest carelessness was permissible. (NZ 257)

She cajoles permission from Mao for her son, who is now serving with the Communist forces, to have leave to visit her. When he arrives she finds that

> He was as wooden-headed, and as wooden-brained, as ever; but when he spoke he seemed to understand much more than before. He did not much care to open his mouth, and so, if he did say something, it had a cold quality as if he were dosing out his words deliberately in fear that he might let something drop by chance.
> This reassured her not a little.
> She had a profound understanding that in this gang it was essential to keep things hidden, and that this was the best means of self-preservation. The boy's naturally dull disposition meant that he did what he did without making great efforts, ... and onlookers had a hard time finding any fault in him. (NZ 257)

Patrimony is embarrassed when he learns how his leave has been obtained. She assures him, however, that no one is going to "chew over his past" or find out how he got his leave. Yet he still stands there tongue-tied, and she reflects—

> Pat's wooden-headedness and wooden-brained nature are not without their historical causes. Ever since he was small he had only had to open his mouth for Old Hua to give him a slap. Later on, when he woke up from his dreaming, the bed-covers would always be flapping up and down [*guanfeng*]. He'd stretch his hand out and it would come up against a different hairy thigh from last time. So he'd be frightened into silence. He'd even choke back his crying into his throat, and not dare let it out. When he was bigger still, and had seen a lot, a lump formed under his heart. And there was the mockery of the other children as well, all of which made him feel he was on a lower level than other people, and that gave him that slight stammer he has when he speaks. (NZ 258)

Then she tells him that there is a way to stop the people of the Liu Family Hamlet from talking, namely "to cover their mouths with the lid of a coffin." "Right!" Patrimony responds, his eyes "suddenly emitting an evil light, ... if we have the chance let's kill them! Kill them every one!" (NZ 258)

They discuss how to work their way higher up the system, and Petite Jade observes somberly:

> "Truth to tell, all of those who follow Boss Mao have emotions that are constrained and repressed. The fire of hatred is an unfeeling fire, a fire

that burns with such extreme ferocity that even the sky may be turned to red." (NZ 258)

We have already seen what happens after this at Liu Family Hamlet. Yet following the massacre there Patrimony becomes "a small boat without a rudder—completely off course." (NZ 265)

> He not only killed people in numbers beyond counting, but smashed up stone stelae on which characters had been inscribed. He dug up the remains of ancient monuments, and destroyed the cultural relics of times past so that not a trace of them was left. It was as if anything old that remained from former dynasties had in it an eyeball, dripping with blood, staring at him, and crying out at him 'Bastard! Bastard! Bastard!' (NZ 265)

Concluding Thoughts

Joseph Conrad observed in *The Secret Agent* that revolutions can take place only if political programs can somehow be linked with the emotional lives of individuals. *The Bastard* is Sima Zhongyuan's way of showing how, in what seems to be his own view, and not just that of his characters, such a linkage occurred in China. His book also gives a specific and circumstantial content to the general idea, which seems to the ordinary Western reader quite bizarre, that a widespread violation of the traditional proprieties in sexual behavior was what led to the calamity of the Communist revolution in China. Improper lust warped the characters of adults, motivating crime directly and linking together chains of cause and effect that led to crimes. Worst of all, it warped children psychologically and morally. Even the horror expressed in his pages at the phenomenon of bastardry, with an insistence that seems exaggerated to the modern mind, takes on a certain practical sense when related to the type of treatment that an illegitimate child was likely to receive in a traditional Chinese social context. Although the interpretation is not even remotely persuasive as serious history, it still has some insights. The generation of hatred was one of the psychological driving forces in the Communist revolution at the popular level, and the portrait the author sketches of cadre psychology, though one-sided, shows considerable perceptiveness.

Sima Zhongyuan is a widely read writer in Taiwan, and his published output has been estimated at over 40 million Chinese characters.[21] It is probable that his underlying assumptions about human nature, and social cause and effect, find a resonance among most of the numerous Taiwanese Chinese who buy his works, though it would not be justified to argue that they necessarily think wholly and simply as he does, or as his characters appear to in this particular novel. What can be supposed, as a minimum case, is that there is enough in common between the thought-patterns of author and readers for his literary work to be able to produce its effect. If this is so, then it may be hypothesized that there is an extensive residue of such late-traditional moral attitudes among Taiwanese Chinese. Maybe even, less visibly, on the Mainland, too. I say 'hypothesized' because, obviously, the examination of one book only raises a possibility. It does not prove, or even—in the strict sense—begin to prove, a case.

A more deeply informed analysis than the present sketch would also place *The Bastard* in the context of Sima Zhongyuan's conviction that often the influence of the past imprisons the present, or that the past can "reincarnate itself" (*lunhui*)—his own term—in the present.[22] But this must be a theme for another place and time.

Taking the last two chapters together, we have to recognize that the *The Children of the Western Sands* and *The Bastard* belong to what is still in many ways a single Chinese psychocultural world. Our conception of this world has therefore to be multidimensional enough to include them both, since—at least at first sight—their perspectives seem to be almost orthogonal. There are, nonethless, a handful of points in common. Both share the belief that how children are brought up determines the future of society. Both are obsessed with some form of pervasive evil running through human life, even if they define it differently. For Hao Ran it is the exploitation of others, driven by an ambition for personal and familial wealth and power; for Sima Zhongyuan it is improper and unbri-

dled sexual lust. Both find a certain thrill in killing. Both are impla-
cably nationalistic. At a deeper level, moreover, both are conceptually closed: neither conveys any sense of questioning about how
events can or should be understood and evaluated. In the following
chapter we turn to the emotions typical of modernity, and find that
two of their defining characteristics are precisely that the stories
that people live in have become increasingly conceptually open,
and—not unconnected with the first point—that to an ever greater
extent they *live in more than one at the same time.*

CHAPTER SIX

Strangers and Sojourners

A 'MODERN' QUALITY in the emotional world of recent Chinese writing is as easy to sense as it is elusive to define. There is an intensified preoccupation with one's own self, and a deepened awareness of the complexities and contradictions within that self, together with the absence of any firm anchorage in a single externally given set of meanings. Implicitly at least, it is accepted that one must try to make one's own meanings, from within a range of externally given but somewhat accidental possibilities that exert pressures and persuasions upon one but carry no necessary conviction. The awareness of conflicting 'stories' being lived out, not only in different cultures and different nations, but also in different groups of people, and even in two individuals who find themselves—perhaps momentarily—as each other's neighbors, and the limited nature of mutual understanding possible, haunts the modern sensibility. Hence, too, there is a feeling of metaphysical loneliness, and an endless testing of any possible truth, which is never thought of as final, but at best as only provisional, that make modern writing almost immediately recognizable as such.

The present chapter considers works by three contemporary writers who are best known in Taiwan, and who represent different aspects of the process of emotional modernization. In the last of them, Yuan Ze'nan, who now lives in the United States, we encounter the self-conscious exploration of a psychological boundary zone, what it means to be, and not to be, 'Chinese'. The Mainland is developing its own patterns, which I must leave to another time or other minds to analyze, but those considered here seem to be in a sense further into the future, even if, obviously, they are also marked by the particular character of their period and geopolitical circumstances.

Alienation and Immersion

The first is Li Ang's *The Husband Killer: Tales of Deerville*.[1] Li has freed herself from the traditional emotional world to the extent that she has become able to look at it with clarity, horror, and a feeling of otherness. But in another sense she is still immersed in it and obsessed by it. Her *nouvelles* show how those who are conventionally 'good' work through a public opinion created by their cliché-ridden, uncomprehending, and maliciously speculative gossip to oppress the sensitive, the nonconforming, and the gifted.

The heart of this processs is the lack of understanding between different individuals and different worlds. Here is the university student Candida Li listening to the self-righteous gossip Publia Cai denouncing Acquabel Lin, a ballet dancer who has returned to Deerville after many years away:

> Her neckline was so low that the cleavage between her breasts was clearly visible, while—behind—her dress left her uncovered as far down as the small of her back....
>
> "Women like her, who do dancing on TV, are no different from dance-hall hostesses, and that's a fact," Publia asserted, concluding her evaluation of Acquabel.
>
> Candida felt humiliated. She had never felt so upset on Acquabel's behalf by any sort of criticism as she did by that coming from this trouble-making old woman. Several times she wanted to explain ... that Acquabel's dancing was nothing at all like the vileness they considered it to be. But as she looked at Publia's dark-hued face, so coldly self-assured, she realized there were some things that there was no way to explain, because people had no desire to understand them, and were even incapable of grasping had they wanted to....
>
> Not a few inhabitants of Deerville praised Publia's clear and conscientious adherence to principle, ... while those of a generous disposition thought it was on this account that she had been obliged to spend most of her life washing other people's clothes. What none of them reckoned

with was that her censorious conscience had provoked any number of quarrels in families in Deerville, inflicted wounds on any number of hearts, and compromised any number of personal reputations. (SF 36–37 and 46)

Two different worlds of feeling lay behind this misunderstanding. Acquabel had had to break free from the confines of small-town conventionality to pursue her art. The personal cost had been high: conflict with her family, the loss of the chance to marry. Now, older, she was finding it hard to maintain the belief in herself that was necessary to go on. Her best pupil had surpassed her, studied abroad, and mastered the mysteries of modern dance that had eluded her. There is an inner tragedy that parallels the unjustified criticism from outside. She is sustained by the memories of the happiness that had first led her to practise dancing in the darkness of the family hall of her best friend, Lotus Chen:

> Far away, at the upper end, she had heard the sound of Chen's mother striking the wooden fish and intoning the sutras, as she herself had moved her limbs and body in short sequences, as the mood took her, enveloped in an obscurity that made it all seem like a waking dream. The faint beams of light that fell from the overhead window, and the flicker of the candles set before the Buddha at the upper end of the hall, had spread vast shadows all around. Pure blackness, they had not kept to their given shapes, but had evolved from their own motions into all sorts of weird configurations. Some had seemed like huge and mindless animals. Others, caught in the corners of the walls, had changed into emaciated, isolated fragments. But no matter what, they had all been *her*....
>
> That she could dance barefoot at the lower end of the Chens' hall, along with the countless shadows of herself, had been the greatest freedom and delight. That in later years she had been able to go on practising under all sorts of different circumstances may have been partly due to the mysterious joy she had experienced at this time. (SF 18–19)

People like this were outside Publia's conception. She came from a family with a celebrated literary past that had fallen on hard times, had married a dissolute husband, and was bringing up her children by doing laundry. She was "a woman who having always, according to her own conceptions, acted correctly with regard to what was required of her station, attributed all the blame to those others with whom she had shared her life."

A different case of incomprehension is that of Solaria, a reformed prostitute, whose husband, Wang Ben, has had the curious habit for more than twenty years of spending the later part of every day tossing bread to wild dogs on the beach and watching them fight:

> She had accepted this custom of his ... It was a long-established principle that, for a woman, marrying was like the broadcasting of the seed of vegetables or flowers. It was a matter of fate whether they encountered a husband like fertile soil or like dried-out ground.... She accepted him, and this habit of his, which was not to say that she approved of it, nor again that she did not approve of it, but merely that, in an all but unconscious manner, she acknowledged fate.... Nonetheless ... now that their everyday livelihood had come under threat she began to be aware of the irrationality of it. (SF 52)

Her trade, which provides for both of them, is making decorative items for the annual round of religious festivals:

> She cherished few memories of the past ... and little by little blotted out a great quantity of her recollections.... Thus, as stitch by stitch, she embroidered or sewed the pretty trinkets that might, one day, provide so many children with countless memories once they had grown up, she gave the matter no thought.... Nor did she allude to what was past, whether it had been in some way bitter or not without its pleasures, and she had become accustomed never to think of the future. (SF 49–50)

Their two lives are doubly meaningless: as individuals (her work, and his pastime) and as a couple who do not communicate with each other.

Solaria's business is now under threat, both from the decline in traditional religion and from the competition of products made in factories. Her husband's real home, moreover, has never been their house, but the sea-wall:

> Having never given any thought to the meaning of this activity of his, he had let it continue for more time than he himself could clearly remem-

ber. But now, on this autumn night, as he sat on the sea-wall, while the waves not far away tumbled and foamed repeatedly, he became aware for the first time of how many years had passed.

He had been sitting for more than forty years on the sea-wall, looking at the silt pile up in the harbor as the shipping trade on which their prosperity had once depended had become the past; and he was still sitting there ... while their family's not inconsiderable share of wealth had all been spent.... And it might even be said that, sitting there forgetfully, he had avoided all of those forty years. (SF 55–56)

At last, on the night of one Mid-Autumn Festival, her tears at his failure ever to come home early turn to anger—after all these years:

Ever since they had been married, she sighed resentfully, they never spent one day together that had been free from hardship.... She had been like an ox or a horse dragging a millstone round, yet they had never had a child. There was nothing to look forward to. If he went on treating her as he did at present, not even coming home early on festival days, being concerned only with his own amusement, and leaving her with no means [on her own] of fixing up all the flower lanterns, she had no idea what their future life held of any interest for either of them. Wang Ben did not utter a word from start to finish, but squatted in front of the heaps of unlit, multicolored flowered lanterns in the corner of the house....

Only when Solaria was clearly growing weary of scolding, and had come to the end of her hurtful abuse, with no more than an intermittent spasm of crying, did Wang Ben stand up. He grabbed hold of his coat and headed out. Solaria, who had already somewhat calmed down, was dismayed to see him making off; and that he was ignoring her provoked her to fresh anger. She pointed a finger at the end of his nose and said venomously: "Go and join your wild dogs! Go and become their companion! Never come back. Never come into this house again!"

.... Once Wang Ben had realized what these words meant, he raised his hand swifly all of a sudden, and with every ounce of his strength knocked away Solaria's outstretched hand. Then he strode to the door, wrenched it open, and left. (SF 54)

He goes to the sea-wall, and at last understands why his wife has so resented him, and what an effort she has made, unappreciated, to keep their household going. For a moment he hallucinates that these forty years of wasted time have never happened. Then the full weight of the unimportance and meaninglessness of his life bears down on him, *and the awareness kills him*. When some fishermen find his body two days later, they can see no obvious other cause of death.

The title-story, "The Husband Killer," turns on the issue of the ambiguity of responsibility. Who killed the pig-slaughterhouse butcher Chen Jiangshui? Was it simply his wife, Sylvia, who wielded the knife, and then dismembered him into pieces, like one of his own animal victims? Or was it her mother, pursuing a post-mortem vengeance on her daughter?—Sylvia had unintentionally caused her mother's death by leading her uncle to where her mother was having illicit sex with a soldier in order to earn a bite to eat. Or was it the pigs in the other world paying back the butcher who had sent them there in such numbers? Or was it perhaps the Hanging Demon, who had been thwarted of his prey when Jiangshui and Sylvia had rescued the old lady Retiaria from her attempted suicide? The characters in the story agree that it must have been supernatural vengeance for some crime.

The reader has to ask himself, or herself, to what extent Sylvia was to blame, if at all. Did the brutality of her husband drive her to it? Was it the doing of the self-satisfied, moralizing gossips who destroyed her self-confidence, and her network of social support, by their untruthful and salacious slander? Or was it society itself? Society, and the conventional virtue that afforded her no help, sanctifying her submission to unending marital torture before putting her to death with all legal solemnity as a warning to other wives who might be tempted to act likewise?[2] Li Ang's central perception is that the patterns of cause-and-effect assumed by society as a matter of apparent common sense are rarely the true ones, and this makes almost every conventional judgement false.

Butcher Chen Jiangshui only enjoys sexual intercourse if his woman screams. He therefore acts cruelly toward Sylvia when they are first married, and as the intensity of her screaming grows less over time, he increases his maltreatment to bring it up to a satisfactory level again. The local gossips think the screaming shows Sylvia's unrestrained lust for sex. Eventually she overhears them destroying her reputation:

She stopped, and listened intently. Yes, it was people talking. Their voices were rasping and cracked. She suspected it was Retiaria, in the middle of saying something indistinct, with the words "Sylvia really is ...," which was followed by a burst of giggling laughter. Sylvia could hear the sharp, high-pitched tones of Verna interwoven with it.

She instinctively checked her forward movement, and darted behind the half-opened back door.... Retiaria was going on:

"If you are like me, you even dare to use death to make your purpose clear! [She is giving a heroic gloss, after the event, to her attempted suicide by hanging, which arose from rage at the disobedience of her daughter-in-law, and from which Sylvia and her husband had rescued her.] If someone's really got a strong purpose, they can do anything."

Then her tone became scornful.

"Why does that creature have to scream every time she does it, fooling people who don't know her into thinking she's having a great time? Sluts like that destroy the good name of us women. If I were to speak to her about it, it would just be a waste of breath."

There was more general laughter.

"Retiaria," said one of the voices, with an abusive giggle, "you get more daring all the time!"

"There's nothing I can't speak about. Women are greedy for men's little roots, as you all know very well...."

... Verna's high, sharp voice broke in next: "Don't dwell on *that*. Let's talk about something else. Butcher Chen only knows how to kill pigs, so how can he afford to feed Sylvia up to look so plump and pale-complexioned, and have such a good time of it?" [They think that since she doesn't have to work, and has no mother-in-law, she is unusually fortunate.]

"Don't you even know that!?" put in Mercatoria. "Butcher Chen goes to the seashore every afternoon and gambles with the fisherfolk, well concealed behind the reeds. I've heard he always wins at Four-Color Cards.... How could he be short of money?" [Up to this moment Slyvia has had no idea that this was what he did in the afternoons. She is dismayed.]

... There was a brief silence. Then Verna's voice began once more, grinding away relentlessly: "You know more about this area than anyone else. Does anyone, by any chance, say anything bad about Butcher Chen?"

"How could they? If he was bad, how could he have saved my life? It's just that Sylvia is greedy. She wants it in the morning, and then again in the evening. She doesn't realize it gets her laughed at. How can anyone do such things in broad daylight?!" Retiaria replied.

There was another roar of mirth. Then a different voice asked: "How do you know if someone does it in broad daylight?"

"Well, well! She screams so loud every time that it can be heard even by someone a mile away."

"It's hard to credit she's like that," said several women together.

"In that case, you don't actually know," [said Mercatoria.] "But I've heard the people over in my aunt's area say that even before she was married, she used to sit outside the door looking at the men. And making a point of staring at just *that part*. Hee-hee!"....

Retiaria lowered her voice in a mysterious fashion: "Perhaps you don't know, but more than ten years ago her mother had illicit sex with a soldier. Her uncle came up and grabbed them in the act. The two of them were crushed together and unwilling to separate."

"Don't they say she was forcibly raped by the soldier?"

"If you're frightened of being raped by someone, you run away. If you don't run, you can still yell, and struggle as hard as you can. Your clothes will get torn to some extent. How can someone whose clothes were all in perfect condition have been forcibly raped?"

Retiaria was manifestly outraged. As she went on speaking her voice became higher, and sharper edged: "And what will make your mouth split open with laughter is this[3]—have you ever heard of anyone who was forcibly raped still happily grunting and snorting while it was happening?"

"So that's how Sylvia learned to scream."

.... When the sound of laughter had died down, Retiaria's creaky voice added something else: "That's right. How can a rotten bamboo ever bear healthy shoots? What the mother in all likelihood forgot was that her daughter was too young to understand these things. She was just in the midst of having it off herself, when her daughter ran away shouting for help, and so killed her mother for nothing."

There was the sound of an explosion. Sylia felt her scalp tingle. Then her whole head swelled up as if it were inflating.... (SF 164–67)

She has just learned that she is—indirectly—her mother's murderer.

This episode destroys her. She absolutely refuses to scream when Butcher Chen has intercourse with her. This drives him to torture her, and starve her, in order to break her will. She cannot talk with the other women any more, because she is so horrified at what they think of her. She becomes psychologically and socially isolated, and loses the sense of what is real and what imaginary. Long after she has murdered her husband, and cut his body into pieces, she is still convinced that she is just living through one more horrendous dream.

Who killed her? And him?

The Winged Puffball

The critic and story writer Yu Guanzhong is from an older generation than Li Ang. His works express that tearing of the soul caused for many of his contemporaries by the tension of having been cut off from the Chinese tradition by the Communist occupation and corruption of the Mainland, and by the sensation of living, while physically on Taiwan, spiritually somewhere in between the culturally incompatible worlds of 'China' and the United States. In "The Seasons of the Dandelion" he puts his experience into the mouth of an unnamed character who is clearly some part of himself. This character is telling his friends how it feels to be about to set off for the United States again:

> He had in some sense the feeling ... that it wasn't he himself who was speaking, but someone else. It seemed as though a curtain were falling on an age, while in the distance a new age, still unnamed, was waiting for him to lift the veil from it....
>
> Every time he spoke of going, it seemed as if he were proclaiming his own death. After he had gone, such matters looked like funeral proceedings. People could still suck and chew on his name, of course, as on a well-flavored olive; but the olive tree was no longer there. To a few others, his departure was like the pulling out of a rotten tooth. It cured a toothache, while leaving an unaccustomed gap in the mouth. In truth, each time he left his country there was a violent pulling out of the roots from the soil, from the climate, and from so many well-known faces and sounds.[4]

It is like looking into three mirrors that create reflections of reflections of one's face, giving "a sense of bottomlessness and fearfulness."

Then, as the jet lifts off the runway in Taipei, "in one fleeting instant one says goodbye to the surface of the land and, at the same time, to China, and an ice-cold surgeon's knife cuts abruptly into the wound of the seasons [of the year]. One's soul becomes a thousand-winged dandelion puffball that flies off in every direction at the first breath of the wind. When the knife is withdrawn, one has already become another person." (FHR 48) And then:

> Even if it is already the third trip, even if the Seattle customs are passed through with no more ado than stepping over the threshold into one's own backyard, even if one has more friends on this side than on that one, even so, one cannot rid oneself of the feeling of being on point of making a parachute jump.
> It is in fact an entirely different world over there.
> This was because, once he had let himself go, his stomach was given over to ice-creams and sodas, his lungs to the fall [air] of the New Mainland [the USA], and his unbounded gaze was fixed on fresh and verdant scenery. This was because, once he had let his eyes close, his ears were filled with nothing but the rhythms of polysyllabic [Western] speech, while he himself was speaking nothing but 'verbs', 'subjects', and 'predicates'.... In the calendars of other countries there was no Spring Visit to the Graves, no Dragonboat Festival, no Mid-Autumn Festival, no Double-Ninth.... *Who* was it that had come back to life at Easter? *Who* was being thanked at Thanksgiving?... Why was the next stop always Tokyo, Chicago, or New York, not Shanghai or Xiamen? (FHR 48)

He has become alienated from the main Chinese story:

> Twenty years ago he had come to the island [of Taiwan], an emotionally passionate young man, with eyebrows and eyelashes and hair that were like the whirlwind beacon-fires brought from the Mainland, with a mind that leapt, and a pulse that pounded as if responding to the songs sung throughout the country during the war against Japan, to the sound of the waves along the Jialing river, to the sound of the historic Yangzi, its billows flowing with a sweep into the ocean.
> Twenty years later, the man setting out from this island was middle-aged. White hairs were invading his temples. Smoke from the wolf-dung beacons [the Communists] burned on the far side [of the Taiwan strait]. The sound of the waves on the Yangzi was confined to the innumerable scrolls in the [Taipei] Palace Museum.... Day by day the Old Mainland was becoming more remote, and the new Mainland nearer. (FHR 49)

Since then he has only seen the Chinese Mainland across the border of Hong Kong's New Territories:

> Below the banks ... one on the northern side, one on the southern, the Shenzhen river flowed as if it were deaf and dumb. A River of Forgetfulness, a poisonous bloody river, a river of tears sung about and wept over to the utmost possible, that wound up tortuously out of the depths of hell, as if unable to bear its burden of terror and ruined hopes.
>
> But on the wide and white expanse of its watery surface, there was nothing to be seen—no boat, no bridge of salvation to cross over, leaving the dead souls to cry for succor in vain.... The boundary between freedom and totalitarianism is a wound that cannot be stitched together, torn across the visage of humankind....
>
> The landscape forgets. Behind the scene of the immense tragedy, the color of the hills is still that same blue-green that it was in the years when the Qing dynasty drew to its close. Yet, except for the partridges on this nearside bank who call, guiltlessly, to the partridges on the other bank, there is silence all around. (FHR 50)

Not only is he "swaying between two worlds," he is aware that the next generation do not feel the situation in the same way that he does:[5]

> What his generation of Chinese had breathed in and out was that immense atmosphere imbued with the particular quality of the Mainland. Their feet had marked its localities as they had passed through them, and across its frosts and snows. The blue skies of its vast heaven had spread above them, and its resplendent white sun.[6] Below them, opened to their fullest, had been the red leaves of the crab apples. Their ears had been attuned to the rhythm of the Yangzi River, to the melody of the Yellow River. The palms of their hands had known the soft pliability of the willow trees, the firm rigidity of the *wutong* [the parasol tree]. South of the Yangzi, north of the border passes, were the windblown sands of the horses they had ridden, were the swallows on the beams, were the pomegranates in the crevices of the teeth that stained the mouth of the eater red—and these were so much more than the worn platitudes of the geography textbooks!... These memories ... had become ... an increasingly heavy burden on their soul.—Yet this weight was something for which the present generation had no feeling.
>
> The Old Mainland, the New Mainland, the Old Mainland ... His life was like the clapper of a bell swinging between the past and the future. He felt that he was a person who was one part Dark Principle, and one

part Bright Principle, one of his faces being in the shadow and one in the light, without any way of looking at them both at the same time. He was an uncanny beast of dark and light, in whose left eye a pagoda was reflected, but from whose right eye shone back a skyscraper. (FHR 52–53)

He thinks of Taiwan as a sort of "Ark on the waters" that is preserving Chinese culture, so that "its people are not so ruined that they become in truth just dandelions." He concludes with a resurgent affirmation of his original national identity:

This was *his* country, whose summer evenings as a child he had known so well. He could not call to mind how many rush-leaf fans he had waved in the course of his existence, nor how many wandering fireflies he had grabbed, nor how many mosquitoes he had swatted dead. He could no longer recall how many cups of cold tea he had gulped down in the course of one all-but-endless summer, or bowls of bitter plum soup, or green bean soup, or iced almond tea. He knew only one thing: air conditioning and Coca-Cola were no substitute for them....

The New Mainland and the Old Mainland ... had ceased their dispute with each other in his heart. *He was Chinese.* This was more important than anything else.... He was not to be imprisoned by the high-piled snows of Colorado. Every time he left his country, it meant a fierce tearing up, a tearing up even of his roots. But his roots were eternally here ... because it was from here that the fragrances spread far and wide forever. (FHR 55–56)

In Yu's case this struggle was a closely fought one, as he was (and is) a connoisseur of Western literature. His perception has been transformed by modern science, and his writings are full of such comments as the following: after a romantic passage in which moonlight is an important element, he continues—"but what we call 'the moon' is only a piece of dead and stupid rock on which laurels, if planted, could not grow, nor even the [fabled] moon-toad survive." (FHR 42) Among his successors, what it really means to declare that one is 'Chinese' is, in a cultural sense, more and more problematical.

Farewell to Immortality

Yu is haunted by a dream of some kind of almost religious ecstasy, outside any formal religion, and at the same time a rationalist awareness of its impossibility. The two feelings coexist in a fusion of this-worldly transcendentalism and a realistic self-mockery. Both are apparent, in counterpoint, in his short story "The Crane Burners." His uncle had once made him a beautiful kite in the form of a crane, the bird on which the immortals of China once rode the skies. Thinking about it long afterwards, he muses:

> Are the people who make kites philosophers, or are they poets? In this business, man does half and the wind the other half. Human beings may plan, but Heaven [also, 'the sky'] brings the matter to its completion. On the surface, man and nature are in opposition. Man wants to pull on the kite to hold it back; the wind wants to push it away. Yet, between this pulling and this pushing, the contradiction between man and nature in fact forms a new harmony. There is something slightly transcendent[7] in this domain, but such a kind of an experience is a poet's experience—or so he thought. At the one end is the limited; at the other end the unbounded. At the one end is the minuscule individual, at the other the entire universe, the whole of space with its vastness and freedom. You release the kite—no, you release your soul—upwards, upwards, and ever upwards into the coldest and utterly transpicuous space, into the blue pathways of the birds, and the multiple mirages of the clouds. Ultimately your feeling is of talking to an angel on the telephone, of playing at tug-o'-war with the wind, or of swift exchanges in your mind with all that vast and vague totality. This is, in truth, the happiest transcendent roaming.[8]
>
> But all these mystical feelings and experiences of transcending the self are only connected to you by a single thread. In that instant it is impossible to tell whether the windswept clouds have seized your heart away, or whether *you* have taken hold of the long and windswept clouds. The windswept clouds are, assuredly, in the heavens above, but one is still standing on the earth. One lets oneself go. Then one brings oneself back. (FHR 27–28)

Yu deliberately undermines this moment of exaltation. He (in his *persona* as the narrator) makes a second attempt at flying a kite. He is no longer a boy with his uncle now, but a father with his young daughters, trying to recreate the magic of a remembered past. It ends in humiliating failure. So he curses the damaged, muddy, object of sticks and paper. "In the high tide of his anger he felt that he could, in good conscience, have murdered every angel there was." Later, when his rage has passed, he sees "the crane-kite's corpse, already broken and spoiled, leaning stiffly against the wall in a dark corner." To save it from spiders and further degradation, he takes it out and burns it. (FHR 35)

He also insists on his own ordinariness, and inadequacies. Out with a friend in the Rocky Mountains, who found the height made him unwell, he notes

> We knew that 'pillowing on the clouds', 'banqueting on the dew', 'riding on cranes', and 'listening to the pines' were activities for the likes of Fei Changfang [a searcher after the Way during the Eastern Han dynasty whose miraculous staff let him move instantaneously from one place to another, and whose amulet enabled him to subdue demons and cure sicknesses], and Wangzi Qiao [an immortal]—beings that commonplace persons like ourselves, who could not throw away our identity papers, or do without specific medicines, would have difficulty in matching!

And he concludes:

> It is in the nature of human beings to be petty and self-enclosed to a lamentable degree. After they have gone up a mountain, and are near to heaven and far from other men, they may on the one hand become extraordinarily excited, and whirl about in their delight, while on the other hand they are gripped by an indescribable fear.... This is because ascending to high places, and crossing abysses, means that one's soul has nowhere to escape a naked confrontation with nature. There is also a limit to a person's capacity to absorb great beauty, and, once one has passed this limit, one feels an insuperable burden. (FHR 60–61)

As living, believable presences to the superior man or woman, the former immortals have died. Yet of course folk religion prospers on Taiwan, and new multicolored temples, obviously well endowed, seem to spring out of the earth between one visit and the next.

A Commonplace Fellow

We end with a book of essays by a still little-known writer, Yuan Ze'nan. His *A Commonplace Fellow*[9] reveals emotions that have reached the limit of what is still recognizably 'Chinese' without his becoming a hyphenated American. He is conscious of the problem of choosing a 'story' within which to live, of the conflicts between the various available Chinese stories, and between the 'Chinese' story in a general sense and the American one.[10] His work has a confessional concern with truthfulness in describing his own feelings. It is secular, sane. There is no hint of a cosmic framework, no quasi-messianic belief in 'progress'. He has a scientific training as a pharmacist, and a taste for accuracy. He believes in freedom of self-expression, admires romantic love even while aware of its dangers, and he tends to respect the young as much as or more than their elders. Throughout, even in his moments of private mystical experience, he exists in a state of existential uncertainty—doubt about his own identity, the validity of his own perceptions, and the nature of human situations—that one recognizes as 'modern'.

Father and Son

In a story with the strange but significant title "I am Nozha," Yuan describes his journey from filial piety to a relationship of mutual understanding with his father. In Chinese fable, Nozha was the son of the Prime Minister of Heaven. He quarreled with his father on account of the crimes that his father felt Nozha had committed against the Dragon King. He nonetheless possessed such filial piety that he committed suicide to save his parents, and after his reincarnation father and son were reconciled.[11] Here is Yuan's father dying in hospital, his son at his bedside, and the same theme emerging as memories run through Yuan's mind:

> My paternal grandfather ... had been a metropolitan degree-holder.... I came from a family steeped in bookish learning. My father was extremely talented, and had learned not a few of his skills from my grandfather. In particular he had picked up a lot about literature, medicine,

and how to divine by looking at stars and faces. But, when it came to passing it on to me, as the eldest son in direct descent, I proved to be useless.

From my earliest years I had no affinity with books. I did not enjoy listening to my father expounding Confucius or Mencius.... I did have a predilection, though, for unofficial histories and anecdotes, and in particular for such tales as *The Enfeoffment of the Gods* and *Wandering West*.... My brain at this time was full of strange thoughts. When I had some spare time, I would make off into the hills and go wild with my sister. My kid sister liked to act the Young Female Dragon, and for the sake of a fight I had no objection to impersonating Li Moqiu on the other side. [Characters from a martial arts romance by the popular Hong Kong author 'Jin Yong', i.e., Louis Cha.] I would hit my sister until her head was bruised and her eyes swollen, and she would run home in tears to tell on me. I was quite vicious in those days. (FFSZ 69–70)

Such memories produce a sense of guilt in him:

"Daddy," [he says in his thoughts] "... in my dreams I am forever seeing myself running away across the snowy ground. Sometimes you have an angry look on your face, and are gripping a cudgel and coming after me.... Sometimes we quarrel. You curse me, and I answer back.— Father, over all these years I have been thinking of you all the time. Don't you know how much I regret all the things I used to do?... Our arguments have come to an end, but the snow keeps falling. There is no way of opening communication between us." (FFSZ 77)

The snow here evokes the scene at the end of the great eighteenth-century novel, *The Story of the Stone*, where Precious Jade, returning after his earthly incarnation to immortality, takes leave—at a distance and across unbroken snow—of his uncomprehending Confucian father, Jia Zheng, who has in the past almost flogged him to death for his immoral behavior.

The deepest dispute between father and son has been over poetry, the older man "considering that a writer has no chance of making his way in life."

How was my father at that time to anticipate that, later, I would in fact be writing new-style poetry. When he did find out, he flew into a thundering rage. My mother always took his side in these violent conflicts. I was lucky to have in my younger sister an ally whose rebellious character was as strong as my own. My mind at that time was full of thoughts about 'struggling for justice'. How could I know what my parents, my elders and betters, were? When I look back on it now, even I am surprised.

After I graduated from high school, though, my father and mother defeated me: if I would agree to study physics or medicine, they would let me go abroad. My mathematics were not good, and I was frightened of blood, so off I went in an aggrieved mood to study pharmacology for a few years. When I was about to leave, my mother ticked off orders to me like Moses reciting the Ten Commandments. My father, however, merely said: "If you don't make a success of your studies, don't come back and see me. That way you won't disgrace our relations and friends." (FFSZ 72)

He takes his degree, as promised, but continues to write poetry; and in the end his father tacitly forgives him. Now he is at the bedside, watching the old man die.

New difficulties arise, trivial at first, then serious. To please his father he has even had a haircut, but his sister says he looks terrible, almost like a monk. (FFSZ 74–75) His mother observes that the pears he has brought for his father are hard and dry. In his distraught state, he has allowed the grocer to trick him. The old man quietly saves his face by saying that they have a sweet taste. Yuan then offers his father some roast duck he has purchased. His sister stops him. It is 'poisonous with heat' according to the categories of traditional Chinese medicine. He explodes: "Someone is on the point of dying and you have to quibble about it's being poisonous with heat!" When he realizes his father has overheard this, he goes white in the face. The old man, however, is in emotional control of the situation, and pretends to have heard nothing. He declines the duck, which he would obviously have enjoyed, in order to avoid a clash. Yuan then reflects:

> I don't really understand why I act the child in this way.... I was well aware that my sister was telling the truth, but I persisted in contradicting her with a nasty turn of phrase, so hurting my father grievously. I recalled that in the past, because I hadn't studied hard, I would be too tense to sleep on the night before an examination, and my father would press lightly with both hands upon my 'sun' acupuncture point[12] so that my nerves relaxed and I went to sleep. Now I had not the slightest iota of comfort to offer to *him*. (FFSZ 75)

A more serious difficulty is how to handle the funeral arrangements in a way that will satisfy both his father's wives. The senior
is estranged from his father, childless, and living on her own; the
second wife is his mother. They are not on speaking terms. The
senior wife reappears in the hospital room, in every sense a visita-
tion from the past:

> The hair on her temples had turned from black to white. Under her
> eyes were two dark and withered pouches. Her body had shrunk till it
> was like a withered tree. Many years of accumulated griefs and angers
> were rising to the surface, emptying themselves into that head of white
> hair, which curled upwards like a flood of resentment. (FFSZ 79)

He wants to talk with her outside, to avoid disturbing his father.
She refuses:

> "What do you mean when you say, 'Move one or two steps away?' *I*
> have not been guilty of illicit sexual relations. Why should *I* go outside
> to speak with you furtively? I have been kept away for several tens of
> years. If I keep away any more, it will be to enter my coffin.—So! I
> want to speak in front of your father. It's all right by me if he hears it.
> There's not one good person in the whole of your family. You, yourself,
> have a little conscience. You know that I've kept myself unsullied, like a
> widow, alone in my bitterness. As for the matters that will have to be
> dealt with in due course [the funeral], ... just be fair, and I will say
> nothing.... Otherwise—you can be sure that when your father skulks off
> to the world of the dead, I shall pull him out there [to judgement] to
> settle our accounts." (FFSZ 79)

With this old-fashioned threat, this apparition embodying the virtues of a past age vanishes.

Yuan's father discusses the funeral arrangements with him, and
the old man's composure in the face of death makes him seem like
"a giant." Yuan says he is sorry he went to the United States. He
should have stayed and learned from his father. But his father
laughs at this, a little bleakly, and says that times have changed. His
store of wisdom is no longer enough for getting along with, even in
Hong Kong. He goes on:

> "Everyone has different periods of good and bad fortune in life, but, if
> you exert yourself, you will always have a chance to rise above the oth-

ers. If you follow others, however, you will sometimes have no prospects. You have the best understanding of yourself. To be a human being, the most important thing of all is first and foremost to establish a harmonious relationship with your own innermost being. Don't be too concerned about the critical remarks of other people. Whatever you do, there will always be people who criticize you. Only try to match up to Heaven and Earth, and to conscience. Do not bring disaster on the country, or misfortune to the people. Then you have nothing to fear." (FFSZ 81)

When Yuan hears these old-style words, for some reason he feels his father has understood him. This speech "opened the fast-tied knots of my heart." (FFSZ 82) His father says to him that he is Nozha: their differences are reconciled. Yuan's exemplary conduct of the funeral some days later shows that his father was right.

Filial piety and obedience have given way to a desire for psychological intimacy with his father, on a basis not far from equality, an emotion that is perhaps more Western than Chinese.

Affectionate Fraud

His relationship with his mother is the reverse of that with his father. The distance between them grows too great to be bridged, so from filial affection he plays a charade, in which he does not believe, to keep her happy. Some years after his father's death he finds that she has taken to sitting at her window in her flat in Taigucheng,[13] and staring at the commuters day after day, until she knows all their faces and clothes. He comments:

> As I looked at her profile, and into the depths of the pupil of her left eye, it seemed to be filling with mists, both eerie and mysterious.... At this time I did not recognize my mother. The mother of my memories could not be like this!...
>
> My deepest impression was of the night before the lunar New Year. I was never willing to go to sleep, but doggedly persisted in helping my mother fold the 'long-life money' and wrap up the 'oil-horn' dumplings. Then about the hour of midnight, as I tugged on the corner of my mother's blouse, we would grope through the darkness to the temple at the end of the village to give our thanks to the gods.

On New Year's eve my mother would invariably have swept the house spotlessly clean. Golden papercuts and red cloth would be in place before the God of the Kitchen and the God of the Locality. In front of the God of War and of Guanyin, Goddess of Mercy, there would be a profusion of new fruits and flowers. Neatly folded tinfoil ingots of long-life money would be stacked in one corner. The indoors would be impregnated with a rich atmosphere of fragrance emanating from the scented candles that were taller than I was, and from the incense-burners....

There was an aroma of peanut oil in the kitchen. The tiny bubbles would have started spitting in the wok, and wafting up in the air, creating a grease-laden smoke that made one muddle-headed and drowsy. The oil-horn dumplings and fried cakes would snap and crackle, while the moon—like a dumpling full of the heat from the wok—hung low outside the window, and my mother's face, perspiring lightly, like the papercuts pasted in the lower corners of the windowpane, would be shining too.

"Mama! What about my New Year's gift money?"

...

"Go to sleep first! You'll have your New Year's money in the morning ...," my mother would say, turning her head and laughing. Her face was a moon, a round moon.

And yet—a moon that was sometimes cold and remote. I was terrified of being beaten by her on occasions such as this. When my father flogged me it was like a rainstorm of blows that numbed me almost at once. My mother's technique of corporal punishment was to give me first one lash, and then to enumerate my misdeeds until I said, 'I know I was wrong.' Then she would inflict a second lash. Just as the pain of the first had passed, a new pain would begin. As this sequence took its course, the fright was extreme. There were times when I couldn't endure it, and ran away. When I came back home my father would batter me within an inch of my life, until his freshly picked length of cane had been reduced to shreds.... The moon at his side would be terrified speechless, and the next day she would take me to see a doctor who specialized in injuries from falls.

In those days the moon, whether it was cold and remote, or warm and soft, was clear and coherent, ... but thirty years later ... this mother of mine by her window in Taigucheng was unfathomable and elusive. Her cloudy expression concealed some domain of which I was wholly ignorant. It seemed as if another woman had emerged from the mists, revealing quite other depths ... At those times I did not recognize my mother. (FFSZ 262–64)

The key to bringing her back to life is her love of jewelry, for which she has had a knowledgeable passion all her life:

> All that was necessary was for her fingers to touch the store of treasures that she had amassed through her questing for them, and her whole person would then be transfigured, her face shining with light. She would seem to have been reincarnated into another reality, into a realm in which she was the empress, and had become dignified beyond measure. (FFSZ 265)

Yuan, being acutely aware of "the vacuity of her life," reinfuses her with enthusiasm by persuading her to buy more pieces of jewelry— not as investments but for company. She is also psychologically transformed by looking at albums of old photographs. (FFSZ 276) When she comes across one of him, which as it happens he doesn't recognize, she comments with a touch of her old tartness, "You were much prettier then than you are now, and a whole lot easier to manage." (FFSZ 277)

His younger sister decides that the old lady is too ill to make a trip to the United States on which she has set her heart, and the matter seems to have been settled. But it has not. Yuan is woken early in the half-light of the next morning:

> When I opened my eyes, I saw a frail human form on the camphorwood clothes chest in the corner of the room. It was sobbing in a faint voice—faint and yet sharp-edged—almost as if it were gasping with suffocation. The feeble body was twisted into a ball, so wrenched about that it no longer resembled a human shape.
>
> "Mother?!" I called out, so terrified that I had to sit up in bed.
>
> Her eyes were welling with tears as she raised her head to look at me. In the dim light, the face was nothing but wrinkled lines, and mists seemed to be swirling up in her eyes.
>
> "I only want to have an outing, to enjoy a change of air. I won't bother you. I won't make any trouble for you.... I'm tired of sitting by myself and watching people. Oh!... and I'm afraid."...
>
> I realized that she was not looking at me at all, but at a space between us where it seemed there was an old photograph from years gone by that was beckoning her to come into it. I knew that, once she had entered it, she would never leave. I couldn't let this happen. I thought with a furious speed.

"I can't wait. I can't.—Do me this one kindness. Take me with you.
I don't care about the others."

As she spoke, her eyes shifted a fraction to look at me directly. Her
beseeching attitude, as she sat there, with no one to rely on, no one to
help her, was like that of a child who has suddenly lost her parents.

I looked down at this weak little woman, and my heart was filled
with love. (FFSZ 282–83)

He promises to take her to America. Once she is there, though,
trouble starts up between him and his sister over how to handle
her. His mother embarrasses them by talking at the top of her voice
in a San Francisco teahouse about a lady with a scar on her face
who is sitting at the next table. He tries to stop her, but she is un-
repentant:

"I only spoke a little. What's so wrong with that?"

... When I asked my younger sister for help, she whispered: "Now it
seems that you're at last going to see just how utterly impervious to
reason she is."

When I turned my head back again my mother was already sitting
sideways on to me. She was not sipping her tea, eating anything, or
paying the slightest attention to me. For a time this made me lose my
emotional center of gravity entirely. I almost wanted to stand up in-
stantly and leave....

After sitting there for seven or eight minutes, immobile, I finally
made my mind up. I took two deep breaths, filled my mother's teacup
from the pot, and said to her: "It was my fault, mother. Please be generous and forgive me."

"What half-witted filial subservience!" snorted my younger sister
contemptuously at my side.

I blushed all over my face, because I had not been in the least sincere in what I said. Nor did I blame my younger sister, as I thought the
matter through that evening. At the time my only concern had been
that I wanted my mother to have a happy trip.

That night I was unable to sleep. I lay on the bed and thought confused thoughts until—in the darkness—the light of inspiration appeared
... and I congratulated my self. I had not acted wrongly. *My mother and
I existed in two different worlds.* The limitations of her background and
period made it impossible for her to cross over to our side. We, on the
contrary, had to make our way across.... I had gone across to her.... By
using her background, and her language, there had been an immediate
rapport. Everything had worked quite perfectly. Once I had explained

everything to her clearly, my mother was not wildly unamenable to reason, but immediately receptive.... As a result, I learned a great deal from her. (FFSZ 269–70)

He is being untrue to his own understanding of the world in order to be true to his heart. But traditional filial piety it is not. In the old cultural world it would have come close to lèse-majesté to have talked about one's parents in such terms, at least publicly.

Idolizing the Young

Just as the attitude to parents has changed, so too has that toward children. Yuan delights in creative insubordination on the part of the young. Here is his account of a lavish Chinese business dinner in San Francisco to which he and his cousin Little Spring are being taken by his Aunt Wang, who "wanted the two of us to see the world, and to have a little of her glory rub off on us." (FFSZ 110) Traditional décor has become an exercise in stultifying cultural nostalgia:

> The restaurant had exerted itself to Chinesify everything. The walls glittered with decorations, as if there were painted beams and soaring ridgepoles. When one was in the midst of it all one had the illusion that one had transcended space and time, and returned to the Old China. (FFSZ 110)

Little Spring asks why so many of the guests are not members of the company, or of the family. Her aunt replies: "Foolish child! These are people who've come to curry favor. They're making use of this occasion to attach themselves to those of power and influence. If they succeed, their prospects will be limitless." (FFSZ 111) But Little Spring is bored by the speechifying and the photographing that precede the meal. When, at long last, a tray of hors d'oeuvres shaped like birds arrives, "she stuffed the multicolored dumplings into her mouth one after the other without any *politesse.*" She has been brought up in America and lacks schooling in old-style manners. This want of delicacy prompts a rebuke from a middle-aged lady:

When Mrs.. Ma, who was sitting opposite, saw the situation, she gave a tight little smile. "Young lady brought by Secretary Wang," she said, "you should eat a little more slowly. Then you will be able to savor as you should the flavors of the various sorts of roast meats rubbed into each of the bird's bodies. If you don't you will not be showing yourself worthy of the kindness of General Manager Chen, who has specially selected for us these hors d'oeuvres of One Hundred Birds Paying Court to the Phoenix." (FFSZ 112)

Little Spring is unruffled by this nasty speech, with its blend of fault-finding and fawning, but Yuan urges her to eat like "elegant Aunt Ma." Little Spring snaps back at him:

"I don't understand why she has to lift those birds in both hands, and then to turn them this way—and that—bestowing her admiration upon them before she devours them. It can't make them taste any better, can it?" (FFSZ 113)

Mrs. Ma pretends she hasn't heard this. She invites the Deputy Manager to sample some Grandly Spreading Fins and some morsels from the Jade Tray of Assembled Jewels. The author comments:

To put the matter bluntly, these were just pretty-pretty names for shark's-fin and a bowl of soup made from assorted winter melons and chosen for their auspicious character.

Mrs. Liang, who was sitting at the same table, was trying to compete in this process of ingratiating themselves with Deputy Manager Chen. She had already seized the ladle with the intention of serving winter-melon soup to him and his wife, but she was trying too hard. Inadvertently she spilt some soup on the table. When Mrs. Ma had this opportunity handed to her, she did not—needless to say—let it slip.

"Mrs. Liang," she observed, "you wouldn't act so hastily if you were picking up jewels. You really shouldn't turn a Jade Tray of Assembled Jewels into 'People Delight When Wealth Is Scattered'."

Mrs. Liang was so incensed at this that she began to tremble. Even Deputy Manager Chen was offended and unhappy. Mrs. Ma knew that she had been wrong to speak in this way, and that she had broken one of the taboos of the business world [by mentioning the scattering of wealth]. (FFSZ 113)

Aunt Wang, who is a "smoother operator than Mrs. Ma," works

dexterously to restore a mood of amiability. Unfortunately the backbiting starts up again:

> Mrs. Ma ... her teeth chattering with hatred, could not restrain herself from picking a further time on Little Spring:
>
> "Young lady! Your chopsticks are criss-crossing in an incorrect way. It is clear that no one at home can have taught you. Look, this is how *I* do it."
>
> "OK. *You* show me. My teacher tells me to 'walk upright and to sit correctly', and that 'the person of gentle breeding keeps three feet from the table when he or she eats'. Is that right? Auntie Ma, you don't seem to me to be three feet from the table, do you?"
>
> [Little Spring is using the ancient scriptures on ritual, and the authority of her teacher, to outbid Mrs. Ma, who tries to double in the same style.]
>
> "I am not like your auntie with her long sleeves—*so* appropriate for someone who is good at dancing—and so, naturally, *I* have to sit a little closer."[14]
>
> Seeing her chance, Mrs. Ma redirected the conversation towards my aunt. But Mrs. Liang was still smarting from her recent tongue-lashing.
>
> "My dear Mrs. Ma," she purred sarcastically, "whenever did you become so modest? You have only to use your tongue, and you can sit, quite firmly, *more* than three feet away."
>
> Everyone couldn't help but start laughing. [A long tongue was the sign of a gossip.] Mrs. Ma's face went scarlet.
>
> "I'm sure you're not implying I said anything wrong," she retorted angrily. "You overseas Chinese! How can one expect you to give attention to the models for good manners provided by China, the land of ritual? Do you think that eating is just a matter of doing as you please? Even the young lady knows that she should 'sit correctly'...."
>
> "If we were to follow Mrs. Ma's views," said Mrs. Liang, who was laughing like a branch of blossoms shaking, "I'm afraid we'd have to take a ritual bath, burn some incense, and select a lucky day before we started a meal...."
>
> "That's right!" Little Spring put in suddenly. "The old teacher who teaches me Chinese says the people of the Qing dynasty wasted their time drinking tea, cultivating flowers, and disporting themselves with birds, and that is how the country was ruined."
>
> We were stunned by her answer. (FFSZ 114–15)

Aunt Wang is furious afterwards with Little Spring for not understanding "the rules" and nearly causing her to lose face. Little

Spring replies that she has no desire to learn such bothersome rules, adding "I'd rather not eat." (FFSZ 115) Although Little Spring made use of a typically Chinese device—authority—in shattering the pretentiousness of the ladies, doing so at all is characteristic of American directness and not Chinese tact. It is clear whose side the author is on.

Yuan is also inclined to idolize childhood as a period of creativity that is all too soon crippled by the stereotypes imposed by adults. He is in no way original in this respect, since it is possible to find this attitude in Chinese iconoclastic thinkers since at least the early 1920s, but it is an important part of the 'modern' emotional pattern. An example is his account of the fairy-tale painting done by his niece in Hong Kong. It is wholly in dark blue, except for the princess's lips, which are dark red. The girl's mother says she is as weird as her uncle, and asks her to draw "a nice picture with the hair colored black" instead. (FFSZ 20) Yuan is saddened by this suppression of the child's "freedom to develop," well intentioned though his sister is. Then he has a dream: his niece is painting a picture of many colors, and explaining to him what they mean:

> "The sun should be red, and the evening sun a pale red, but when it sinks level with the sea, and the blue water of the sea is reflected in it, it beomes purple. So I've used purple for it. I've used grey for Grandpa's face, because he's ill, but green for his hair, because I hope he's like a green hill and lives forever. I've used red for mother's face because, since Little Flower [the cat?] has stolen her fish and eaten it, she's about to get angry and chase her to spank her." (FFSZ 25)

Still in his dream, Yuan comments that "there's no way I would have thought of such colors, so far am I removed from the age of childhood." Later, he says to his niece: "You are a child full of imaginative power. Perhaps *you* can open the way for *me* into many things?"

Only in the present century have children begun to be experienced by adults in the Chinese world as being in a certain sense 'people'. And only begun.

Who Is Chinese?

Yuan is fascinated by Chinese, including himself, who—whatever their surface appearance—are no longer wholly 'Chinese'. Writing in Hong Kong, he says that "the tragedy of a person like me is that where there are Chinese, I feel like an American, and that where there are Americans, I feel like a Chinese." (FFSZ 188) His younger sister tells him that "sometimes the point of view from which you speak would terrify many Chinese people to death." He answers, "Let them die then!" To himself, he reflects, "surely more things have died in my heart than theirs?" (FFSZ 203)

Elsewhere he observes:

> In these last few years in America, I have, without being quite fully aware of it, learned to forget. I no longer think at all of Chinese traditional culture.... I am, I think, someone who has cut the umbilical cord of China with a relative degree of success, though I will not discuss, at the present juncture, whether I have gained by doing so, or lost. I have become imbued through and through with the disgusting habits of the foreign devils.... The one benefit I obtain is that I don't suffer from homesickness. (FFSZ 202)

But of course he is ambivalent, and this emerges from "Story Angle," in which he imagines the thoughts going through the mind of a young Chinese mother who is talking to her five-year-old son—they are too distant for him to hear what she is actually saying—as they try to come to terms with living in an American suburb:

> "Like father, like son. When the elders are no good, the young don't make a good showing either. Our family was getting on fine in Taiwan, but we would have to make every last effort to move to the States. Once we'd come, the old man had nothing to do all day. Couldn't find work, so he made off to the bar, in desperation. Even my wedding ring was pawned, and then—just like that—off he goes with a foreign woman. If I'd known this was going to happen, I'd never have come in the first place. And now, even the kid's like this." (FFSZ 131)

It seems that the boy won't eat his rice, but is demanding a hamburger. "Chinese people all eat rice," says his mother. "Whoever ate a hamburger?" When her son names two Chinese who do, she snaps back: "They're not Chinese! Anyone who eats a hamburger isn't Chinese!" "Don't kids in Taiwan eat hamburgers, too?" he asks. Of course they do, so she has no answer, but she thinks:

> "I've got no right to make him act like a Chinese in America. Even grown-ups can't resist the temptations, how much less a youngster like him? Poor kid, his father's run away with someone else, but he's still in the dark about that. Let's take it one step at a time. First, I'll ask that Mr. Zhang if he can lend me a little money ... but I'm afraid he's casting a roving eye at my body." (FFSZ 132)

Her son says she's to stop crying. He'll do as she says. But she tells him she's going to phone 'Uncle' Zhang, after which they can go and buy a hamburger. (FFSZ 133) We know, with a rueful smile, that they are going to adapt—and survive.

Yuan's relationship with his friend Dawei (David) shows the ambiguities in 'Chineseness' at a deeper level. Dawei has grown up in the States, made a fortune, and conceived a belated passion for things Chinese. He has had his house redone by designers in a Chinese style, throwing out even his family photographs, and "hanging up things of which he had no understanding at all." Some are fakes, some genuine, like a painting by Liu Guosong, a Taiwanese who has adapted traditional brushwork techniques to an abstract style. Seeing this painting makes Yuan happy on his friend's behalf. But— when he looks more closely—he sees that "the basic nature of the fittings was still wholly Americanized." (FFSZ 40–41) For example:

> The vertical lines were as straight as the handles of writing-brushes, the horizontals absolutely level.... There was not the slightest sense of personal warmth. Splendor, yes, but no feeling. (FFSZ 41)

A cockroach then appears, and to Yuan's amazement, Dawei lets it escape. This is true Buddhist magnanimity, he thinks. He feels inferior to his friend when he himself kills a cockroach that evening in his own home. But appearances have deceived. He learns over the phone that Dawei has called in professional pest exterminators, who have destroyed even the eggs. "The undertone of oppression in his happy-sounding voice on the phone made me think of the design plan of his home, and a sudden cold shiver ran through me."

This unwillingness to give any quarter was probably what lay behind Dawei's success in business. He learns the reason the first cockroach was spared was because Dawei feared "it might make a mess of the carpet." (FFSZ 43–44)

Dawei quotes the Confucian *Analects* to justify himself: "If the gentleman is not heavy-handed, his authority will not be felt." This is a misinterpretation: it should be taken as "if the gentleman is not dignified."[15] With mock modesty, Yuan declares himself to be "a lesser sort of man," but he recalls another of Confucius's sayings: "clever phrases and good appearances are seldom found among those who have true fellow-feeling for others."[16]

On another occasion, his friend says to him: "We're all Chinese," an assertion that sets Yuan on edge. He rejects total extinction:

> "My cockroach problem is not serious. It can be dealt with in any old way [a very 'Chinese' attitude]. For full-scale mobilization, the objects should be a little larger."

When Dawei asks how much larger, Yuan won't answer. "Tell me!" his friend insists. "We're all Chinese! Don't treat me as an outsider in this way." Provoked, since he does not consider Dawei to be 'Chinese', Yuan replies: "As big as you." (FFSZ 46)

Another friend, who is ethnically Chinese but cannot even speak the language, shows him three glass paperweights he has bought in the People's Republic, believing them to be "antiques" dating from the 1920s. Yuan tells him they are recent fakes:

> The workmanship was extremely coarse. A fair number of air bubbles had been enclosed in them, like the sighs of an afflicted person that had risen halfway up inside before being held fast by the high pressure. They formed rounded full stops. They did not even imitate the shapes of question marks or exclamation points. (FFSZ 63)

This is of course a symbolic comment on Chinese Communism. He looks at his friend, and thinks that "for all his yellow skin, black hair, and black pupils in his eyes, he had not the least flavor of China." (FFSZ 64) He goes on, "just for the sake of arguing":

> "It's not an antique, I'm afraid. It's a witness to present-day blood and tears. Look at those flowers. They make me think of the tragic events of

the Hundred Flowers. The flowers are still there, but where are the people who grew the flowers?"

"What was the Hundred Flowers?"[17]

"Have you heard of the Great Cultural Revolution?"[18]

"No."

"That, too, was 'Made in China'. It could also be thought of as being an antique. Only this antique was a dormant volcano—one that erupts from time to time."

"What are you talking about? I don't understand anything." (FFSZ 64–65)

One may be an ethnic Chinese, but untouched by China.

When he returns to his home city, Hong Kong, he finds he has become a psychological tourist. He is repelled by the pressures the inhabitants exert on each other, and the lack of concern for other people. It seems to him a world built on his elder sister's philosophy: "Human life is a dream.... Eat first, pay afterwards" (FFSZ 172–73) He watches the crowds on the dance floors "twisting fiercely in time with the beat ... as if they wanted to break free from something in their fates." It was a world, he says, "into which I could not force my way." (FFSZ 179) "Spiritual hunger and thirst" cannot be assuaged in Hong Kong, though the melancholy sentimental lyrics of the popular singers who create so much of the city's atmosphere still move him:

> Do you understand or not
> Life is changing, never stops,
> Changes we never can foresee
> Being the only constancy?
> (FFSZ 190–91)

It is Westerners who ultimately move him most. He shares Jack London's contempt for life that "keeps going for a long time by means of being economical." He admires Richard Burton's contempt for public criticism, seeing "the pointlessness of defending an empty reputation."(FFSZ 144) He praises Truman Capote for "holding firm to your own ideals and style of life", including his sexual deviation, so that, even if his writings have not moved peo-

ple as much as they might have done, "at the very least your *life*
had éclat." (FFSZ 150–51) Yuan has come to see the individual as a
self-justified and self-justifying entity.

The Authenticity of Experience

Yuan is always testing the validity of his own sensations, perceptions, and interpretations. This artistic agnosticism, which always
doubts itself, is akin to science in its fundamental modesty. He uses
the form of jottings (*sanwen*—unsystematic pieces), he says, because "they are totally naked." "These minute joys and angers,
griefs and delights, have all been personally experienced." Not
many people write, in his view, "without erecting some defences."
He is obsessed with "the truth of the confessional." Writing these
reminiscences has strengthened his awareness of "the elusive nature
of human life and character." Above all, he has learned that "the
hardest thing of all to understand is my own self." (FFSZ 1–4)

The visual artist "is always trying for all he is worth to grasp
something that is absolutely ungraspable." "To have grasped a single
scale, or half a claw, already makes one a great master." Yet he
hates Audubon for having killed specimens of birds in order to
make his great paintings. "This method of disregarding everything
else for the sake of art disgusts me every time I think of it." (FFSZ
4) The illusion-creating deceit behind art also worries him, since,
he says, "I strongly believe in real things." (FFSZ 4–5)

He responds to the details of everyday experience:

> I put the old newspapers ... soaked through with rainwater, into the
> garbage can. The blurred printed characters seemed to have already be-
> come history, like the mildewed volumes in libraries. Future genera-
> tions will make the same mistakes, for people forget things swiftly in
> our hurried world. (FFSZ 14)

Or again:

> My senses have grown duller these days. For me a rainy day is—
> simply—a rainy day, when one has to remember to carry an umbrella
> when going out. Yet I still love the spattering sound—*plink! plink!*—on
> the umbrella, urgently tapping out the rhythm of our lives. (FFSZ 15)

But the moment he has said something that, as here, borders on the sentimental, he undercuts it:

> The rain fell through a hole in the umbrella and slid onto my neck. Nothing is wholly perfect or beautiful—an umbrella, a rainy day, or life. A chill thought is trickling down my neck.   (FFSZ 16)

His writing is a remedy, and one that has to be perpetually renewed, to an existential crisis. He will write about "any little something that will let me get hold of it, to prove to myself that I have existed."

And yet, he goes on, "my brain is like a prism that is devoted to refracting the light from other people into a multicolored spectrum, while I myself merely play the role of a transparent medium, empty and utterly devoid of content." (FFSZ 194) The meaning he infuses into the material of experience is transient, provisional; there is no fixed interpretation.

He has moments of matter-of-fact mysticism. In the past, he says, he used to get out of his car and feed the birds that sat on the pylons by the roadside in the morning mists. Now he drives past, pretending to himself that he doesn't want to disturb them, but

> Strange to say, as time has gone by, those iron-black shadows have actually begun to shine with light, so that every day when I cross the bridge my eyes are always sparkling. Yet, having reached the stage in life that I have, I really find it hard to believe that miracles can happen. (FFSZ 118)

He stresses that he has lost his youthful romanticism and credulity, "and yet I really can see birds that give off light, which startles me, and has puzzled me for quite some time."

On one occasion this 'miracle' recurs in a furniture shop, when a mildewed old carpet shines, so that even its rotten parts appear beautiful. This gift is a source of "stolen happiness." He has come to feel, he says, that "the more commonplace things are, the more chance there is of finding one among them that gives out light," whether books, flowers, squirrels, or records of popular music.

It is even true of people. When my mother came to visit, I never imagined that her face, which was wrinkled like a face from Chinese history, would have been able to give off light. But her face, when she laughed, or spoke, or—most of the time—scolded me for all my inadequacies, actually shone. But from beginning to end, I never dared to tell her of this. (FFSZ 120)

He thinks that anyone who really makes an effort to look can see things that shine with light, and "they can make one happy."

Love

In its original form, in the European Middle Ages, romantic love combined a sexual passion with feelings of a religious nature, in the sense that the person whom one loved was felt to give life its essential meaning. It is a profoundly un-Chinese sentiment, and Yuan is fascinated by it but still wary enough of it to keep a certain distance.

He talks to a Chinese-American woman called Fanny who describes herself and her husband as "two dried grasshoppers tied to a red thread" in allusion to their traditional arranged marriage. The drabness of their day-to-day existence frustrates her:

"Love should contain romance, and a startled delight unattainable by thought! Love should not be stereotyped and dull of wit like this!" (FFSZ 30)

Yuan tells her there's no security in romance, but she rejects this:

"I must have romantic love! A feeling of security without romance would be like reading the same book over and over again. Even if it were a masterpiece, the feeling that it was great would have vanished after the tenth reading." (FFSZ 30)

He lectures her, a little piously, on the need for "everlasting love" to develop from "romance" and hence to "security" and "mutual understanding," but she explodes:

"I must have love! I want love in an afternoon where the sunlight spreads everywhere, love on a plain where there are no shadows, love in a place where there is room for me to grow!" (FFSZ 32)

She is trapped in her marriage:

> "At present my love is dead. It's a dead love that suffocates me. It's like—this hill, this stone, this lake—an expanse of dead water. If it were demanded of me that my heart should be utterly brave and daring, I could rise to that. But I can't bury everything inside me in order to embrace a love that has never had a breath of love in it." (FFSZ 34)

For her, "there's nothing to be afraid of in death itself, but I cannot endure the limitations it imposes. I want the spark of my life to burn brightly." So, she swings back and forth between a kind of infinite self-expansion and immediate self-extinction. She doesn't care about ordinary familial or social relationships. Her dreams are not of sexual release of tension, nor of material or social advantage, but of some kind of individual, almost transcendental, exaltation. "Either success or failure would be all right," she declares. "I can't wait any longer. I'm not afraid of people's mockery, or their abuse. I want to pay the price." (FFSZ 35) The author, a little wiser, comments on her helplessness when she tries to control the impulses that have taken hold of her:

> "Fanny!.... This is only *a love-story that, by some chance of fortune, has taken place in your body*. What's more, you won't be the first person to be so sacrificed." (FFSZ 35)

People can be possessed by stories almost as if by a form of demonic possession.

He has a strong sense of determinism. In another piece he describes his feelings as he talked to another woman, this time in Hong Kong:

> As we walked forwards through the dark in the silence, all at once my feet stubbed against seaweed and pebbles. Looking at these fine, rounded, pebbles, I suddenly perceived that each one was almost identical in size but had a different pattern from the others, that it was carved from a different experience. You and I, both of us, were only two small pebbles moved along by the waves and currents regardless of our wills, more than busy enough with our own affairs, let alone having time to talk idly of more distant prospects. (FFSZ 53)

The metaphor is interesting, especially in the sense of the sense of the unbridgeable separation of each individual existence from all others.

When Yuan writes of the end of one of his own love affairs he is clinically lacking in self-pity:

> More than two years of living together now seem so superficial, like politics, or an autumn papercut, or buildings reflected in a puddle of dirty water. All that was once so real has become so superficial, collapsing at the first blow. It appears that you had only to nod your head for a waiter to pick it up and whisk it away on a tray. (FFSZ 162)

It was an affair whose end will attract no notice, "like a quilt tossed off a bed after a weekend's delirious lovemaking, that even at its most pathetic will hardly draw a glance." Then he speaks to her in his imagination:

> "I could almost leave my body and tell you, peacefully, about the surging and crowding that goes on inside, where there are power failures, or too much rubbish, or where a door has gone missing, or a window. But you, placed in the middle of it, are neither bigger nor smaller than you are in fact. You are—just you. The city does not change. Space and time do not change. Merely, from time to time one or two specks of dust alter their positions.
>
> ... It was I myself who shut my eyes, and then felt resentment at the darkness. It was I myself who forced the light to be lit, and was astonished at the shadows around me." (FFSZ 161)

It is this internal drama of the emotions, evoked here, that more than anything else is accepted in the 'modern' world as guiding and validating a person's actions in life, as being the essential and distinctive part of that life. It must have existed in traditional China in some form or another, but it was, if so, barely visible, and never acknowledged as being at the heart of what should direct, or be, a life. It probably first appeared openly in the Chinese world in some of the writers of the 1920s—such as Yu Dafu—but Yuan Ze'nan, a generation or so later, now accepts it without question as the norm.

The Problem of Happiness

A self-conscious searching for happiness, together with uncertainty about its nature, seems to be characteristic of the 'modern' mind.[19] We can find this at two levels in Yuan's pages.

First, he is appreciative of the minor but not negligible art of being content. Thus he says: "If one reckons honestly, a person does not really own many things in the course of a lifetime. Enjoying what one has, and not quibbling over every last item, is a way of compromise that avoids pain." (FFSZ 12) A little later he adds: "I have learned in the course of the last two or three years to be satisfied with an ever more restricted scope." (FFSZ 14) "My capacity for delight goes no further than the commotion made by a single cricket, or a single honeybee humming and soaring, these things so full of vital force." (FFSZ 16) One day he is enjoying being lazy, since he has finished some work, and so "has not the slightest qualm of conscience," but is unsettled to find that the international news in the newspaper is ominous. He comments: "Well, then, let me at least eat an orange. When the newspapers do not satisfy one's spirit, eating is a sort of compromise solution. Even if the orange is sour to the taste, at least it's natural, not man-made." (FFSZ 94)

Besides this emotional minimalism, he also possesses a wry sense of the unacknowledged pleasures of life. On his return to Hong Kong, for example, he has "an extremely happy meal" with his younger sister at which they "laughingly consigned vast numbers of people to hell." (FFSZ 167) On another occasion he observes that the pleasure his old mother derives from contemplating the past by browsing through an album of photographs is "as if she were plugged into an electric current." (FFSZ 276)

The second level is a more desperate matter, full of ambiguities. The last story in the book, "When Debts Are Settled," is a discussion of this level of happiness. The scene is San Francisco, on Market Street, where endless muddy repairs to the roadway resemble "a wound bursting open." Yuan is in a café frequented by "nighttime hunters ... each fighting on his own, each harboring different dreams." (FFSZ 288-89) He meets a young man called Alan:

He was an American male, massively built, with the upper half of his body bare, and wearing nothing but a pair of white workman's overall trousers that hung straight down his frame, trousers that were mottled on every part of them with grease stains. His thick curly hair covered his head in a tangled disarray, but could not conceal the exceptional quality of his face. A worn-out feeling could be detected in the corners of his eyes; that there was weariness in his expression was beyond doubt. But—when he smiled—his half-mocking spirit seemed to warn one not to be too pleased with oneself, for the life that he had led had been so much more spectacular than one's own. (FFSZ 289)

Yuan wonders if Alan, who used to live in Los Angeles, had once been "a star." The young man answers that in a certain sense he had been, and adds: "The life I led was not unlike the life of the [real] stars. Even the brilliance of the real stars, once they were off the silver screen, was no match for mine.... When I was in my heyday, it was no use *my* relying on studio lights, or on make-up, to establish my reputation. My acting technique was rather more demanding. In this world of ours, knowledge and hard work have little value compared to that intangible something called 'the charm of youth'. The charm of youth is like a forest. It has a kind of primeval force. When one has 'firewood' to peddle, and knows how to go about selling it, then one has a natural resource beyond any reckoning." (FFSZ 292-93)

So he had been a boy prostitute. Alan goes on to describe his life:

"Like the stars, I made my living by selling the charm of youth. They sold their faces. I sold my flesh. If, some time, a star didn't have a handsome face to turn to, he'd come to me to buy mine. And it wasn't only the stars. It was well-known socialites, famous businessmen, even important personalities from the churches, all of them people playing important roles in society. When they came to me, there was no difference between any of them, except clothes and gestures. I never turned anyone away in those days. I was drunk on their fawning over me. I was happy to respond in the same ingratiating way....

"I earned a lot of money then. At the same time I consumed a lot of drugs. My clients liked to get me befuddled first by taking peculiar drugs. Then they could take possession of my body in any way they liked. It seemed that by doing this a sense of emptiness didn't return to them when they had finished with me and went off elsewhere.

"But the money went out as fast as it came in. It was like the happiness after taking drugs. You can't hold onto it.... I sought material enjoyments in a frenetic pursuit. It was the only thing to be done to avoid going out of my mind." (FFSZ 293–94)

He had fled to San Francisco to save himself from going to pieces entirely. He now worked as a locksmith, and found life "even if not altogether as I would like it to be, still much more regular." (FFSZ 294)

"I looked at the lightning flash tattooed on his burly arm," says Yuan, "and wondered—into how many other people's empty loneliness the illumination of that emblem had suddenly blazed, and left behind on his own body a dull black stain?" Alan comments that among those in "the trade of selling smiles" there is a saying that "when you're young you sell, when you're old you buy." And he adds that "emotion and wealth that one earns in one's youth have to be repaid many times over in old age." (FFSZ 294)

Yuan thinks that in its different way his own life has been not unlike Alan's, squandered to no purpose. "I had caroused in wine bars, charged about the dance halls, smoked, drunk, and been debauched, ... becoming an object of admiration in others' eyes. They thought that since I was young, and my circumstances not too bad, with a secure job and no family burdens, no overwhelming griefs, and no excessive moving about from one place to another, I ought to be happy.—And in fact I *was* always smiling. But they could not see, behind my cheerful smiles, that feeling of being taken possession of while in a state of befuddlement." (FFSZ 295–96)

His friends tell him that all he has to do is make a few friends, go to church, marry and have a few kids, and that will blunt his feeling of being an outsider. "Regrettably," he observes, "my perverse nature lacked the determination for this and, on the contrary, took no delight in these things." (FFSZ 297) He concludes that "being busy, being insensitive, and overindulgence in consolations are the most effective painkillers of our generation;" but, he adds, "I fear the feeling of befuddlement that comes when the pain is stopped in this way." (FFSZ 298) His writings are a means of relief, and perhaps also "preparation for settling the debt" when he is old. He hopes that if ever he has one day to wear trousers stained with grease and repair locks, he may be a little happier than Alan.

The soul no longer has any sense of being in others or for others.

Notes

Notes

Introduction

1. Mark Elvin, "The Collapse of Scriptural Confucianism," *Papers on Far Eastern History*, 41 (1990). Reprinted in id., *Another History: Essays on China from a European Perspective* (Sydney: Wild Peony, 1996).

2. Geremie Barmé and John Minford, eds., *Seeds of Fire. Chinese Voices of Conscience* (New York: Hill and Wang, 1988) and G. Barmé and Linda Jaivin, eds., *New Ghosts, Old Dreams* (New York: Times Books, 1992).

3. An illustration of this may be found in Prys Morgan, "From a Death to a View: The Hunt for the Welsh Past in the Romantic Period," in Eric Hobsbawm and Terence Ranger, eds., *The Invention of Tradition* (Cambridge: Cambridge University Press, 1983). Wales was "a national community that was not a political state" (p. 92) in which, after the union with England, the "loss of Welsh history had a debilitating effect" and "a heroic act of salvage was needed" (p. 47). The result was the re-creation of a Welsh 'story', a significant part of it being invented (p. 56). The process had "a great healing function at this difficult juncture in Welsh history" (p. 100), though in the early nineteenth century "[t]he nonconformist take over of Welsh culture created a new image. It weakened Welsh interest in the far-distant national past, replacing it with an interest in the past of the Old Testament ... and emphasized the new puritanical Sunday as 'The Welsh Sunday', the new 'Welsh way of life' being that of the chapel, the singing school ..., the temperance assemblies, ... the mutual improvement societies [etc.]" (p. 95).

4. Consider in this respect the view of Harold Bloom, with respect to the 'Yahwist' component of the Torah, that "Yahweh in the Book of J, *is a literary character*, just as Hamlet is. If the history of religion is the process of choosing forms of worship from poetic tales, in the West that history is even more extravagant: it is the worship, in greatly modified and revised forms, of an extraordinarily wayward and uncanny literary character, J's

Yahweh." Harold Bloom and David Rosenberg, *The Book of J* (1990. Reprinted, London: Faber and Faber, 1991), pp. 11–12.

5. For instance, Richard Stremski, *Kill for Collingwood* (Sydney: Allen and Unwin, 1986), p. 12: "Pride was inherent in the Club because of its origins as the representative of a suburb that required redemption.... [T]he Club institutionalised the aspirations of the community."

6. See Michel de Certeau, *L'invention du quotidien*, I, *Arts de faire* (New edition, presented by L. Giard. Paris: Gallimard, 1990): "the stories [*récits*] of what-is-going-on constitute our orthodoxy" (p. 270). "[T]aken hold of by the radio the moment he wakes ... the listener walks all day in the forest of the telling of tales [*narrativités*] by journalists, by advertising, and by television.... Even more than the God of whom the theologians told stories yesterday, these stories [*histoires*] have the function of providence and predestination: they organize in advance, our work, our festival days, and even our dreams. Social life multiplies the acts and forms of behavior *imprinted* by narrative models. Our society has become a story-told society [*une société récitée*]...." (p. 271).

7. See, for example, Terence Ranger, "Taking Hold of the Land: Holy Places and Pilgrimages in Twentieth-Century Zimbabwe," *Past and Present* 117 (1987). According to Ranger, p.159: "[B]y far the greater part of the African past ... was expressed ... in oral traditions and myths, in rituals and ceremonies, which claimed the land for particular peoples and chiefs and spirits. The 'rocks and stones and trees' on which white settlers looked incomprehendingly were all incorporated into an African oral historical geography. Hardly a hill or cave existed ... which did not have a religious or political historical significance."

8. One example: for an account of the immense depth of the story that lies behind the Jewish festival of Tabernacles (Sukkot) see Joseph Rykwert, *On Adam's House in Paradise. The Idea of the Primitive Hut in Architectural History* (1972. Reprinted, Cambridge, Mass.: MIT Press, 1981), esp. pp. 154–60, and Leviticus 23.33–39.

9. It is not easy to judge *a priori* which beliefs have a Social Darwinian capacity for survival. Many of the ideas and rites of late rural Catharism in the Languedoc, for example, would seem at first sight to have been ill-suited to self-perpetuation, including such practices as virtually obligatory suicide by starvation (the *endura*) after taking the ultimate sacrament of purification (the *consolamentum*); but E. Le Roy Ladurie has shown in his *Montaillou, village occitan de 1294 à 1324* (Paris: Gallimard, 1975) that the system as a whole had many socially valuable functions. See especially chapters 14 and 23.

10. The term 'fictional' is incorrect as the selection, interpretation, and

emotional loading of facts can often be as important as outright invention. The philosophical problems relating to what is or is not in some sense 'objective truth' are outside the present discussion. For a discussion of some of the issues, see Richard A. Schweder, *Thinking Through Cultures* (Cambridge, Mass.: Harvard University Press, 1991). The approach that he recommends, namely "constantly moving from one objective world to the next, inside and then out, outside and then in, all the while standing back and trying to make sense of the whole journey" (p. 68) is quite close to that which I have adopted here, but I would say 'story' rather than "objective world." Elsewhere (p. 188) he comes quite close to story theory, observing, for example, that "for orthodox Hindus a major way to prove a point is to recount a historical or personal narrative, and a central body of evidence about what the causal structure of the world is like consists of 'historical' experiences recorded in the Hindu scriptures."

11. Salman Rushdie, *The Satanic Verses* (New York, London, etc.: Penguin Group, 1989). This is concisely illustrated by the way in which Salman the Persian, the Prophet's mischievous amanuensis, who at times records his inspirations a little wrong on purpose (pp. 367-8), observes on p. 363, "The closer you are to a conjurer, ... the easier to spot the trick." The idea that religious life is lived as a story is often present: "... without warning, Hamza says to Mahound [Muhammad]: 'Go ask Gibreel [Gabriel],' and he ... feels his heart leaping in alarm, who, me? *I'm* supposed to know the answers here? I'm sitting here watching this picture and now this actor points his finger out at me, who ever heard the like, who asks the bloody audience of a 'theological' to solve the bloody plot?.... Gibreel...'s not just playing the archangel but also him, the businessman, the Messenger, Mahound.... Nifty cutting is required to pull off this double role, the two of them can never be seen in the same shot, each must speak to empty air ... and trust to technology to create the missing vision, with scissors and Scotch tape.... *Mahound comes to me for revelation, asking me to choose between monotheist and henotheist alternatives, and I'm just some idiot actor having a ... nightmare, what ... do I know ... to tell you, help. Help.*" (pages 108-9)

12. For example, his description of Louis XV as "gazing dubiously, the absurdest mortal extant (a very Solecism Incarnate) into the absurdest confused world." Thomas Carlyle, *The French Revolution* (1837. Reprinted, London: Chapman and Hall, n.d.), p. 18.

13. See Edward Timms, *Karl Kraus—Apocalyptic Satirist, Culture and Catastrophe in Habsburg Vienna* (New Haven and London: Yale University Press, 1986), who describes Kraus's satire as based "on the contradiction between the given social structure and the forms of consciousness in

which it was apprehended" (p.18): a situation where "ideological contradictions created states of mind that were self-evidently absurd" (pp. 27–28).

14. Miguel de Cervantes Saavedra, *El ingenioso hidalgo Don Quijote de la Mancha* (1605–15. Reprinted Madrid: Espasa-Calpe, 1993). Trans. P. Motteux, rev. Ozell, as *Don Quixote* (New York: Modern Library, 1930).

15. Motteux, *Quixote*, p. 9; Cervantes, *Quijote*, p. 23.

16. Motteux, *Quixote*, p. 113; Cervantes, *Quijote*, p. 94.

17. Thomas Carlyle, *The French Revolution*, p. 7.

18. Ibid., pp. 333–34.

19. Quoted in Leonie Sandercock and Ian Turner, *Up Where, Cazaly? The Great Australian Game* (Sydney, London, New York, etc.: Granada, 1981), p. x.

20. Sandercock and Turner, *Up Where, Cazaly?*, p. 230.

21. Ibid., p. 200.

22. Quoted in Bruno Bettelheim, *The Uses of Enchantment: The Meaning and Importance of Fairy Tales* (1976. Reprinted, London: Penguin, 1978), p. 35 (no source given).

23. Bruno Bettelheim, *Uses of Enchantment*, p. 7.

24. For example, gods, demons, and consciously aware animals and artefacts.

25. The Mbya believe that the world they live in is Evil, and that this is not their fault, but rather because everything in it is one-sided, finite, and changeable. Only in a duality in which everything is also what it is not, and hence impossible to name, is there Good. The great events in their history were religious migrations eastwards to try to find a Land Without Evil, and their horror at being stopped in this quest by the ocean, which confirmed them in the view that the eternal land lay on the other side. Convinced that, in the past, some of their ancestors were answered by the gods and found their way there, the Mbya seek by right living and meditations to overcome their own imperfections and so break the silence of the gods and find the way across. According to Clastres there is probably no people more religious. See Pierre Clastres, *Society Against the State* (1974. English edition, New York: Zone Books, 1987), pp. 157–75.

Chapter 1

1. The two recent books by Paolo Santangelo, *Il 'Peccato' in Cina* (Bari: Laterza e figli, 1991) and *Emozioni e Desideri in Cina* (Bari: Laterza e figli, 1992) provide an indispensable background to this topic.

2. Li Ruzhen, *Jing hua yuan* (Hong Kong: Zhonghua shuju, 1958). As there are numerous editions of this book, I give both the numbers of the

chapters and the pages. Cited as JHY. On the author see Hsin-sheng C. Kao, *Li Ju-chen* (Boston: Twayne, 1981).

3. Zhang Yingchang, ed., *Guochaoshi-duo* (1869. Republished as *Qing shi-duo* [The Qing Dynasty Bell of Poesy]: Beijing, Zhonghua shuju, 1960), 2 volumes. Cited as GCSD.

4. A list of the main sources of Li Ruzhen's fantasies is given in Tamori Noboru, *Kyō ka en* [The Destinies of the Flowers in the Mirror], 2nd ed. (Tokyo: Heibonsha, 1961).

5. In the loose sense of 'the appropriate moral consequences of one's past actions', including those in a previous life.

6. He Bingyu has documented the background to Li Ruzhen's knowledge of mathematics, and suggests that his value for the speed of sound was derived indirectly from Western Europe through the Jesuits in China. As a general thesis this is likely, but the specifics of He's argument attempting to link Li indirectly with Mersenne, though he makes an important point about the difficulty in choosing an appropriate modern value for the conversion of the Chinese 'mile' (i.e., *li*), are not convincing as they stand. See He Bingyu, "Cong *Jing hua yuan* shitan shijiu-shiji chuqi kexue zhishi zai yiban shiren-zhong-de puji" [An exploration, based on *The Destinies of the Flowers in the Mirror*, of the spread of scientific knowledge among the generality of scholars in the early nineteenth century], in Yang Cuirong and Huang Yinong, eds., *Zhongguo keji-shi lunji* [Essays on the history of science and technology in China] (Taipei: Academia Sinica and National Jinghua University Institute of Historical Research, 1991). His figure (on p. 28) for Mersenne's upper estimate of the speed of sound does not match that in A. C. Crombie, *Styles of Scientific Thinking in the European Tradition* (London: Duckworth, 1994), II, 827.

7. The Chinese term *Tian* can cover a range of meanings from 'day' and 'the sky' to 'Heaven', 'God', and 'Nature'.

8. The Chinese term *qi* covers the senses of 'matter' and 'vitality', as well as that of 'energy'. Its central meaning is that of 'breath' or *pneuma*. It is the primal substance of a universe in which there is nothing dead or at least without something resembling the force of life.

9. See Barbara Shapiro, *Probability and Certainty in Seventeenth-Century England* (Princeton, N.J.: Princeton University Press, 1983).

10. The Chinese term *xin* conveys the sense of a faculty that both feels and understands; hence 'heart-mind' is a common scholarly translation.

11. New York: Revell, 1900. See especially pp. 65, 269, 273, and 277.

12. This point has been most effectively established by T. B. Stephens, in his *Order and Discipline in China: The Shanghai Mixed Court 1911–27* (Seattle: University of Washington Press, 1992), especially chapters 1 and

2. Though they use different language, this basic outlook is shared by most of the contributors to K. Bernhardt and P. C. C. Huang, eds., *Civil Law in Qing and Republican China* (Stanford: Stanford University Press, 1994). Thus the "Qing code was administrative and penal in its original approach and intent" (p. 165), and "(t)he imperial state threw ... its weight behind ... the traditional family system in order to reinforce the legitimacy of both institutions." (p. 130). After one complex case that had led to a riot, the provincial governor even declared that "it did not matter whether the local magistrate was right or wrong or crooked or straight. There was opposition to the official." (p. 101) This book is rich in valuable details, and in theoretical discussions of other themes, but to some degree misguided in thinking it a novelty to show that late-imperial Chinese courts regularly handled cases of a type that the Western tradition would label 'civil' (already noted, for example, regarding commercial contracts in Elvin, *The Pattern of the Chinese Past* [Stanford: Stanford University Press, 1973], p. 295). Likewise, the heavy emphasis almost throughout on the dichotomy between 'civil' and 'criminal' is not congruent with late-imperial Chinese legal thinking, and analytically problematic if taken as indicating any line of clear operational division, as some of the contributors point out (for example, Mark Allee, on p. 141, or even Huang himself with respect to sexual offences, on p. 165).

13. The text will also support the interpretation that they resembled the Chinese type of horizontal, wind-driven, sail-mill.

14. A commonplace of modern sinology, although the precise reconstructions are not yet entirely certain.

15. She is said to have succeeded.

16. See J. Z. Young, *Doubt and Certainty in Science* (Oxford: Clarendon Press, 1951), pp 92–99 and 119.

17. See P. Clastres, "What Makes Indians Laugh," in his *Society Against the State* (1974. Translation, New York: Zone Books, 1987).

18. Lee Siegel, *Laughing Matters, Comic Tradition in India* (Chicago: University of Chicago Press, 1987), pp. 84, 176–77, 232.

19. See, for example, the *Lettres persanes* (1721. Paris: Éditions Garnier Frères, 1975), pp. 152–53: "Dieu met Adam dans le Paradis terrestre, à condition qu'il ne mange point d'un certain fruit: précepte absurde dans un être qui connaîtrait les déterminations futures des âmes."

20 The Lilliputians "will never allow, that a Child is under any Obligation to his Father for begetting him, or to his Mother for bringing him into the World; which, considering the Miseries of human Life, was neither a benefit in itself, nor intended so by his Parents, whose Thoughts in their Love-encounter were otherwise employed. Upon these, and the like Reasonings, their Opinion is, that Parents are the last of all others to be trusted

with the Education of their own Children." *Gulliver's Travels* (1726. Ed. R. Greenberg. Norton: New York, 1970), p. 41.

Chapter 2

1. According to Qu Dajun, *Guangdong xinyu* [New Comments on Guangdong] (circa 1690. Reprinted, Hong Kong: Zhonghua shuju, 1974), pp. 1:7–8, these stars were "below Canopus," which has the declination 52°40' South. They would only have been visible in the Canton area for a short period early in the year. It was believed that rice-seedlings would die or wither if they were out.

2. Qu Dajun, *New Comments*, 6:210–11.

3. Qu Dajun, *New Comments*, 24:606.

4. Qu Dajun, *New Comments*, 22:551–52. 'Smirr' is a (West) Scottish word for a mist-like rain.

5. The eighth was the date when the post-solstice sacrifice was made to all the gods, and a drum beaten to drive away epidemics.

6. The *yin* and the *yang*.

7 Xue Ruolin, *You Tong lungao* [Draft discussion of You Tong] (n.p.: Zhonghua qiju chubanshe, 1989), p. 128, gives a variant text that shows You as slightly more sympathetic to the old peasant than the GCSD version.

8. 'Hypatotheism' means a 'belief in a dominant but not a unique deity', who somewhat resembles the ruler of a human society.

9. See Hatada Takashi, *Chūgoku sonraku to kyōdōtai riron* [The Chinese village and collectivity theory] (Tokyo: Iwanami, 1974), esp, ch. 5, and S. Gamble, *North China Villages: Social, Political, and Economic Activities Before 1933* (Berkeley and Los Angeles: University of California Press, 1963), ch. 5. Only after the late nineteenth century did village-based forms of crop watching begin to emerge.

10. Probably white artemisia and *Marsilea quadrifolia*. Though humble plants, these had been traditionally offered to the spirits. See *Zuojuan* [The commentary of Zuo], Yin, 3. The Tang poet Bo Juyi thought them only appropriate for a wife "unworthy of the full sacrifices" however. See *Bo Xiangshan shiji* [Anthology of poems by Bo Juyi] (Taipei: Zhonghua shuju, 1963), p. 42.

11. This refers to the hexagram Kun. "It represents nature in contrast to spirit, earth in contrast to heaven, space as against time, the female-maternal as against the male-paternal. The Receptive must be activated by and led by the Creative; then it is productive of good." R. Wilhelm, trans. C. F. Baynes, *The I Ching or Book of Changes* (New York: Bollingen/Pantheon, 1950) I, 10–11. Likewise, "the Earth must receive the Heaven, and the wife must follow her husband." *Zhou Yi Yao-shi xue* [Mr

Yao's study of the *Changes of the Zhou*] (Taipei: Shangwu yinshuguan, 1965) I, 40.

12. The sage's mother cut the fabric to symbolize the effects of weakening in one's continuity of purpose. She moved house to find a neighborhood that had a better influence on him. See J. Legge, *The Chinese Classics, II, The Works of Mencius* (London: Trubner, 1861), proleg., pp. 18–19.

13. See Sheng Dashi, *Selling off a Grandson*, in GCSD 17:570.

14. The crows were birds of ill omen in this poem that describes the legendary beauty Xishi and her lover, the king of the state of Wu, enjoying each other's company on the night before the ruin of his kingdom by the armies of Yue. The concluding lines are:

> The silver pointer's sinking, inside its silver basin,
> As the water through the water-clock drips down apace.
> They arise to watch the autumn moon sink downwards toward the
> waves.
> When, in the East, climbs the slow sun, *what pleasures will they take?*

See *Li Taibai quanji* [Complete works of Li Bo] (Beijing: Zhonghua shuju, 1977), I, pp. 176–77.

15. The bride's past, present, and future incarnations.

16 For example, Gu Kuizhang's *Buying Her Costly False Hair* (GCSD 23:839–40).

17. Liu Zhen, an official under Cao Cao, at the end of the Later Han dynasty, was punished for looking straight at the wife of Cao Cao's son during a drinking party instead of prostrating himself. See *Zhongguo renming da cidian* [The large Chinese biographical encyclopedia] (Hong Kong: Taixing, 1931), p. 1473. Shunyu Kun tried to trick Mencius into admitting that if it were wrong for men and women who were not married to each other to hold hands, a man would be morally justified in letting his sister-in-law drown rather than helping her. See Legge, *Mencius*, IV.I.xvii, p. 183.

18. A. P. Wolf and C-S. Huang, *Marriage and Adoption in China, 1845–1945* (Stanford: Stanford University Press, 1980), esp. chapters 7, 11, 12, and 13.

19. Consider Du Fu's *Song of the Firewood Carriers*, which refers to a part of what is today Sichuan province during the eighth century. His fascination with the exceptional is evident:

> The unwed women of Kuizhou have grizzled hair on their heads.
> They have still not entered a husband's home, though some are forty or
> fifty.

It's more difficult finding spouses now, because of the present
rebellion,
So all of a lifetime they'll nurse this grudge, and sigh at their affliction.

By regional custom the men work sitting, the women obliged to work
standing,
So the women's domain is the world outside, while the men stay in as
house-husbands.
Almost all of the women stagger home, toting the bundles of faggots
They must sell for money and so provide a base for the family budget.

Till they're old the virgin's double plaits still fall against their necks.
For them wild blooms, and hill trees' leaves, do duty as silver clasps.
Reckless of life, they quest for profit, and boil salt brine from wells,
Their energy spent on climbing cliffs, and hauling their goods to market.

Rouge and cheap ornaments intersperse with the channels their tears
have cut.
They are thinly clad in this walled-in land where it hurts to walk on raw
rock,
But how can you say these Shaman Hills girls are in any sense unlovely?
For north lies the hamlet of Zhaojun, who became the Shanyu's
consort!

See Chou Zhaoao, ed., *Du Shaoling ji xiangzhu* [Collected Works of Du
Fu with notes] (Beijing: Wenxue guji, 1955) 15:110–11.

20. Probably bronze rings used to make the rope taut. See the poem by
Liang Yusheng in GCSD 25:949.

21. The essential physical soul (*jingpo*) was linked to the body as its
form or essence, remaining with the body after death. The spiritual soul
(*hun*) was part of the vital energy (*qi*) of the person and was liberated from
the body when the latter died.

22. The land where, in the dawn of the Chinese race, the Yellow Emperor married his wife Leizu.

23. I have used the old Spartan term to convey the derogatory tone of
canghuo, which originally implied enslavement for a crime.

24. A fictitious animal said to have such short forelegs that it could
only move by straddling the back of a wolf, which, it was said, had corre-
spondingly abbreviated hindlegs. The two animals symbolize mutual inter-
dependence.

25. *Dharma* is right conduct, and the Buddha's teaching of it is likened
to rain that falls upon all equally.

26 The 'haling-way' = 'hauling way' is an old English term for a towing
path.

Chapter 3

1. M. Elvin, "The Gentry Democracy in Chinese Shanghai, 1905–1914," in J. Gray, ed., *Modern China's Search for a Political Form* (Oxford: Oxford University Press and Royal Institute for International Affairs, 1968), reprinted in M. Elvin., *Another History: Essays on China from a European Perspective* (Sydney: Wild Peony Press, 1996); J. Fincher, *Chinese Democracy* (2nd ed., Monumenta Serindica #20. Tokyo: Institute for the Study of Languages and Cultures of Asia and Africa, 1989).

2. The most important dissenting voice is T. G. Rawski, *Economic Growth in Prewar China* (Berkeley and Los Angeles: University of California Press, 1989), who takes a more optimistic view of the performance of agriculture. The increase in population between 1850 and the 1930s was of the order of at least 100 million persons, perhaps slightly more.

3. Sketched in M. Elvin, "The Double Disavowal: The Attitudes of Radical Thinkers to the Chinese Tradition," in Y. M. Shaw, ed., *China and Europe in the Twentieth Century* (Taipei: Institute of International Relations, 1986), and the shortened version in D. Goodman, ed., *China and the West. Ideas and Activists* (Manchester: Manchester University Press, 1990); on Confucianism, see M. Elvin, "The Collapse of Scriptural Confucianism," *Papers on Far Eastern History* 41 (March 1990), reprinted in id., *Another History*.

4. See, however, Lung-chang Young, "Literary Reflections of Social Change in China, 1919–1949" (Ph.D. thesis, New School for Social Research, 1964. Ann Arbor: University Microfilms, 1978), who surveys this theme and notes on p. 51 that "traditional society was portrayed as a grotesque mixture of mutually conflicting ideas."

5. E. Timms, *Karl Kraus, Apocalyptic Satirist. Culture and Catastrophe in Habsburg Vienna* (New Haven, Conn.: Yale University Press, 1986), p. 10.

6. "A man is always someone who tells stories. He lives surrounded by his stories and by those of others. He perceives everything that happens to him through their medium, and he endeavors to live his life as if he were telling it." J. P. Sartre, *La Nausée* (Paris: Gallimard, 1938. 1954 ed.), p. 57.

7. See the passage in *La Nausée*, pp. 163–65, in which the narrator contemplates the root of an old chestnut tree: "Absurdity was not an idea in my head, ... but this dead snake extended at my feet, this snake of wood."

8. 'Wangzhu-sheng', *Renhai chao*, hereafter RHC, (Shanghai: Zhongyang shudian, 1935), 5 vols. On the author's identity and other literary activities, see Zhu Zijia, *Wang zhengquan-de kaichang yu shouchang* [The

political regime of Wang Jingwei from its first to its final scene] (Hong Kong: Wuxing jishu baoshe, 1974) VI, 169–70. Ping also wrote under the name of 'Qiuweng' [Old gentleman of the autumn-time]. The book has been reprinted, using simplifed characters, in the series *Shanghai-tan yu Shanghai-ren congshu* (Shanghai: Shanghai guji chubanshe, 1991).

9. The device has been adopted here of using Latin roots, as a sort of substutite for literary Chinese units of meaning, in order to convey the half-meaningful quality of the names of many of the imaginary places and characters in *Tides*, rather than always transliterating or translating into English. 'Pax' = 'peace' is, as is often the case with Ping Jinya, ironic.

10. Explanations enclosed within parentheses, as here, are Ping Jinya's own.

11. The story is set in the years immediately following the revolution of 1911. The wearing of a pigtail, though no longer mandatory, as it had been under the Manchus, was still relatively common.

12. Though it happens that what Brightstrider has said is true. See the next section.

13. See the section *Murder by Slander* below.

14. Literally, 'to blow on the cow's hide' (*chui niupi*), which usually has the sense 'to talk big' but here is certainly obscene. The original phrase was the vulgar *chui niubi*—see *Mathews' Chinese Dictionary* (second edition), p. 209.

15. That is to say, making a fortune.

16. RHC *xuwen*. I am indebted to Sam Rivers for pointing this out to me.

17. Yuan Shikai's.

18. The title of Imperial Academy Student was a purchased one under the Qing dynasty. The traditional civil-service examinations had been discontinued in 1905, but those with the old degrees still commanded a substantial measure of respect.

19. 'Southern Darkness Village'. The reference is to the first chapter of the *Zhuangzi*, the famous work of Daoist philosophy from the third century B.C.E., but the reason for the allusion is unclear. It may refer to the astonishing transformation of one thing into another.

20. It was not unknown for a village to have a 'city god' (*chenghuang*). See E. Werner, *A Dictionary of Chinese Mythology* (1932. Reprinted, New York: Julian Press, 1961), p. 48.

21. One interpretation of *wei pogua* is 'under sixteen', since the character *gua*, meaning 'melon', can be visually subdivided into two graphs of *ba* meaning 'eight'.

22. That is to say, using rituals that were thought to be partially modernized.

23. Literally, 'to take a percentage from the winnings at gambling'.

24. *Biru*, that is 'like a jade amulet'. 'Bullatus' means both 'wearing an amulet' and 'bombastic'.

25. His *membrum virile*.

26. Used by Buddhist monks to tap out time when chanting.

27. The *Gaowang jing*, revealed to Sun Jingde between 534 and 537 in a dream. He was in a prison, under sentence of death. The executioner broke three swords trying to behead him, after which the prime minister of the day, Gao Huan, petitioned for his release. Gao's surname may be referred to in the title.

28. A procession of idols.

29. The *xianren*: those who did not work or work regularly, either because they were well off or because they chose not to.

30. Jiangxi bowl-riveters were said to guard their professional secrets so jealously that they would not even reveal them to members of their own family.

31. The phrase 'broken shoes' is a vulgar term for a loose woman.

32. Without knowing it, he is referring to his own son.

33. Heaven in anthropomorphic form.

34. For Jade Ego's mildy dissolute side, see RHC 36 on his visit to a Buddhist nunnery.

35. "Where every prospect pleases, / And only man is vile." Bishop Heber, "From Greenland's Icy Mountains," a once-popular hymn.

36. His Chinese name means 'Raiment of Clouds'. 'Cirrus', besides being a kind of cloud, also denotes the fringe of a garment or curly hair.

37. That is, 'north of the Yangzi river', hence a migrant. People from the Jiangbei region tended to be looked down upon by the inhabitants of Jiangnan as being somewhat uncouth.

38. *Tupo yu*. I have not identified this fish, and the translation of the name is literal.

39. The belief that Heaven rewards the virtuous with good weather and punishes the wicked with calamities. In late-imperial China this was often regarded as applying to collectivities, such as particular counties, rather than to individuals.

40. There were approximately six *mu* per acre.

41. There is a phrase to this effect, which has now become a proverb, in the 'Biaoji' section of the scripture *Liji* [Records of ritual], and it can also be found in the 'Shanmu' [Mountain trees] chapter of the *Zhuangzi*.

42. An insect that eats books, clothes, and wood.

43. Not identified.

44. In mid-winter.

45. The parasitic fungus *Cordyceps sinensis* that grows inside certain

insects and arachnids during the winter. In the summer it manifests itself in the form of extruded grass-like hyphae.

46. The author may be in error here. Horses were probably not ridden in China at so early a time.

47. I have not been able to find this expression in any other source to date.

48. Bullatus has just married, as his friends are aware. His wife is furious when she later learns about this episode.

49. "Things fall apart; the centre cannot hold; / Mere anarchy is loosed upon the world." W. B. Yeats, "The Second Coming," in *The Collected Poems of W. B. Yeats* (London: Macmillan, 1950, 2nd ed.) p. 211.

50. To the best of my knowledge it is discussed in no history of Chinese literature, though its existence is occasionally mentioned. For its popularity, see Zheng Yimei's *yinyan* or foreword to the recent reprint in the *Shanghai-tan yu Shanghai-ren congshu* mentioned in note 8 above. This pattern of popularity followed by oblivion accords with what I was told by the bookseller from whom I bought my copy in Hong Kong in 1965, and by Mr. Lim Choo Hoon (RSPAS, Australian National University), whose late uncle was a bookseller.

Chapter 4

1. Hao Ran, *Xisha er-nü* (Beijing: Renmin chubanshe, 1974), 2 vols. Hereafter XSEN.

2. How A-bao was weaned, in effect from one day to the next, is not explained.

3. Landlords, rich peasants, counterrevolutionaries, and others.

4. For an account of the emotional life of the inmates of these camps, read Zhang Xianliang, *Half of Man Is Woman*, trans. M. Avery (London: Viking, 1987).

Chapter 5

1. *Niezhong* (Taipei: Huangguan [Crown], 1980). Hereafter NZ.

2. On Mao's sexual proclivities and, more importantly, the interweaving of his political and emotional lives, see Li Zhisui, *Mao Zedong siren yisheng—huiyi-lu* [The memoirs of Mao's personal physician] (Taipei: Shibao wenhua, 1994), the Chinese version of id., *The Private Life of Chairman Mao* (New York: Random House, 1994). This book is also an account of one individual's initial enthusiasm for Communism and his sense of its betrayal by the leadership.

3. The Nationalist army officer who recounts the tale to the author is

made to declare: "If bastards are in the seats of power even for a single day, what sort of world will our world become?" (NZ 269)

4. See their writings in Editorial Board of the Modern History Division of the Chinese Academy of Sciences, and the Editorial Team of the Ming/Qing Archives Section of the Central Archives, eds., *Yangwu yundong* [The Foreign Affairs Movement] (Shanghai: Renmin chubanshe, 1961), 7 vols.

5. Patrimony's name has a double meaning, 'Much Wealth' (Duofù) and 'Many Fathers' (Duofù), which the English translation is an attempt to evoke by means of the pun 'Pater-many'. One of his aims is also to lay hands on the property of Old Liu, who was his nominal father until his mother's adultery was revealed.

6. Another reading would be: "has badly damaged his prospects in the underworld [when he comes to judgement]."

7. 'Hua' may be taken as suggesting 'China', as indicated in NZ 269. 'Lascivus' means 'playful, wanton, licentious, or insolent'.

8. *Poxie*, a woman who has already slept with other men.

9. *Macbeth*, III.iv.

10. As Monkey could not leap off the Buddha's palm. See Wu Cheng'en, *Xiyou ji* [Wandering West] (Hong Kong: Shangwu yinshu-guan, 1961), *hui* 7.

11. *Lian* = (all-or-nothing) moral credit-worthiness, as opposed to *mianzi* = (incremental) prestige. See Hu Hsien-chin, "The Chinese Concept of Face," *American Anthropologist* 46 (1944).

12. D. Gillin, *Warlord: Yen Hsi-shan in Shansi Province, 1911–1949* (Princeton: Princeton University Press, 1967), notes that "every year the authorities seized tons of opium and imprisoned or shot hundreds of people caught dispensing narcotics." These "attempts to prevent the manufacture or sale of opium in Shansi simply caused the price ... to rise so steeply that vast quantities of drugs were attracted into his domain from other provinces." (pp. 38–39) In the mid-1930s, however, Yan "proceeded to make the manufacture and sale of opium in Shansi an official monopoly, under the guise of selling medicine to addicts." (p. 137)

13. See NZ 117 for these identifications.

14. On Li and Zhang see J. B. Parsons, *Peasant Rebellions of the Late Ming Dynasty* (Tucson, Ariz.: University of Arizona Press, 1970). The sobriquet 'Eight Great Kings' (*sic*) is discussed on page 18.

15. On this ideal, see M. Elvin, "Female Virtue and the State in China," *Past and Present* 104 (Aug. 1984), pp. 138–39.

16. For a partial parallel to this theme of a husband's seeming friend making a public display of virtue and generosity as a cover for a murder

motivated by his lust for the wife, followed later by self-betrayal after he has married her, see the tale recounted by Xu Ji in the eleventh century, and partly summarized in Elvin, "Female Virtue," p. 140.

17. The word translated as 'prick' is written 'X' in the Chinese. Comparison of the other contexts where it occurs (such as pp. 130, 145, and 154) suggest that this interpretation is probably correct.

18. The *zouma deng*, or zoetrope, is a toy, usually made of paper, that uses the hot air rising from a candle to turn the angled blades of a small rotor mounted horizontally, on which is set a pattern of horses, or other animals, that spins round with the rotor. Seen behind a paper or glass shade surrounding the rotor and candle, the horses appear to be racing round. Professor Mabel Lee, personal communication; and J. Needham et al., *Science and Civilisation in China*, 4.1, Physics and Physical Technology (Cambridge: Cambridge University Press, 1962), pp. 124–25.

19. His real identity is a mystery, as the 'He', meaning 'who?' or 'what?' suggests. Hence the rendering 'Ignotus' = 'Unknown'.

20. This attitude was well founded. See L. P. Van Slyke, *Enemies and Friends: The United Front in Chinese Communist History* (Stanford: Stanford University Press, 1967), pp. 130–42.

21. Sima Zhongyuan, *Sima Zhongyuan zi-xuan ji* [Sima Zhongyuan's own selection of his work] (Taipei: Liming wenhua shiye gufen youxian gongsi, 1975), p.1. This may be the best place to mention the interesting comments made to me in an email (11 June, 1997) by Mr Roger Wu, who is Sima Zhongyuan's son, about his father's motives in writing *The Bastard*. The book, he says, "does more or less illustrate most (Asian) people's moral stand—one deserves [the consequences of] what he does. My father himself, on the other hand, is somehow neutral on this kind of moral issue. He believes everyone has the right to do whatever he likes to do so long as no one gets physically or emotionally hurt." His father wanted to inflict a measure of deserved "humiliation" on Chinese leaders who had "messed up the whole country," but at a deeper level, "like most of my father's books, [it] reflects the ironical cruelty of modern China." Those who joined the Communists had "suffered[,] ... were full of resentment ... [and] wanted to take revenge.... The future of the country was not of their concern.... They just wanted to get back at the people they overthrew." The tale of Petite Jade is "just a cover" for this purpose. Sima Zhongyuan told his son he wanted his "real intention" in publishing *Niezhong* put on record, and this note I hope meets his request.

22. See the postface in volume 2 of his *Kuangfeng-sha* [Storm-blown Sand] (Taipei: Huangguan, 1967), p. 4.

Chapter 6

1. Li Ang, *Shafu. Lucheng gushi* (Taipei: Lianhebao, 1983). The title-story is drawn from a real event, cited on pp. 203–7. Hereafter SF.

2. As in the newspaper editorial cited on SF 76.

3. Often, in Li Ang's tales, laughter is the sign of an evil disposition.

4. Yu Guanzhong, *Fen-he ren* [The crane burners] (1972. Reprinted, Taipei: Chunwenxue, 1985), hereafter FHR, p. 39.

5. Yu was born in 1928.

6. Note the implied reference to the flag of the Nationalist republic.

7. *Xing-er-shang*, that is 'above the forms [of the physical world]'.

8. *Xiaoyaoyou*—the term used by Master Zhuang, the Daoist mystic in the fourth century B.C.E.

9. *Fanfu suzi* (Taipei: Erya, 1985), hereafter FFSZ. His second book of essays, *Buwang zi-sheng* [Not a life to no avail] (Taipei: Erya, 1989), seems to lack the spark that sometimes sets its predecessor alight. The four novellas in Yuan's *Yanhua yinxiang* (Taibei: Lianhe wenxue, 1987) focus on the complexity underlying the surface banality of interpersonal relations. Life is not easy to live, and often seems to be "escaping from one" (p. 100). Most people live in a fog of puzzlement about others, a puzzlement broken by moments of startling lucidity. Motives are usually ambiguous; and least-bad solutions to human dilemmas—such as the survival of a marriage—often require weakness and even emotional dishonesty. Realism dissolves at rare moments into dream and surreal illusion, which heighten the sense that the meaning of what is happening is elusive. The ambiguity of the cultural-emotional orientations of Chnese surviving in West Coast America is likewise a recurrent theme. Maoist rule—physically remote, but psychologically close—also touches their lives now and again with the effect of a nightmare not really understood. What is perhaps more evident here than in the essays is Yuan's vision that people have a period in their lives when possibilities are open and they can become one sort of person or another, after which comes a moment of decision, or a twist of fate, that determines the rest of life, almost as an aftermath.

10. He was born in Hong Kong in 1949, spent some time in Taiwan, and now lives in the United States.

11. The full story is more complicated. See E. T. C. Werner, *A Dictionary of Chinese Mythology* (1932. Reprinted, New York: Julian Press, 1961), pp. 245–49, 456, and also 59–60, 63–64. On the Buddhist legend see the *Bukkyō daijiten* IV.3995.

12. Taiyang. Located about an inch back from the lateral tip of the eyebrow, it is believed to alleviate headache, migraine, the common cold, trigeminal neuralgia, and toothache.

13. A district on the northeast edge of Hong Kong island.

14. A reference to the legalist philosopher Master Fei of Han, from the third century B.C.E., who said that those with long sleeves were good at dancing and those with plenty of money good at business. See *Han Fei-zi*, 19, "Wu du."

15. *Lunyu* [Analects] I.8.

16. *Analects*, I.3.

17. A campaign in 1956–57 in which the encouragement given to intellectuals to voice their true feelings and ideas led large numbers incautiously to say things for which they were harshly punished in the subsequent Anti-Rightist campaign.

18. A highly complex movement, whose principal phase ran from 1966 to 1969, though it nominally lasted longer. Mao mobilized the resentments of teenagers against the bureaucratic totalitarian system in order to break his political enemies. Numerous talented people were killed or destroyed, and a generation of higher education all but lost. See 'Simon Leys' (P. Ryckmans), *Les habits neufs du Président Mao* (Paris: Champs Libre, 1971).

19. See T. Zeldin, *Happiness: An Exploration of the Art of Sleeping, Eating, Complaining, Postponing, Sympathizing, and, Above All, Being Free* (London: Collins Harvill, 1988).

Library of Congress Cataloging-in-Publication Data

Elvin, Mark
   Changing stories in the Chinese world / Mark Elvin
       p.   cm.
   ISBN 0-8047-3090-3 (cloth: alk. paper)
   ISBN 0-8047-3091-1 (pbk.: alk. paper)
   1. Chinese literature—Ch'ing dynasty, 1644–1912—History and
criticism.   2. Chinese literature—20th century—History and
criticism.   3. Chinese literature—Social aspects.   4. China—Social
life and customs.   I. Title.
PL2297.E48   1997
895.109'0048—dc21   97-37179
                                                                CIP

This book is printed on acid-free, recycled paper.

Original printing 1997
Last figure below indicates year of this printing:
06   05   04   03   02   01   00   99   98   97